the Unofficial Guide™ to Managing

Your Personal Finances

Stacie Zoe Berg

D0898480

Macmillan • USA

Macmillan General Reference
A Pearson Education Macmillan Company
1633 Broadway
New York, New York 10019-6785

ISBN: 0-02-862921-3

Manufactured in the United States of America

10 9 8 7 6 5 4 3 2

First edition

To my family

Acknowledgments

I would like to thank my husband for his support, assistance, and generosity. I'd also like to thank my parents for their support and for bringing me up to care about the welfare of others—more specifically, my mother, who grew a few gray hairs worrying about my deadlines so I wouldn't have to, and my father, for teaching me to be meticulous about details and accuracy.

I'd also like to thank everyone at Macmillan: Jennifer Perillo, managing editor, and Nancy Mikhail, senior editor, for asking me to write this book; Randy Ladenheim-Gil, senior editor; Sandra Birnbaum Wagman, developmental editor; Laura Poole, copy editor; and Scott Barnes, production editor, for their guidance and hard work.

Thanks to the technical editors at Debt Counselors of America: Judy Branzelle, Esq., Elizabeth Parker, Esq., and Wayne Ruckman, CFP; as well as Mark Eppli and Steve Landau, who also served as technical editors, for all their hard work and dedication to this project.

Lastly, thanks to all the experts interviewed for the valuable information they provided.

The *Unofficial Guide* Reader's Bill of Rights

We Give You More Than the Official Line

Welcome to the *Unofficial Guide* series of Lifestyles titles—books that deliver critical, unbiased information that other books can't or won't reveal—*the inside scoop*. Our goal is to provide you with the *most accessible, useful* information and advice possible. The recommendations we offer in these pages are not influenced by the corporate line of any organization or industry; we give you the hard facts, whether those institutions like them or not. If something is ill advised or will cause a loss of time and/or money, we'll give you ample warning. And if it is a worthwhile option, we'll let you know that, too.

Armed and Ready

Our hand-picked authors confidently and critically report on a wide range of topics that matter to smart readers like you. Our authors are passionate about their subjects, but have distanced themselves enough from them to help you be armed and protected, and help you make educated decisions as you go through your process. It is our intent that, from having read this book, you will avoid the pitfalls everyone else falls into and get it right the first time. Don't be fooled by cheap imitations; this is the *genuine article Unofficial Guide* series from Macmillan Publishing. You may be familiar with our proven track record of the travel *Unofficial Guides*, which have more than three million copies in print. Each year thousands of travelers—new and old—are armed with a brand-new, fully updated edition of the flagship *Unofficial Guide to Walt Disney World*, by Bob Sehlinger. It is our intention here to provide you with the same level of objective authority that Mr. Sehlinger does in his brainchild.

The Unofficial Panel of Experts

Every word in the Lifestyle *Unofficial Guides* is intensively inspected by a team of three top professionals in their fields. These experts review the manuscript for factual accuracy, comprehensiveness, and an insider's determination as to whether the manuscript fulfills the credo in this Reader's Bill of Rights. In other words, our panel ensures that you are, in fact, getting "the inside scoop."

Our Pledge

The authors, the editorial staff, and the Unofficial Panel of Experts assembled for *Unofficial Guides* are determined to lay out the most valuable alternatives available for our readers. This dictum means that our writers must be explicit, prescriptive, and above all, direct. We strive to be thorough and complete, but our goal is not necessarily to have the "most" or "all" of the information on a topic; this is not, after all, an encyclopedia. Our objective is to help you narrow down your options to the best of what is available, unbiased by affiliation with any industry or organization.

In each *Unofficial Guide* we give you:

- Comprehensive coverage of necessary and vital information
- Authoritative, rigidly fact-checked data
- The most up-to-date insights into trends
- Savvy, sophisticated writing that's also readable
- Sensible, applicable facts and secrets that only an insider knows

Special Features

Every book in our series offers the following six special sidebars in the margins that were devised to help you get things done cheaply, efficiently, and smartly.

1. "Timesaver"—tips and shortcuts that save you time.

2. "Moneysaver"—tips and shortcuts that save you money.

3. "Watch Out!"—more serious cautions and warnings.

4. "Bright Idea"—general tips and shortcuts to help you find an easier or smarter way to do something.

5. "Quote"—statements from real people that are intended to be prescriptive and valuable to you.

6. "Unofficially..."—an insider's fact or anecdote.

We also recognize your need to have quick information at your fingertips, and have thus provided the following comprehensive sections at the back of the book:

1. **Glossary:** Definitions of complicated terminology and jargon.

2. **Resource Guide:** Lists of relevant agencies, associations, institutions, Web sites, and so on.

3. **Recommended Reading List:** Suggested titles that can help you get more in-depth information on related topics.

4. **Index.**

Letters, Comments, and Questions from Readers

We strive to continually improve the *Unofficial Guide* series, and input from our readers is a valuable way for us to do that. Many of those who have used the *Unofficial Guide* travel books write to the authors to ask questions, make comments, or share their own discoveries and lessons. For lifestyle *Unofficial Guides,* we would also appreciate all such correspondence, both positive and critical, and we will make our best efforts to incorporate appropriate readers' feedback and comments in revised editions of this work.

How to write to us:

Unofficial Guides
Macmillan Lifestyle Guides
Macmillan Publishing
1633 Broadway
New York, NY 10019

Attention: Reader's Comments

The *Unofficial Guide* Panel of Experts

The *Unofficial Guide* editorial team recognizes that you've purchased this book with the expectation of getting the most authoritative, carefully inspected information currently available. Toward that end, on each and every title in this series, we have selected a minimum of three "official" experts comprising the "Unofficial Panel" who painstakingly review the manuscripts to ensure: factual accuracy of all data; inclusion of the most up-to-date and relevant information; and that, from an insider's perspective, the authors have armed you with all the necessary facts you need—but the institutions don't want you to know.

For *The Unofficial Guide to Managing Your Personal Finances,* we are proud to introduce the following panel of experts:

Judith Branzelle

Mark Eppli

Steve Landau

Bussie Parker

Wayne Ruckman

Debt Counselors of America

Judith Branzelle is a staff attorney at Debt Counselors of America, Inc. Judith frequently appears on radio talk shows and speaks to consumer groups on financial matters. In previous positions, Judith was a consumer advocate to the White House Conference on Families and a staff attorney to the American Health Care Association. In addition to her law degree, she holds a Masters Degree in Family Studies from the University of Maryland and has counseled many families on personal finance.

Mark Eppli is Associate Professor of Finance and Real Estate in the School of Business and Public Management at George Washington University, where he directs the MBA program in Real Estate and Urban Development. Prior to obtaining his doctorate, he was Manager of Research and Investment Analysis with the Pacific Financial Companies (PM Realty Advisors) where he approved the acquisition of $85 million in commercial real estate assets and supervised a $300 million real estate portfolio.

Steve Landau works for IntelliChoice, Inc., one of the most respected automotive information providers in the United States. IntelliChoice publishes *The Complete Car Cost Guide,* among other publications. IntelliChoice has been praised by publications such as *Automobile, Autoweek, Booklist, Changing Times, Consumer Digest, Money, Road & Track, Success, U.S. News & World Report* and others.

Bussie Parker is a staff attorney at Debt Counselors of America, Inc., where she examines debt and credit issues, including credit scoring, identity theft, payday loans, title loans, pyramid schemes, debt in the military, electronic fund transfers, banking, and credit reporting. Previously, she worked at the American Association for Retired Persons as Legal Counsel for the Elderly, and as a law clerk for an Administrative Law Judge at the Commodity Futures Trading Commission. She received her J.D. from American University in 1995.

Wayne Ruckman is a Certified Financial Planner and is employed by Debt Counselors of America, Inc. He has experience in lending, loan administration, and loan collections, and was formerly employed as an AVP and Loan Review Officer for a multi-billion dollar bank in Virginia. He also has experience in retirement plan administration. Wayne spent five years as a Volunteer Financial Counselor for the Cooperative Extension Service in Virginia. Wayne has a B.S. in Finance from Frostburg State University, where he graduated Magna Cum Laude in 1987.

Debt Counselors of America, Inc. is a non-profit Internet organization which assists consumers who have questions or difficulties with credit and debt issues. Debt Counselors sponsors a weekly webcast call-in radio show called "Get Out of Debt" and provides special programs to help consumers resolve difficult financial issues. DCA can be reached through its Web site (www.getOutOfDebt.org.) or by calling (800) 680-3328.

Introduction

Money can't buy everything. Money can't buy happiness. Money can't buy self-esteem. Money can't buy good health. But money can buy a sense of security, the best doctors, and a sense of peace.

Many people spend as much as they make. They fill their lives with stuff. They buy expensive clothes and sporty cars. They look great. But those who really can't afford it don't feel so terrific. They have everything, and a little bit more—they have the stress that goes along with having everything their hearts' desire when they really can't afford it. Every day they go to work just to pay the bills, which takes some of the enjoyment out of their jobs and makes working a bit more of a chore.

For others the situation is worse. They have spent themselves deeply into debt and cannot find a way to get out.

The problem is, the clothes go out of style, and the car gets nicked and dented, costs a bundle to maintain, and eventually wears out. In the end, they have nothing to show for their money except debt.

This is not to say you shouldn't enjoy your money. After all, it is yours. But if you put your money to work in the stock market or in other investments, you won't have to work so hard for it. It can work for you.

It's ironic that we spend at least 12 years in school (with many spending 16 years or longer) learning how to make money, but we're never really taught how to deal with personal finances. Many of us don't know how to set up a budget—or stick to it. There are plenty of us who don't know how to save money or invest it, nor do we realize the importance of saving and investing.

Certainly, you can live paycheck to paycheck, but if you don't save for your retirement, you may end up spending your golden years in the rat race. At age 70 you just might want to spend your mornings on a golf course rather than in rush-hour traffic. You may want to spend your day at the pool with your friends rather than at the office dealing with conflicting personalities. Maybe you really do want to sit in a booth and eat an early bird dinner. But you won't have that choice if you don't start saving now. You'll still be at work.

The amount you'll have to save to live your life in the style to which you have become accustomed is staggering. Think amassing a whopping $500,000 will make your retirement years secure? While half a million dollars is a lot of money, you'd only get $22,202 a year (after taxes) if you withdraw principal and interest for 25 years. (These numbers are based on a 3.5 percent inflation rate, a 6 percent average interest rate, and assumes you're in the 28 percent tax bracket.) Forget about that cruise to Europe. (Worried? For more on saving for retirement, see Chapter 12.)

Besides providing for retirement, money can buy some very important things. It can buy a sense of well-being. Just knowing you have money set aside can give you a feeling of empowerment and a sense of security. If you're trying to buy self-esteem by owning fancy clothes, cars, and homes and by going on extravagant vacations, think again: You're more likely to have those things—and enjoy them—by putting your money away now. Having it, rather than wearing it, driving it, or living in it—especially when you can't comfortably afford it—seems to work better. Plus, once you have a six-month emergency fund (essential in a good financial plan), you'll no longer work just because you have to, but because you enjoy your job. If you get fired or are laid off, you won't have to panic. You can consider it an opportunity to get a better job and move up the career ladder.

And what if you get sick? If you have money saved, you can buy the world's best medical care, regardless of what your health plan covers.

You can see that money buys a certain type of freedom.

But this type of freedom takes a lot of money. How do you get that kind of money if you don't earn that much? Think it's impossible? Just by saving a few dollars a week and investing them slowly over time can make you wealthy. Chalk it up to the miracle of compounded growth. Compounded growth has a snowball effect. Here's how it works: You start with a few flakes, make a ball and roll it in the snow to pick up more flakes, and soon you have a big enough snowball to build a snowman.

For example, if you make a one-time, lump-sum stock market investment of $2,000 at age 25 and reinvest all your dividends, by the time you're 65 years old, you'd have $99,570, assuming an annual average market return of 10 percent on your investment.

If you need more incentive to save, you can use the "Rule of 72" to figure out how much time it'll take to double your money in different investment scenarios. For instance, it will take you 7.2 years to double your money if it's earning a 10 percent rate of return. (See Chapter 1 for the equation and examples.)

Of course, you also have to take inflation into account. It can take a significant bite out of your spending power over time. To see how it works and how you can combat it, read Chapter 1.

So, how do you get started? How do you begin to save money if you can barely make ends meet? First, you have to take a good, hard look at where you've been spending. Then, if you want to save money, you'll have to cut back. The best way to do this is to set up a budget and set financial goals. (It's easier to give up small things when you know what you're saving for, whether it's a house, a car, or a college degree.)

The financial planners interviewed for this book report that many people feel confined and restricted by the idea of setting a budget. Take comfort— even if you have a budget, you can still have some flexibility so the budget doesn't become a burden in and of itself.

Of course, you're going to have to cut back somewhere if you want to buy financial freedom. Such freedom doesn't come cheaply, but it's well worth spending a few bucks on.

Cutting back on spending doesn't have to be painful. It doesn't mean you have to give up your social life, and it doesn't mean you'll have to wear out-of-date clothes. There are plenty of ways you can reduce your spending without feeling too deprived. Tips on cutting back are covered in Chapter 1, too.

Once you start saving more than you make you must "buy" yourself out of debt, because rarely does an investment return as much as credit cards charge in interest.

Debt can be devastating. If you try to consolidate your debt with a home equity loan to get your payments "under control," you may end up in foreclosure if you miss payments. If you're in debt, you need to read Chapter 9. There are practical ways to dig out of it.

And there are fun ways to make your money work for you. You can use credit cards to get frequent-flier miles, free gas, cash back, and more. And there are other creative ways to make credit cards work for you—read about these strategies in Chapter 2.

Investing is one of the keys to financial success. You must choose investments that match your risk tolerance level, and you must select a balanced portfolio—that is, you must not put all of your eggs in one basket.

Investors have different levels of tolerance for risk. Some investors get nervous when the market moves south. They pull their money out at the slightest downward movement to save what they can. As a result, they end up selling at lower prices, guaranteeing a loss. Then there are those who invest their money and walk away. No matter if the market tumbles, sleeps like a hibernating bear, or peaks and dives day after day, they hold on to their purchases. In the long run, based on market history, it is these investors who eventually come out ahead.

Not everyone has nerves of steel; in fact, market volatility is often a result of investors pulling out of the market to calm their frazzled nerves. It's important to assess your personal risk tolerance so you can build a portfolio that you can keep in both good and poorly performing markets. Holding on is key to getting ahead.

Besides the risk impulsive actions may pose, you should consider some additional risks when choosing your investments. They include inflation risk, that is, the loss of purchase power. The trick is to make sure your investment earnings keep up with or exceed the pace of inflation. Then there's credit risk. Just like a lender checks to see if you're a good credit risk before loaning money to you, you must make sure the companies you invest in are sound. There are several other types of risk you should consider before choosing your investments. And then you need to learn a little about the main types of investments. Learn more about risk as well as stocks, bonds, and mutual funds in Chapter 4. How to diversify your portfolio and how to find an investment advisor is covered there, as well.

But what good is all the money if you turn around and throw it out the window of your new home or car? Get the "inside scoop" on how to buy or lease a car in Chapter 6, how to buy a home in Chapter 7, and how to "buy" a mortgage in Chapter 8.

You'll probably buy a car or truck before you buy a home. Chapter 6 is filled with ways to save money on this major purchase, from how to negotiate to what really makes a vehicle a good buy. Sometimes buying a new vehicle isn't the best financial move. In some cases it's cheaper to lease. Learn how to make the distinction in Chapter 6.

Perhaps your budget isn't big enough for a new car. Read this chapter to find out tips on how to get the best buy on used cars as well.

While you can lose hundreds or even thousands of dollars on a car, you can lose a lot more money buying a home if you aren't a savvy consumer. Many people mistakenly believe that if you buy a home for $200,000 and you sell if for that much the next day, you break even. Far from it! Add in 6 percent for real estate commissions, and another 4 percent or so for closing costs, attorneys fees, moving expenses, and so on. Cost to move: $20,000—not exactly breaking even.

So you've got to take home buying seriously. Many people spend just a few days or a few weeks house hunting, only to realize later that they're stuck in a house that may no longer suit them because it's too expensive to move. Part of the problem is that home buying is another important aspect of personal finances you don't learn about in school. Another part of the problem is that real estate agents are salespeople, plain and simple. They work on commission. Their job is to get you into (or out of) a home as quickly as possible. That's what you're paying them to do.

So it's your job to learn about such an expensive purchase. In Chapter 7 you'll learn about the home-buying process, strategies for buying a home "on sale," and how to find a good real estate agent to help you buy or sell your home. We also give you tips on how to use the Internet to help buy or sell a home.

Though many real estate transactions take place without the aid of an attorney, we strongly advise you to retain legal representation when buying a home, especially if you're buying a new home. Both new and resale contracts are filled with fine print, and you need to fully understand what you are signing. An attorney can help you add in contingencies (though some buyer's agents will, as well) to protect your assets in the deal.

In Chapter 8 expert attorneys, who specialize in residential real estate transactions, give insight, understanding, and tips.

The home-buying process doesn't end when your bid is accepted. You must find a mortgage to finance your home. Mortgages are complicated loans. In Chapter 8 we'll tell you about the different types of mortgages and how to compare mortgage rates.

The last thing you probably want to do is pay a little extra in taxes. After all, according to the Tax Foundation, you had to work, on average, 129 days to pay off your tax bill in 1998. Read Chapter 10 to find out how to make your taxes a little less taxing.

Many people don't want to work their entire adult life to leave the bulk of their estate to the federal government in the form of estate taxes. But estate planning isn't just about money. Did you know that if you have children and die without a will, a court judge will decide, based on state law, who will raise your children? Did you know that if your estate goes through probate court your personal finances become public record? In Chapter 13 we share advice from financial planners on estate planning.

Though earning money and investing it is important, you must also protect your assets. An easy way to do this is with insurance. If you don't have health insurance and you or members of your family get sick or suffer an injury, you can lose everything and incur great debt. If you don't have auto insurance, one accident can wipe out all of your savings and put you into debt. If you don't have homeowners or renter's insurance, one violent storm can wash away all your savings. Read more about insurance coverage in Chapter 5.

Sometimes things happen that you don't expect and can't predict. You lose your job. You and your spouse divorce. Both of these events can have a significant impact on your finances. In this book, we give you expert advice in dealing effectively with these events. There are ways to cope. Neither of these events needs to be financially devastating.

Downsizing has become a common business strategy. Although it may increase your company's profit, if you're the one who gets the pink slip, it may have an adverse impact on yours.

But it may not. Job loss can be used as an opportunity to climb the corporate ladder (though not at the company you just left) or an opportunity to change careers. Either way, you must be prepared for job loss to protect your finances. It is not an infrequent event. Have an emergency fund and a plan. While you're "in between jobs," you may have to change your investment strategy or tap into your assets. Chapter 14 covers all this and more.

Sometimes, after spending a long time with your spouse, your finances are joined, but your hearts are not. Divorce can take a huge emotional and financial toll. Any way you look at it, divorce is expensive. However, there a many ways you can limit the costs. In Chapter 15, expert financial planners and psychologists give tips on limiting the financial and emotional costs of divorce. They also talk about how women differ from men in their approach to divorce and how each can learn to protect their financial interests. The experts also give the inside scoop on methods some spouses use to hide assets until after the divorce is final. If you're in a situation where you think your spouse might cheat on you (financially), read this chapter.

Sometimes, things just plain don't go right. You also need to protect your assets from fraud. Thieves are savvier than ever. Some are using the Internet to set up shop to take your money, while others are stealing identities and using your good name (and credit) to buy big-ticket items. Read Chapter 16 to find out more about that.

Managing your personal finances may be a chore. But if you watch your money closely, you may see it grow before your eyes.

Managing Your Money

PART I

GET THE SCOOP ON...
How compounding your interest can build your
principal ▪ How the "Rule of 72" can work for
you ▪ How dollar cost averaging can make
investing easier and more profitable ▪ How you
can figure out how much you're really spending
▪ Painless ways to save money ▪ How to set up
a budget that you can stick to

The ABC's of Counting Your Pennies

No doubt about it—managing your money is time-consuming and frustrating, especially when you don't know where it's all going.

But if you continually let your pennies slip though your fingers, you will not be able to put them to work for you. You will have little or nothing to invest so that you can eventually buy a new car or home, pay for your children's education, or build a nest egg for your golden years.

You don't have to give up every luxury you enjoy to reach your financial goals. You can simply learn to spend more efficiently once you get a handle on your current spending habits.

In this chapter, I'll show you how you can save big bucks by making a few small changes. I'll teach you how to expand your savings through investing, no matter how little you have to start with. And I'll tell you what the experts say about designing a budget to meet your everyday needs and your financial goals.

3

Why it's so important to save money

It's very easy to spend money. What's hard is *earning* it—and what's even harder is saving it. But if you learn how to save money, you can put it to work for you.

Ironically, most people spend at least 12 years—and many spend 16 years or more—in school gearing up for the working world, but they rarely learn about personal finance, that is, how to take care of their earnings. As a result, many people don't know how to save and invest, let alone make ends meet, and end up living paycheck to paycheck. Others live in debt. These financial lifestyles often come with a price tag of their own: stress and low self-esteem.

Being in debt or living from paycheck to paycheck can make you very reliant on your employer. If you fear making your boss angry and losing your job, that may take away some of your power and can limit your choices in life. By necessity you may become a "yes" person. Losing an income, even for a relatively short time, can lead to losing your car or even your home or both. The effects of one wrong financial turn or one unexpected expense can be devastating. You need only consult the list of foreclosures in the real estate section of your local newspaper to see that this tragedy really does happen to hard-working people.

Not having enough money at retirement can tarnish your golden years, too. "There are a lot of people in Florida who are working at McDonald's because they have to, not because they want to," says Pam Senk, director of retirement planning at Retirement Foundations in Tampa. "There are no answers at 75," she says. "The time to take care of it is when you're still working."

"It takes a substantial amount of money to retire comfortably today," Senk adds. Because of inflation and increased life expectancy, retirement funds that appear to be large—$500,000 or so—may be difficult to live on during retirement years. According to IRS Publication 590, a single 62-year-old person can expect to live another 22.5 years; couples, age 62, have another 27.8 years. (See the IRS Web site—www.irs.gov—or call them toll-free at 800/829-1040 to obtain a copy of this publication.)

If you take control of your finances—if you handle your money well and routinely invest a small percent of your earnings—you can ease some of your worries and probably prevent financial disaster. If you lose your job, you'll have something to fall back on. If you decide to buy a home or a car, you'll be able to afford it more comfortably. When your children get ready to graduate from high school, you'll have their college bills covered. And when it comes time to retire, you'll have a nest egg to sit on.

Put your money to work for you

There are several investment strategies that can make investing easier and more profitable. These strategies include:

- Compounded growth
- Dollar cost averaging
- The Rule of 72

Compounded growth

For some people, saving for their goals, like owning a home or a car, or even obtaining financial independence, seems impossible. That's where the power of compounded growth can come to your rescue. By investing in the stock market—whether through individual stocks or stock mutual funds—over a long period of time, you can let your money make money.

Unofficially...
Based on historical averages, the S&P 500 index, which is one of the more popular stock market indices, has returned more than 10 percent annually on investments since the 1920s.

In terms of actual dollars, if you had $100,000 invested, earning 10 percent each year, after the first year you would have $110,000.

Therefore, if you add that $10,000 to your principal, theoretically the next year you'd have an $11,000 return (10 percent of $110,000 equals $11,000). Each year, based on historical stock market performance, you'd have 10 percent more to add to your principal. This phenomenon is referred to as *compounded growth.* It's putting your money to work for you. (Note: These numbers don't account for capital gains taxes and investment fees.)

To reap the benefits of compounded growth you must have patience and some tolerance for risk. The stock market can be quite volatile at times; it can also stagnate like a hibernating bear. But then there are those times when it rages like a bull; these are the periods when growth usually outpaces losses from previous years.

For example, if, at age 35, you make a single investment of $2,500 in a stock mutual fund and reinvest all of your dividends thereafter. Assuming that the market returns an annual average rate of 10 percent on your investment, by the time you reach age 65, you'll have accumulated $43,624.

Assume instead that you had made that $2,500 investment and reinvested the dividends starting at age 25. By age 65, you would have a pot totaling $113,148. That's a 159 percent gain over that accrued by waiting 10 more years to invest.

If you had started even earlier—at age 15—by age 65 that $2,500 would have grown to $293,477.

Now imagine you hadn't taken control of your finances while you were younger and had waited until age 45 to invest; your return would be only $16,819. At age 55 that same $2,500 investment would reap only $6,484.

The stark contrast in these accumulations (as shown in Table 1.1) illustrates the power of compounded growth. To reap the benefits of compounded growth, however, you must have time for the compounding to work. The earlier you begin to save and invest, the longer your money has to grow. The length of time your money is invested also plays a significant role in reducing risk. The longer your money is invested, the longer it has to ride out any dips in the market. If you invest routinely, a practice called *dollar cost averaging,* and reinvest your dividends as well, you'll be able to take advantage of buying at market lows.

TABLE 1.1 HOW COMPOUNDED GROWTH WORKS

Starting age	Investment return in today's dollars
15	293,477
25	113,148
35	43,624
45	16,819
55	6,484

← Note! This table illustrates the value of a one-time investment of $2,500 at a 10 percent average rate of return starting at ages 15, 25, 35, 45, and 55 and ending at age 65, according to Quicken Investments Savings Planner calculations.

Dollar cost averaging

Another useful investment strategy is called dollar cost averaging. Dollar cost averaging is a method of investing routinely in order to catch market lows when you can buy more shares for a dollar. This method of investing helps take the worry out of timing the market.

Here's how it works. Assuming you start at age 15 and invest $2,500 every year at a 10 percent annual average rate of return, by the time you're age 65, you will have invested a total of $125,000, but your stockpile will be worth $2,909,771—yes, almost $3 million!

Likewise, if you start at age 55 and invest $2,500 every year for 10 years, again at a 10 percent average annual rate of return, you'll have invested $25,000, which will have compounded to a mere $39,844.

Note! ➜
This table demonstrates the accumulation of wealth by investing $2,500 every year, at a 10 percent annual rate of return, until you reach age 65, according to Quicken Investments Savings Planner calculations.

TABLE 1.2 DOLLAR COST AVERAGING

Starting age	Total invested	Total return in today's dollars
15	125,000	2,909,771
25	100,000	1,106,481
35	75,000	411,235
45	50,000	143,188
55	25,000	39,844

The beauty of dollar cost averaging is it increases your chances for a better return over time because when you buy at market lows, you're actually purchasing more shares than when you buy at higher market positions. So when the market rises, you in turn have more shares to rise in value.

For example, say you had $1,000 to invest. On March 17, a certain stock's shares were priced at $1 each, so you bought 1,000 shares. On March 18, the market soared. Now shares were selling for $2 each. If you had waited a day, you would have gotten only 500 shares for that same $1,000 investment. Meanwhile, the value of your 1,000 shares doubled. That's the benefit of buying at market lows. With dollar cost averaging, you end up buying at highs and lows, as well as everywhere in between. Because the market historically has risen, you typically end up ahead. If you try to time the market and invest lump sums (as opposed to smaller amounts routinely) you may, from time to time, hit the jack pot, but more often you'll walk away with "empty pockets." Even the pros have trouble predicting market direction.

Rule of 72

If you need more incentive to save, or have saving goals in mind and want to know how long it will take you to reach them at different interest rates, you can use the Rule of 72 (a mathematical computation used to estimate the time it will take a given amount of money to double in value at a given interest rate) to try out different investment scenarios.

The mathematical formula for the Rule of 72 is simple: 72 divided by the rate of return or interest rate on your investment equals the number of years it will take for your money to double, if earnings are reinvested.

How inflation reduces your spending power

Many people are afraid to invest in the stock market because of the risk of loss. Ironically though, they are guaranteeing a loss on their money by tucking it "safely" away in a passbook savings account or under their mattress because of the impact of inflation.

Consider this: If you have $1,000 dollars at a 5 percent inflation rate, one year later your $1,000 would be worth $950. In this example, each dollar today buys 5 percent less one year from today. Or, you can look at it this way: Essentially, everything increases in price by five percent. The Rule of 72 can be used to see the impact that inflation has on your money. At 4 percent inflation, the prices of goods and services double in 18 years: 72 ÷ 4 percent = 18.

> **"**
> Let me tell you the secret that has led me to my goal: My strength lies solely in my tenacity.
> —Louis Pasteur
> **"**

Note! ➡
Use this table to
see how many
years it will take
your investments
to double at a
given rate of
return. Or, you
can use it to see
what rate of
return you'll
need to double
your money in a
specified number
of years.

TABLE 1.3 RULE OF 72

Rate of return	Number of years to double your investment
1 percent	72.0
2 percent	36.0
3 percent	24.0
4 percent	18.0
5 percent	14.4
6 percent	12.0
7 percent	10.3
8 percent	9.0
9 percent	8.0
10 percent	7.2
11 percent	6.5
12 percent	6.0
13 percent	5.5
14 percent	5.1
15 percent	4.8
16 percent	4.5
17 percent	4.2
18 percent	4.0
19 percent	3.8
20 percent	3.6
21 percent	3.4
22 percent	3.3
23 percent	3.1
24 percent	3.0
25 percent	2.9

For instance, if you invest $20,000 in a mutual fund whose performance mirrors the S&P 500 index and want to know how long it will take to double your money at a 10 percent rate of return, set up the math equation as follows:

$72 \div 10$ percent = 7.2 years

How long will it take to double your money at 8 percent?

$72 \div 8$ percent = 9 years

How long will it take to double your money at 15 percent ?

$72 \div 15$ percent = 4.8 years

The current average annual inflation rate is 1.7 percent, according to the most recent U.S. Department of Labor (DOL) statistics (June 1997 to June 1998) available. But inflation rates vary among sectors, like college tuition and real estate.

Another way to look at inflation is to *compare purchasing power*, which measures "the change in the quantity of goods a dollar will buy at different dates," according to the DOL definition. For instance, a dollar in 1980 bought 57 cents worth of goods in 1993. Likewise, you'd have had to spend $1.75 in 1993 to buy something that cost $1 in 1980.

You also can see the effects of inflation by examining income levels. With the exception of those industries that have exceeded the average annual inflation rates, to have the same amount of purchasing power if you were earning $25,000 in 1980, you would have needed to earn $43,850 in 1993.

Because cost-of-living salary increases often don't keep pace with annual inflation rates in some industries, you'll be able to afford less, even if your salary increases keep pace with the general inflation rate. To keep pace with all industries, you'll either have to get big promotions (and substantial pay raises) or invest your money to keep up with or exceed the highest inflationary rates among the sectors.

Figuring out how much you actually spend

Do you really know how much you spend? Probably not. "When you ask [clients] how much [they] are spending, they don't have any idea, nor do they know how much is coming in sometimes," says Elizabeth Jetton, CFP, and president of Financial Vision Advisors, Inc., in Atlanta, Georgia. While they know how much they earn, they don't know how much they actually *net*, that is, how much they take home after taxes—federal, state, Social Security—are taken out, she notes.

Furthermore, many people don't know what they spend their money on. Mortgage and utility expenses account for only about 40 percent of expenditures, Jetton says, although that percentage varies; the more money a household makes, the higher that percentage rises. For those who have less, much more goes to the basics.

"More money doesn't correlate, necessarily, with greater wisdom or knowledge about where that money is going," Jetton says. The more people have, the less they tend to know, she adds. The well-to-do are not living on the edge of financial ruin, so knowing where and how every dime is spent is not a necessity. But higher-income earners tend to think that there are no alternatives to certain "extras," like cleaning services, dog walkers, and gardeners. The list of these services continues to grow, and pretty soon the higher-income earner has lost track of how much money he or she is actually spending on a day-to-day basis. This type of spending can ultimately stop even the wealthiest people from getting what they really want in the long run. (This is not to imply that people of lesser means keep close tabs on their income. Many lose track of how much they've charged on credit cards, spending themselves into debt.)

If you're in that situation, what action should you take to get out? Begin to make conscious decisions, Jetton says. She asks her clients three key questions:

- What is it about money that is important to you?

- What brings you happiness?

- How do you use money to achieve happiness?

Her clients usually don't respond that they'd be happier if they could go out to dinner more often. Rather, they say that they don't want to have to worry about money, and they don't want to have to work so hard. They also want to spend more time with their loved ones. These intangibles are the things that really are of greater value to them, she says. So how do you change your spending habits in order to meet your goals?

Setting up a budget

The best thing you can do keep your spending in check is set up a budget and stick with it.

In order to create a budget, you need to figure out where you've been spending all your money, and differentiate between what's *necessary* and what's *discretionary*. An easy way to do this is to see what you've spent over the last three months—to capture the quarterly bills, suggests Carrie Coghill, CFP, senior vice president/financial advisor at D. B. Root & Company in Pittsburgh, Pennsylvania. Seeing how much you spend is often an eye-opening experience and a source of motivation. Changes in your lifestyle should be made slowly to be successful, Coghill adds.

To get a handle on your spending, Martin W. Thurman, a CFP and registered investment advisor in Wichita, Kansas, suggests drawing a line down the middle of a sheet of paper. Write down the amount of money you have coming in on one side and the amount going out on the other side.

You can use tools to help you keep track of your cash flow, including:

- Software like Quicken or Microsoft Money

- Debit cards, which send monthly statements to you and which function like checks

- Credit cards, which also send statements to you each month (However, do not use this tracking method if you are tempted to overspend or you do not pay off the balance each month.)

Keeping track of your expenses is important. All financial planning comes out of cash flow, says Adam Rosier, CFP and senior financial advisor with American Express Financial Advisors, Inc., in Southgate, Michigan. He suggests two ways to set up a budget:

1. Set target spending levels for different spending categories, which come under the umbrella of fixed and discretionary expenses. Save the rest. (Either place it in a savings account or, better yet, invest it if you already have an emergency fund.)

2. Figure out what you need to save for different goals, like buying a home or saving for college. Save that money and spend whatever is left over.

If you decide to use the first method, you can divide a sheet of paper in half. On one side, list all of your fixed expenses, like rent or mortgage payments, gas, electricity, and water, insurance payments, and the like. On the other side, list discretionary expenses, like dining out. This method offers a lot of flexibility in discretionary spending for those who don't like the idea of having a "budget."

The second method particularly will help you stay out of debt because one of the "savings" pots is set aside in a liquid account for emergencies, like unexpected medical bills or car repairs. By setting up an emergency fund, you'll always have quick and easy access to cash, should the need arise. And you won't have to dip into your investments, which can be costly. (For more on emergency funds, see below.)

Goals, like buying a car or home and paying for a college education, need to be saved for in conjunction with one another, not one, then the next. Take whatever amount you have to invest and divide it into pots: A pot for a new car, a pot for a new home, and a pot for tuition, for example. Your specific investment strategies will come from the specific purpose of each pot. Money for longer-term goals should be invested in more aggressive mutual funds, which often produce higher returns over time than conservative investments like bonds. This is a good savings strategy for those who can avoid the temptation to dip into the pots.

No matter which method you choose you must stick with it. Coghill says that people often feel that they're going to be too restricted on a budget and avoid setting one up for that reason. However, just starting the process by becoming aware of your spending habits is productive. If you find out that you're spending more on dining out than on your mortgage, that awareness, while distressing, can help you make changes.

Timesaver
Most mutual fund families allow you to set up automatic monthly deductions from your paycheck. Invest this way and you'll save on the time and money it takes to write a check and mail it, plus you'll take advantage of dollar cost averaging.

Bright Idea
Look into taking
a course on per-
sonal finance.
Debt Counselors
of America,
Inc. (www.
GetOutOfDebt.
com) offers 25 to
30 self-help arti-
cles on a variety
of subjects,
including per-
sonal finance.
Also, groups
such as
Cooperative
Extension,
universities and
colleges,
women's groups,
or religious orga-
nizations often
hold seminars on
personal finance.

Just say no

Eventually, you must adapt your lifestyle so that it is in line with reaching your financial goals.

Thurman gives clients the following advice to help them protect themselves against splurging:

- Shop with a list and stick to it. Include only those items you need or that are in your budget.

- Leave your credit cards at home. "We all know what happens when we say we will pay the entire amount when the bill comes. [There's] always something else for the money to be spent on," Thurman notes.

- Place a Band-Aid on your credit card. "When you go to peel it off to use your card, it will give you one last chance to ask yourself if this is really what [you] want to do," Thurman says.

- Focus on your goal. "It's easier to say 'no' to an impulse purchase when you're focused on a financial goal [like] saving for a home, car, etc.," Thurman says.

- Identify what triggers your spending (boredom, loneliness, anger, stress). If you know what your triggers are, you can be on guard against them, which may help with self-control.

"Some of these [strategies] may sound silly, but you will be surprised how effectively they can work," Thurman says. But before you begin saving for your long-term goals, start saving for a rainy day.

Establishing an emergency fund

The first goal of a good financial plan, as noted earlier, is establishing an emergency fund. This fund should be accessible and should have at least enough money to cover expenses for six months.

Your emergency fund, according to Rosier, should consist of three tiers:

1. A bank checking account to cover short-term needs. This gives you the cheapest access to your money. Find one with no fees, if possible.

2. A money market account to gain a higher yield/interest rate. (Note: These accounts often have restrictions on the minimum amount for which a check can be written, typically, $250, and sometimes they restrict the number of checks you can write per month.)

3. Certificates of Deposits (CDs) from banks. (A CD is an investment that guarantees a specific rate of return for a specific period of time. CDs are offered by banks and are FDIC-insured.) Stagger the maturity dates. You can opt to rollover the money at maturity.

An emergency fund is not only important for when you have unexpected expenses or a job loss but it is also a way of preventing you from being forced into making poor investment decisions.

The idea of dollar cost averaging works in reverse when you are forced to sell your investments. For example, it is more likely you'll lose your job when the market is low, reflecting an economic decline; if you didn't have an emergency fund set up, you might have to sell off some of your stock market investments to meet your living expenses. Because share prices are relatively low in a depressed market, you'd have to sell more shares than you would at a market peak to get the same dollar amount. For instance, if you needed $1,000, at a market high you might have to sell 10 shares of stock. But at a market low you might have to sell 15 shares to get the same amount of money.

Watch Out!
Be sure to diversify your investments among aggressive and conservative stocks as well as among different sectors to reduce market risks. There's not much investment sense in putting all of your eggs in one basket.

When the market rises again, you will have lost out on the increase in value of those "extra" shares you sold. Also, unlike withdrawing money from a bank savings account, if you sell shares of stocks or stock mutual funds, you may have to pay sales commissions or other fees, plus a capital gains tax on any profit, which in turn may force you to sell even more shares to cover those added expenses. (See Chapter 4 for more information on investing.)

"When I'm sixty-four..."

No matter which method you decide to use for budgeting, after you've established an emergency fund, you should start saving for retirement in conjunction with or, initially, in lieu of, saving for a home, car, college education, or luxuries, because retirement is probably going to be your biggest expense. You need to allow time for your money to compound.

One way to invest for your retirement is to take advantage of investments that grow tax-deferred or tax-free. While it is hard for some young people to understand why starting early is important, the younger you are when you begin saving for retirement, the less you'll have to save to reach your goals, because compounded growth will typically work in your favor. (See the discussion on compounded growth presented earlier in this chapter.) If you have a 401(k) retirement savings plan at work, you should take advantage of it. Where else can you earn an instant 100 percent (dollar for dollar) or 50 percent (50 cents on the dollar) return on your investment but through your employer's match of your contribution?

There are many other tax-advantaged ways to save for your retirement. See Chapter 12 for details.

Figuring out where you can cut costs

Thurman has quite a few clients that want to invest, but don't think they have any money to spare. "Sitting down with them and finding some [places to cut] can be a chore," he says. "For example, one couple had HBO, Cinemax, etc. I asked them how much they really watched TV. Come to find out they hardly ever watched TV. They just got so used to paying the bill they never really thought about stopping the cable [service] and using the money for other means."

"Look at some of the small things you do, and you will not be surprised the next time you ask, 'Where did all of the paycheck go?'" Thurman says.

There are always places to tighten your belt. Here are a few of Thurman's cost-cutting ideas:

- Dining out. While it's more convenient to eat out, it's also more costly. If you spend $25 five times a week, you're spending $625 a month. Compare that with what it costs to buy groceries. Cut down on dining out and invest the leftovers in a mutual fund.

- Transportation. Plan your outings efficiently so you don't end up retracing your path and wasting gas.

- Taxes. Start preparing for the current year's tax season on January 2 each year. Invest in software like Microsoft Money or Quicken. These programs will print out tax-deductible expenses. While it takes time to enter expenditures and deposits, you'll end up saving the $150 per hour you may have paid to an accountant to do the same thing.

There are countless other ways to cut back. For some, it may simply be a matter of thinking before

Moneysaver
Shop around for long-distance phone service. Some will pay you $50 dollars or more to switch service providers. You can also find a plan that will save you money based on your calling patterns.

spending. While small things help—like using less water and electricity—the biggest cuts should come from your discretionary income.

Cutting down does not mean eliminating everything. It's simply doing some things *smarter*. Here are some examples of small changes that can save big bucks:

Bright Idea
At the end of each day, place your spare change in a jar and watch how fast it adds up.

- Rather than buy books or rent videos, borrow them from the library.

- Go on day trips rather than staying overnight at a hotel.

- Buy store and generic brands; they're usually cheaper, and you'll often find that they contain the same ingredients or are of the same quality as name-brand items.

- Don't overbuy produce and other perishables.

- Stock up on canned goods and frozen foods when they're on sale.

- Make your own baked goods from scratch; divide dry ingredients into plastic bags and make your own cake mixes.

- Buy classic styles, not faddish clothes.

- Run your dishwasher at night or on weekends when electricity is less expensive; don't use the heat-dry cycle.

- Rinse clothes in cold water rather than in hot water.

- Buy a bag of popcorn kernels and pop it yourself instead of buying the microwaveable kind.

- Eat in rather than dine out; brown bag it to work.

- If you do eat out, catch the early bird special or "free meal for kids" deal.

- Buy furniture from North Carolina or other outlets by phone.

- Save hundreds of dollars by using airports with more competitive airfares.

- Use e-mail instead of regular postal mail to save the cost of postage and stationery.

- When traveling by car, carry a cooler of soda and food.

- Stay at motels and hotels that offer free breakfasts.

- Increase your deductible on your insurance (and hope you don't have to collect on insurance too many times).

- Buy things when they're on seasonal sale, such as summer clothes in August.

Sometimes people don't think about how small expenses can add up over time.

66

Seasonal sales can save you a mint. It means planning ahead a little, but time flies. Year-end sales are fabulous.
—Carrie Coghill, CFP, senior vice president/ financial advisor.

99

TABLE 1.4 HIDDEN PLACES TO FIND MONEY

Activity	Cost per item/ frequency	Cost per year
Cup of coffee	65¢/workday	about $170
Car wash	$5/week	$260
Two movie passes	$12/twice monthly (Add in munchies and the cost skyrockets)	$288
Vending machine snack	60¢/workday	$156
Two CDs	$28/month	$336

← Note!
This table reveals five places to "recover" more than $1,000. Source: Martin W. Thurman, CFP and registered invest-ment advisor in Wichita, Kansas.

Getting motivated and staying on track

Some people find it difficult to save just for the sake of having an extra few dollars. Setting goals, like buying a home, will give you something tangible on which to set your sights. If you have trouble sticking to your budget, create smaller goals, or keep milestones in mind. For example, resolve that in one year you'd like to have $2,000 set aside for a down-payment on a house, and in two years you'd like to have a total of $5,000 in that pot.

"Seeing the distance you have to travel can be very disheartening," Thurman says. Consider starting with "a small goal that will be accomplished quickly so you can see that the process does work and goals can be obtainable," he suggests.

Thurman gives some helpful hints on how to stay on track:

- Place pictures of your goals (a new house, car, or boat, for example) around your house, office, and car for a constant reminder of what you're trying to achieve.

- Set a certain amount of money aside to invest for each goal. Choose an investment tool for each goal, like a bank savings account, CD, mutual fund, stock, or bond. If you invest in a mutual fund or stock, you may reach your goal faster, depending on market performance and your investment time horizon.

- Monitor the growth of your "stash." Sometimes that will give you the incentive to keep saving or tighten your belt another notch or two.

The closer some people get to their goal, the harder they try, Thurman says.

Many financial goals will not be achieved quickly. Many goals take years to reach. "Know this, and don't get discouraged when all the money is not there overnight," he says.

Just the facts

- Many people don't know how much money they spend per month, or even what they're spending their money on.

- Understanding compounded growth, the Rule of 72, and dollar cost averaging can go along way to making your money work for you.

- There are many small ways to cut back on discretionary spending without feeling the pinch too much.

- The first goal you should meet is setting up an emergency fund.

- If you are forced by circumstance to withdraw funds at market lows you will end up paying more in lost opportunity when the market rebounds.

GET THE SCOOP ON...
How interest rates and charge calculations work
▪ The different types of plastic cards ▪
How to make credit cards work for you ▪ The
new types of credit cards hitting the market

Credit Cards

C redit cards can be a powerful tool in your financial toolbox. They allow you to keep your money invested during the grace period offered by most credit cards each cycle, and they can provide protection when purchases break or when you're not satisfied with your purchase or when you have been cheated. These plastic cards also provide convenience. But to take full advantage of credit cards, you must pay off your debt every month. Otherwise, this powerful tool can help you dig yourself into deep debt.

In this chapter I'll tell you how credit cards can work for you and against you. I'll tell you about creative ways you can use credit cards to take full advantage of all they can offer. I'll also tell you about the different types of cards and some of the pitfalls you should watch out for.

Using credit

"Cash or credit?" These are familiar words to consumers. The Consumer Federation of America reports that the average household has 11 credit

Chapter 2

cards. In 1998, credit card charges in the United States topped $1 trillion for Visa, MasterCard, Discover, and American Express combined, according to CardWeb, a credit card research organization based in Frederick, Maryland. Visa alone crossed the $1 trillion mark worldwide in 1998.

Fifty to sixty percent of what's charged is paid off each month, avoiding interest charges, according to CardWeb. But not all consumers are using credit so wisely. In 1998, consumers owed $440 billion to Visa, MasterCard, Discover, and Optima, according to CardWeb, and there was $518 billion in revolving credit balances. See Figure 2.1 below to see where you fit in.

Note! ➡
How do you rate
with paying your
credit card bills?

Paying Credit Card Balances

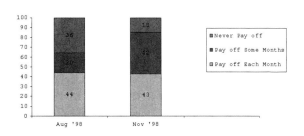

Source: American Bankers Association Education Foundation

Adam Rosier, CFP and senior financial advisor with American Express Financial Advisors, Inc., in Southgate, Michigan, recommends using credit cards (those without an annual fee) to charge almost everything you buy, paying balances off in full each month. The benefit of charging everything you buy is twofold:

- It helps you keep track of expenses. (Use the monthly statement as a record).

- You can earn rewards, like cash back bonuses, free air travel, hotel stays, and car rentals.

Shopping for a card

Terms and conditions, as well as interest rates and incentives, vary from card to card. To get the best buy, you need to shop around and compare. Key terms to consider when selecting a credit card are spelled out in the disclosure form and include:

- Annual percentage rate (APR)—the cost of the credit, which includes interest and may include other charges such as the annual fee, expressed as a percentage.

- Annual fee—an yearly fee similar to a membership fee.

- Grace period—usually about 25 days, this is a period of time during the billing cycle when you can pay your credit card bill without incurring a finance charge. Typically, the grace period applies only if you pay your balance in full each month. The grace period doesn't apply to cash advances. A few credit cards have no grace period.

Additionally, you should also compare:

- Cash advance fees
- Late payment charges
- Over limit fees

Take all of these costs into consideration when you select your cards.

Unofficially...
The collective credit limit is $2 trillion, according to the Consumer Federation of America.

Watch Out!
Credit card interest rates can change over time. Variable rate cards are tied to changes in other interest rates, such as the prime rate, Treasury Bill rate, federal funds rate, cost of funds rate, or Federal Reserve discount rate, which, in turn, are tied to certain indexes.

Credit cards often come with other bonuses including:

- Rebates on purchases
- Reduced introductory interest rates
- Extensions on manufacturers' warranties
- Purchase protection and/or security
- Car rental insurance
- Travel accident insurance
- Travel-related discounts
- Medical and legal services
- Credit card registration to protect you if your cards are lost or stolen

Compare all of these factors and features, and choose a card that offers the ones that best meet your financial needs.

How credit cards can work against you

If you're paying interest on them, credit cards are working against you. While they are a nice convenience, accruing interest can make using credit quite costly. For instance, if you bought a $4,000 stereo on a credit card with 20 percent interest and made only the minimum payments, that $4,000 stereo would end up costing nearly twice as much—$7,400. (For more on credit card debt see Chapter 9.)

If you can't eliminate interest payments by paying off your credit card debt, at least shop around for the lowest interest rate. Sometimes credit card issuers offer low introductory credit interest rates. Also, in general, when comparison shopping, look at the interest rate: What is it based on, and how often does it change?

If you have a variable interest rate and you don't always pay off your balance, take note of the periodic rate used to calculate the interest. There are primarily two formulas used to get the periodic rate:

1. The prime rate, the 1-, 3-, or 6-month Treasury Bill rate, the federal funds rate, or Federal Reserve discount rate, plus a number of percentage points, also called the *margin*, equals the interest rate.

2. The issuer multiplies the chosen index or index plus the margin by a *multiple*, a specified number, to calculate the interest rate.

In addition to being aware of how much interest your card is charging, you should also take note on how that interest is calculated. Interest calculations are very confusing to consumers, says Robert McKinley, president of CardWeb Inc. Eighty-five percent of the industry uses *average daily balances*, including new purchases, to calculate interest, he explains. Using this method, credit card companies add new purchases to your balance each day for the billing cycle and divide the total by the number of days in the billing cycle to come up with an average. They then multiply the average by the interest rate to get the interest charge. Because new purchases are included, you don't get a grace period on them if you carry a balance forward into the next cycle.

You should also watch out for the *previous balance method*, or two-cycle average daily balance (including new purchases) calculations, McKinley says. Using this very complicated method for calculating interest, interest is charged retroactively. The credit card issuers charge interest for two billing cycles if you carry a balance. Here's how it works: If you didn't pay interest in the previous month because you paid your balance in full but the next month you don't pay the balance in full, you'll be charged interest for two months, the month you didn't pay the balance in full and the previous month, as if you didn't pay off that balance. If you carry a balance continuously, you'll be "double-charged" once. But every time you go from a zero balance to any balance and don't pay the balance off the second month, you'll incur an interest charge. If you pay your balance in full each month, this calculation method won't affect you.

Credit cards can cost you in fees as well. While once upon a time, banks used to lure customers by giving away free toasters, credit card issuers are now raking customers in with perks and rebates. Don't bother fretting about what it's costing them to do this. Consider what it may be costing *you* to use these cards.

Credit card issuers are finding more ways to get their customers to pay for the loans they're receiving. Possible fees includes:

- Annual fees
- Late fees
- Over limit fees
- Inactivity fees
- Account closing fees
- Balance transfer fees
- Cash advance fees
- Fees for paying all your charges each month
- Maintenance fees

From the second half of 1996 to the end of 1998, the cost of fees went up 60 percent, McKinley says. The average late fee was a little over $21 and the average over limit fee was $20 at the end of 1998. Eighteen months prior, those fees were $13 on average.

Besides increased fees, new fees are popping up everywhere. One such fee is an inactivity fee. Stay charge-free for six months and it might cost you $16. Close an account with some issuers, and you'll pay for it—$25 for processing. One bank, McKinley says, charges a balance transfer fee in the form of a 3 percent cash advance fee—and it's not required by law that this fee be disclosed to you.

If you use your credit card to get cash, you may pay a big price for it. Cash advance fees are very expensive, McKinley says, as high as 5 percent of the amount of the advance. And the interest rate on cash advances might be higher than that for charging, another little tidbit that's not necessarily disclosed in disclosure documents, he adds. Be sure to call the credit card issuer and ask about all the fees and charges that may be assessed against you.

In addition to hiking up interest rates and charging more and more extraneous fees, credit card issuers are also making big bucks lending consumers money by shortening *grace periods*, the interest-free period from when the billing cycle closes to when the bill is due. Grace periods used to be 25 to 30 days, but now they're typically 20 to 25 days, according to McKinley. For those who pay their balances in full, those extra 5 to 10 days of carrying a balance without paying penalties (the float period) is lost. (A few cards have no grace periods at all.)

Watch Out!
If you miss a payment or two, your credit card issuer may hike up your interest rates. Be sure to read the fine print.

How credit cards can work for you

It may seem that with over limit fees and inactivity fees, you simply can't come out ahead. No so! Here's how you can make credit cards work for you.

Timesaver
You can research credit card rates and more on the Web at sites like www.bankrate. com, www. cardweb.com, and www.bog. frb.fed.us/pubs/ shop/tablwb.pdf.

First, try to get rid of the fees. Some you can eliminate yourself—don't charge beyond your credit limit and pay your bills on time. Others, like the annual fee, you may be able to eliminate just by asking. You do have leverage, especially if you charge more than $3,000 annually, McKinley says. The same is true if you carry a balance of $2,000 or more. If you charge more than $10,000 a year, you also have leverage to get fees waived.

If your card earns you frequent flier miles, however, don't expect to get award program membership fees cut or eliminated. The credit card issuers are firm about those fees, he says. And there are no guarantees. "[The credit card issuers and program sponsors] can yank the rewards [programs]," McKinley says.

Another way to save cash using credit is to time your purchases. By charging purchases early in the cycle you can increase the grace period float, McKinley notes.

Creative credit card money saving strategies

It may take a little juggling, but you can make credit cards work for you. Here are some creative strategies provided by McKinley:

Peter, Paul, and Marry—In this scenario, you can charge all your expenses to a rebate card, which tends to carry higher interest rates than the no-frills credit cards. Using a balance transfer check, shift the unpaid balance on the rebate card to a lower rate card. The balance transfer is treated as a purchase, and you get a second grace period if you didn't have a previous balance. (For some consumers, this might be more trouble than it's worth. For those people, there's another way: Have two cards. Use a rebate card to buy purchases that you know you'll pay off, and then use a low-rate card strictly for major purchases you can't pay off right away.) You will get more bang for your buck if you can rob one card with the other, that is, by robbing Peter to pay Paul and then "marrying" the two cards.

Churning the Balance—Using this strategy, you move the balance of one credit card, using balance transfer checks, to another card in order to reap the incentive from the "transferred to" card. Then you can move it again to reap more benefits. If you have a couple thousand dollars on your balance, this can add up to big rewards, which is why many credit card issuers limit the number of transfers they'll allow per year.

Buying Down—Consumers can lower interest rate points on credit cards as they can with mortgage loans by paying a modest ($15 to $25) annual fee in exchange for an interest rate several points lower than the lowest perk card.

Squeaky Wheel—Call your bank and complain about a high interest rate or fee. Ask to have it reduced.

Rate Hopping—Take advantage of introductory teaser rates, which usually last between 3 and 12 months. Mark your calendar, though, so you'll know when the introductory rate expires. There is a downside to this strategy: You must stay on top of credit reporting agencies to make sure each account you close is reflected accurately in your credit report so it doesn't look like you have too much credit available.

There are quite a few reward cards that have no annual fees. But good ones (like ones that offer frequent flyer miles) carry high fees. Whether or not those types of cards will pay off for you depends on your annual charges (the more you charge, the more frequent flyer miles you earn, for example), whether or not you pay off your balance each month (if you don't pay your balance, these cards can become expensive), and whether you can take advantage of the incentive earned—for example, whether you can fly during the periods that are not blacked out or use the miles before they expire. Also, make sure the rebate is worth it. It won't pay to use a gas station rebate card if that brand of gas is the most expensive, or use an automobile manufacturer's rebate card if you don't end up purchasing one of the manufacturer's cars or trucks.

Find a rebate card that fits your needs and one with low enough fees to make it worthwhile. Then charge everything (a pack of gum, a candy bar—a mile is a mile!) to rack up the rewards. But, remember to keep costs down you need to pay balances in full each month. If you travel on company business and you can you use your own credit card (and get reimbursed!), you can benefit even more, McKinley says.

Look for promotions. For instance, from time to time the American Express waives the annual fee for its corporate card for one year for the primary cardholder. Your boss won't let you have one? No problem. Become a sole proprietor of your own small business where you can sell your hobbies. It costs a few dollars to register your company with the county, but it will save you $55 on the annual fee for one year. American Express has one of the best frequent flyer rewards programs available. Cost? Another $25.

TABLE 2.1 THE COST OF ONE ROUND-TRIP TICKET VIA A REBATE CREDIT CARD

Airline	Card	Annual fee	Max miles per year	APR	Cards	Telephone
Alaska Airlines	Alaska Airlines MasterCard	$45	Unlimited	v*17.99%	MasterCard	(800/552-7302)
Alaska Airlines	Alaska Airlines Gold MasterCard	$45	Unlimited	v16.49%	MasterCard	(800/552-7302)
American Airlines	Citibank AAdvantage Card	$50	60,000	v18.4%	MasterCard/Visa	(800/FLY-4444)
America West	FlightFund Visa	$45	60,000	v18.49%	Visa	(800/678-2632)
Continental Airlines	Chase OnePass Classic	$45	80,000	v17.9%	MasterCard/Visa	(800/245-9850)
Continental Airlines	Chase OnePass Platinum	$65	Unlimited	v16.9%	MasterCard/Visa	(800/245-9850)
Delta Airlines	Classic Delta SkyMiles	$55	60,000		American Express	(800/SKY-MILE)
Delta Airlines	Gold Delta SkyMiles	$85	100,000		American Express	(800/SKY-MILE)

Besides credit cards, there are additional ways to earn frequent flyer miles such as using certain car rentals, hotels, long-distance service providers, florists, and more.

continues

Airline	Card	Annual fee	Max miles per year	APR	Cards	Telephone
Northwest Airlines	WorldPerks Visa Classic Card	$55	50,000	v18.25%	Visa	(800/360-2900)
Northwest Airlines	WorldPerks Visa Gold Card	$90	80,000	v18.25%	Visa	(800/360-2900)
Southwest Airlines	Rapid Rewards Classic	None First Year	75,000	v17.9%	Visa	(800/SWA-VISA)
Southwest Airlines	Rapid Rewards Gold	None First Year	Unlimited	v17.9%	Visa	(800/SWA-VISA)
TWA	TWA Aviators Card	$50	50,000	v17.4%	MasterCard/Visa	(800/501-6428)
TWA	TWA Aviators Gold Card	$75	80,000	v17.4%	MasterCard/Visa	(800/501-6428)
US Airways	Dividend Miles Platinum	$125	Unlimited	v17.9%	Visa	(800/335-4318)
US Airways	Dividend Miles Gold	$70	Unlimited	v17.9%	Visa	(800/335-4318)
US Airways	Dividend Miles Classic	$50	Unlimited	v17.9%	Visa	(800/335-4318)
United Airlines	Mileage Plus Classic	$60	50,000	v18.4%	MasterCard/Visa	(800/284-9173)
United Airlines	Mileage Plus Gold	$100	50,000	v18.4%	MasterCard/Visa	(800/284-9173)

*v indicates a variable interest rate.

Research rates and perks. CardTrak (800/ 344-7714) provides a summary of credit cards with the best interest rates nationally. The cost is $5 per subscription. Or, you can use the Internet. You can find CardTrak's Web site at www.cardtrak.com, where you can find the same information immediately and free. While you're surfing the Web, head over to Washington. The Federal Reserve System collects and publishes a report on credit card plan terms every six months. You can find the survey at www.bog.frb.fed.us/pubs/shop/tablwb.pdf. The site includes information on credit card institutions, annual percentage rates, indices, grace periods, phone numbers, and more.

So much plastic

In addition to the many perks available, there are also several different types of cards available.

The newest type to hit the market are gift cards, which function like debit cards. These cards look like credit cards, complete with embossed numbers and a magnetic strip. Retailers like Sears, Wal-Mart, Home Depot, and Blockbuster are offering this type of card as an alternative to gift certificates. The cards come loaded with money, usually $50 and up, though some are less. The user can make purchases at the store from which the card was purchased.

If you don't want to limit the receiver to just one store, you may have another choice soon. Visa and MasterCard are piloting gift card programs of their own. MasterCard's Swift Gift Global Gift card denominations start at $25. Visa's Gift Card starts at $50 denominations. Additional fees may be involved. These cards can be used anywhere MasterCard and Visa are accepted, except at ATMs.

Moneysaver
If you pay a lot in interest, avoid these perks and instead use credit cards with low interest rates. The people who benefit from rebate cards are the ones who pay their balances in full each month.

Then there are the standard, or classic, cards—Visa and MasterCard. Typical credit limits start at $100 and go up to $10,000. These cards generally don't come with a lot of perks, though some offer travelers' insurance.

Then there's the gold card, which is rapidly being replaced by another "precious metal" card—the platinum card, discussed below. The gold card starts with a $5,000 credit limit and has a lower APR than the standard card. The fees tend to be higher than those for standard cards, however, assuming the bank is charging fees. Gold cards have a package of benefits that includes insurance products for air travel, collision damage waiver for car rentals, purchase protection coverage, and assistance services for legal and medical troubles, according to McKinley. But the higher credit limit is the main attraction, he says, noting that you must have at least a $25,000 annual income to qualify for one.

Unofficially...
You may be seeing one more metal soon—one company, McKinley reports, is issuing a titanium card. It'll be similar to the platinum card, but with different perks.

The platinum card has been around for just a few years, McKinley says. There's not much of a difference between these and gold cards, except with platinum cards banks must have 24-hour services, he says. Platinum cards also have a minimum $5,000 credit limit. They may have a higher level of travel accident services than the gold cards, as well as a range of other extras. Most platinum cards have $50,000 or $100,000 credit limits, according to McKinley, but in reality, most people don't qualify for those high limits.

Besides card colors, which designate credit limits and extras, there are other card categories. One is the hybrid card; this card is offered by both Visa and MasterCard via the Visa signature card and the World MasterCard, respectively. These cards have both charge (which requires you to pay the balance at the end of the billing cycle) and credit (which allows you to carry a balance) features. The choice of how to use the card—as a charge card or credit card—is determined by the consumer upon receiving the bill. McKinley expects this choice to be at point of sale in the future. Many of the consumers who use these cards pay off their balances in full each month. These cards generally carry an annual fee of $50 and are geared toward more affluent customers, particular those that travel, McKinley says. They compete with the American Express Platinum charge card, which has an annual fee of $300 and is by invitation only.

All three of the above-mentioned cards have special features such as automatic upgrades in certain hotels and car rentals. Some also offer preferred seating at restaurants.

Visa announced another product—the Visa Infinite card—which is designed for the upscale, technology-bound traveler. In addition to other perks, this card features an exclusive Web service. It offers 24-hour access to personalized travel information, retail and travel offers, an online concierge service, and more.

Other product types include:

- Subprime
- Secure

Both subprime and secure cards are geared toward consumers with poor credit records and those with no credit history. Both have a lot of fees involved. With the secure card, you must make a deposit, on which you may or may not receive interest. Fees can be as high as interest assessed, McKinley says.

Rewards (or rebate) cards, discussed earlier in this chapter, are another category. These are the cards that give you something back, like cash or frequent-flier miles.

There are also debit cards like the Visa check card and MasterCard debit card, which you can use in place of checks. Unlike credit cards, these cards have no credit line. The money to pay off the balance comes directly out of your bank account, but not immediately, like with an ATM card. They're somewhat confusing to use because you sometimes must push the "credit" button on store keypads to use them, McKinley says. These cards only need a signature, no PIN necessary. Consumers like the convenience these cards offer, so much so that their numbers grew 60 percent a year between 1995 and 1998, according to McKinley.

Smart cards are relatively new in the United States and are still in pilot programs. These cards (Visa Cash and MasterCard Mondex) are like credit cards, but have an embedded computer chip. (Currently, cards use magnetic strips.) Computer chips give the card more capacity. They can be interactive; for instance, the Mondex can be used to transfer cash from one card to another, so you can pay back a friend for a small loan. The current application is to use them as cash for small purchases, like candy from a vending machine. Users can download money from their bank accounts at the ATM. One day you'll be able to use these cards from your computer, McKinley predicts. Currently, chip applications are being developed for storing your health records, including x-rays, on these cards. Pilot programs, according to McKinley, also include multicurrency products, which are great for international travelers.

Charge cards essentially have no credit function. You generally have to pay off the balance in a maximum of 30 days, though there may be some options to extend payments, according to McKinley. The idea of forcing consumers to pay off the balance is good for some and not for others, McKinley says. The two most popular charge cards in the U.S. are American Express and Diner's Club, both travel/entertainment cards.

Charge cards generally carry high annual fees because you're not paying any interest on the charges. Annual fees for the American Express card start at $55 (plus $25 for the rewards program) and those for the Diner's Club card start at $80. Typically, charge cards have no preset credit limits.

Charge cards offer some of the best rewards programs. Both American Express and Diner's have flexible frequent flier programs. You can apply Diner's points to any airline and earn miles at a faster rate than you can with other rewards programs, according to McKinley. American Express also has a flexible frequent flier program, though not all airlines are included. The American Express rewards program also allows you to use your points to purchase vacation packages and retail items.

Just the facts

- You can increase the value of your money by taking advantage of credit card rebate programs, like purchases that earn you frequent-flyer miles.

- You must read the fine print carefully to know under what circumstances you'll incur fees or an increase in the interest rate, especially because there are many new fees being charged by credit card issuers, even to those consumers who pay their balances in full and on time each month.

- Jumping from card to card in order to get the best interest rate may be detrimental to your credit rating.

- Grace periods are getting shorter, which leaves less time for savvy credit card users to float their balances.

GET THE SCOOP ON...
What products and services banks offer ▪ What
products and services credit unions offer ▪
The differences between banks and credit
unions ▪ How to get the best of both

Taking Care of Business

Chapter 3

After you've made a budget and created a financial plan, you need to make some decisions about where you're going to stash your cash for emergencies and for paying bills. You may also need other financial services and products, like home and auto loans and credit and debit cards.

In this chapter, I'll tell you what banks have to offer their customers and what credit unions can offer their members. I'll give you comparisons between the two types of financial institutions and pose some questions you can ask yourself to help you make decisions regarding when to use a bank and when to use a credit union. I'll also offer you tips on how to choose a bank. Finally, I'll tell you how to get the best deals from these financial institutions.

Taking advantage of banks

Banks offer an array of products and services, including savings and checking accounts, trust management, credit cards, debit cards, safe deposit boxes, loans, and investment services, as well as business banking products and services to business customers.

These services will cost you, sometimes a lot. Banking isn't free, even though in cases of savings accounts and Certificates of Deposit (CDs) you're giving the bank your money and it's investing it to make a profit for itself.

Banks are charging for more and more of their services. In addition, many banks don't pay interest on checking accounts and pay only nominal interest rates on savings accounts, so by keeping your money there, you may be losing out to inflation, too.

Unofficially...
If you live in a community property state, community funds deposited in the individual names of each spouse and those in joint accounts are each insured up to $100,000.

You may be wondering, then, why not just keep your money safely tucked away in your mattress where it won't cost you a cent? Well, first, imagine how difficult and inconvenient it would be to pay all your bills in cash. Second, your money's not insured there. If someone takes it, it's gone. Deposits in most banks, however, are insured—up to $100,000 per depositor—by the Federal Deposit Insurance Corporation (FDIC). (To tell if your deposits are insured, look for an FDIC sticker on the bank's door or at the teller's window.)

Though you'll no longer get a free toaster when you open an account, banks still offer their customers useful services. In addition to those offered by credit unions—savings and checking accounts, mortgage loans, and car loans—many banks offer investment services, including stock brokerage services. At these banks you can typically invest in mutual funds and buy annuities and insurance.

To get the best deal for your money, you should shop around. For savings accounts, the choice is easy. Compare interest rates and interest rate calculations. For checking accounts, compare the following:

- Monthly maintenance fees
- ATM fees, especially those assessed for using an ATM other than the bank's or one outside its network
- Fees for transferring money between deposit accounts (checking to savings and savings to money market, for example)
- Check processing fees
- Fees assessed if your balance drops below the required minimum
- Cost of printing checks
- Cost of bouncing a check
- Cost of stopping a check ("stopping payment")
- Cost of a copy of a canceled check
- Loan application processing fee
- Overdraft charges
- Cost of cashier's checks
- Debit card cost per use

Try to find a bank that has low fees and that will pay you interest on your checking account balance. If that bank pays higher interest rates for higher balances, try to keep your balance at least that high, unless, of course, that money would be better invested in the stock market or other security.

There are other things you should consider when shopping for a bank:

- Is the bank conveniently located near your home or office? If it isn't, does it have electronic banking services, such as a nearby ATM, and does it have free telephone banking or online access through your personal computer?

- Are there other branches near shopping centers so you can run more than one errand at a time?

- Are the hours of operation convenient? Does the bank have evening and weekend hours?

- Are the tellers and managers friendly and help-ful? Are they people with whom you can form a business relationship?

- Does the bank offer all of the services you need now and those you will need in the future? Are the services priced competitively?

- Does the bank offer investment services, like mutual fund investments and stock brokerage services? Can you buy annuities and insurance through them? (Watch out—you'll probably pay a hefty commission for this added convenience.)

- Does the bank offer overdraft protection, free check printing, and similar perks?

- Does the bank have safe-deposit box rentals available or will you have to travel to another location?

- Is the bank insured by the FDIC?

- Is the ATM in a well-lit area? Is there a camera installed? A panic button?

- Is there a drive-through teller window with extended hours of service?

Answers to questions like these will help you choose a bank wisely.

As with any consumer service, sometimes things go wrong. If you want to complain about your bank, and you've already written to its president, there are several other places to turn to:

Moneysaver
If your bank offers insurance coverage to cover the con-tents of your safe-deposit box, don't purchase it if your valuables are already fully insured via a rider on your home insurance policy.

- State bank regulators (www.pueblo.gsa.gov/crh/banking.htm lists state banking authorities)
- State bankers association (listed separately on the Web)
- American Bankers Association (www.aba.com)

Taking advantage of credit unions

At the end of 1997, there were 11,658 credit unions with a total of 73.5 million members, according to the Center for Credit Union Research at the University of Wisconsin-Madison. Total assets were $360 billion. Credit unions hold 8.3 percent of consumer savings, 22.3 percent of auto loans, and 11.9 percent of consumer installment credit.

Credit unions provide services to their members, who in turn own the credit union. A credit union is a nonprofit group run by a volunteer board elected by the credit union's members. As such, credit unions are considered financial cooperatives. They vary in terms of size and number of services offered, as well as membership, because they serve different groups or communities. Deposits are insured up to $100,000 (on each separately named account) by a government agency called the National Credit Union Administration (NCUA).

According to the Center for Credit Union Research, there's been a 30 percent drop in the number of existing credit unions since the mid-1980s. Interestingly, membership in credit unions has risen by that same amount, and shares and deposits have risen more than 93 percent. These numbers can be explained by the fact that the number of small credit unions has decreased while the number of large credit unions has increased.

Credit unions offer savings and checking accounts, usually at higher interest rates and lower fees than banks do. Credit unions also offer loans for buying homes and cars, as well as home equity loans, generally at lower rates than banks. Credit unions also commonly offer credit cards with much lower interest rates than those offered by banks, except for special promotional rates. Credit unions, however, don't offer business loans or investment services, as do many banks.

If you want to join a credit union and you don't already qualify for membership through your employer, contact NCUA (www.ncua.gov) to find out where you might qualify for membership in your state. Not everyone can take advantage of credit unions. To join one, you must be eligible for membership. Credit unions serve particular groups—for instance, Navy Federal Credit Union serves members and former members of the U.S. Navy and the U.S. Marines. Other groups include associations, groups of employees, and unions.

If you want to file a complaint against a credit union, contact the National Credit Union Administration.

Credit unions versus banks

There are some distinct differences between banks and credit unions. In addition to the differences in the way each is run as noted earlier, banks have to meet Wall Street demands to increase profits and often do so by reducing and eliminating services while adding and increasing fees. Credit unions, on the other hand, are run by their members and have no shareholders demanding personal gain. Instead, any profit made by a credit union is returned to their membership through the payment of higher interest rates on savings, lower interest rates on loans, and bonus dividends.

The contrast between credit unions and banks is also apparent in costs and availability of services. According to a *Bank Rate Monitor* survey in July 1998, credit unions had better rates and fewer fees than most banks and thrifts (i.e.: savings and loans, or S&Ls) when it came to car loans, credit cards, CDs, and money market accounts. (*Bank Rate Monitor* (www.bankrate.com) is an online publication of Intelligent Life in North Palm Beach, Florida.)

On the other hand, you can find more services at banks, there's a shortage of credit union ATMs, and some credit unions don't offer cashier's checks or certified checks. Plus, low-income home buyers may find it difficult to get a mortgage loan from a credit union because credit unions are exempt from the Federal Community Reinvestment Act, which mandates that financial institutions help serve people living in low-income communities.

Unfortunately, banks can be too expensive for low-income families to use for general banking services. In fact, an estimated 12 million households don't have a bank account, according to Consumers Union, an advocacy group and the publisher of *Consumer Reports* magazine. This is because many people simply can't meet the minimum monthly balances required by banks to avoid fees.

Credit unions are nonprofit, so they are not taxed. If security is a part of your banking decision, credit unions by law can only invest in U.S. government securities, while banks invest in both large and small businesses in the form of loans, which may pose risks. Banks also put their funds in other nongovernmental investments. Because banks are

Unofficially...
Banks hold 94 percent of all savings and deposits in financial institutions, more than 12 times the amount America's credit unions hold. (Source: Credit Union National Association, Inc.)

commercially owned, they are supposed to make profits and therefore must take some risks.

In comparison to banks, many credit unions have limited accessibility and a limited number of services, says Keith Leggett, senior economist with the American Bankers Association. Commercial banks are usually full service. On average, commercial banks are larger and more sophisticated financial institutions than credit unions, though there are some credit unions that rival commercial banks. Navy Federal is the largest credit union, and it is comparable in size to a regional bank, according to Leggett. However, regardless of size, credit unions do not offer business banking services.

Furthermore, most credit unions are small and can't offer large loans, Leggett says. The average credit union has $25 million in assets. (Navy Federal has $10 billion in assets.) More than 5,000 credit unions have less than $5 million in assets. So roughly half of all credit unions have only $5 million in assets, he says. In contrast, the average commercial bank has $78 million in assets.

There are almost 9,000 commercial banks, which tend to be larger institutions with greater levels of financial sophistication and offer more products and services, Leggett says. If you add S&Ls to those, the number increases to almost 11,000. Branch locations (for banks and S&Ls) totaled 72,326 as of December 1997. Many credit unions tend to have just one branch. The following figures demonstrate the growth in assets and in the number of banks over the years.

Now that you have some knowledge about banks and credit unions, which should you use? Here are

Unofficially...
S&Ls were principally formed to do mortgage lending, but the difference between S&Ls and commercial banks has been blurred.

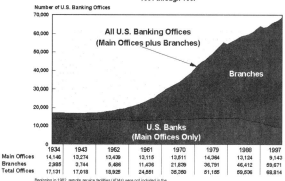

Number of FDIC-Insured Commercial Banks
1934 through 1997

Number of U.S. Banking Offices

	1934	1943	1952	1961	1970	1979	1988	1997
Main Offices	14,146	13,274	13,439	13,115	13,511	14,364	13,124	9,143
Branches	2,985	3,744	5,486	11,436	21,839	36,791	46,412	59,671
Total Offices	17,131	17,018	18,925	24,551	35,350	51,155	59,536	68,814

Beginning in 1982, remote service facilities (ATMs) were not included in the count of total branches. (At the end of 1981, there were approximately 3,000 such facilities.)

Includes U.S. Territories and Possessions.

← Note!
Number of FDIC-insured commercial banks
(Source: FDIC)

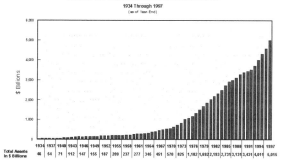

Assets of FDIC-Insured Commercial Banks
1934 Through 1997
(as of Year-End)

	1934	1937	1940	1943	1946	1949	1952	1955	1958	1961	1964	1967	1970	1973	1976	1979	1982	1985	1988	1991	1994	1997
Total Assets In $ Billions	46	54	71	112	147	155	187	209	237	277	346	461	570	825	1,182	1,692	2,193	2,731	3,131	3,431	4,011	5,015

← Note!
Assets of FDIC-insured commercial banks
(Source: FDIC)

some questions you can ask yourself to help you determine the answer. You may decide to use both—one for checking and savings accounts, another for loans, or other combinations of services. Use Worksheets 3.1, 3.2, and 3.3 while you comparison shop among and between banks and your credit union.

WORKSHEET 3.1—COMPARISON SHOPPING: SERVICES

Goal: *Save money*

Compare	Bank A	Bank B	Bank C	Credit union
Interest rates	____	____	____	____
Checking fees and interest rates	____	____	____	____
Loans	Interest rates, closing costs and other fees, special promotions, discounts for using other services			
	____	____	____	____
Investing	Services offered: brokerage for stocks, mutual funds, annuities, insurance, bonds, other securities			
	____	____	____	____

WORKSHEET 3.2—COMPARISON SHOPPING: FEES

Service	Fee
Checking account (monthly maintenance charge)	$_____
Cost per check	$_____
Overdraft charge	$_____
Check printing	$_____
Copy of canceled check	$_____
Cashier's check	$_____
Money order	$_____
ATM in-network charges	$_____
ATM out-of-network charges	$_____
Account transfers	$_____
Account closing fee	$_____
Charge for dropping below required minimum balance	$_____
Bounced check	$_____
Stopping payment on a check	$_____
Loan application processing fee	$_____
Debit card cost per use	$_____
Safe-deposit box rental	$_____

WORKSHEET 3.3—COMPARISON SHOPPING: GENERAL QUESTIONS

How much money will you be able to keep as a minimum balance? $_____

Will that balance be high enough to meet any minimum balance required to avoid a fee?

_____

What is the current interest rate on checking accounts?_____

Savings accounts?_____

What is the minimum balance you must maintain to earn interest?

Savings? _____Checking? _____

How much interest, if any, will your account earn each month? $_____

How many checks per month will you need to write and how much will this number incur in charges, if any? $_____

How many times per month will you use your debit card and how much will you incur in charges, if any? _____

How many visits to an ATM that will incur fees will you need to make each month?_____

How much will it cost? $_____

How many ATMs are in the network and can be used at no charge?   _____

Can you bank by telephone? _____

Can you bank online? _____

What is the interest rate on car loans and how is it calculated?   Interest rate _____
Method of calculating interest?
Simple _____Compounded _____

What is the interest rate on mortgage loans and how is it calculated?Interest rate _____
Method of calculating interest?
Simple _____Compounded _____

What is the interest rate on savings accounts?

_____

What is the commission rate on investment tools?   Mutual funds _____
Stocks_____ Bonds _____
Annuities _____
Other insurance products _____

What are the hours of operation?
_____ to _____

Did employees answer your questions quickly and accurately? _____

Is the institution federally insured? _____

Does its ATMs have bright lights? _____

Does its ATMs have cameras, rearview mirrors, and panic buttons? _____

How to get the best deals

You must do a little legwork to find the best deal. Sometimes the best deal is in the form of a special promotion. Wait for a promotion to run and you may, for example, avoid closing costs on your home, saving hundreds of dollars.

If you use more than one service offered, some banks will give you a break. For instance, if you have a checking or savings account and your home is mortgaged through the same bank, you may be able to get a discount later on a home equity loan at that bank or get your savings and checking account fees waived.

Some banks offer express checking, a feature that permits you to save money by eliminating or reducing monthly checking account fees, allowing low minimum balances, and giving you unlimited check writing—if you're willing to do all of your banking electronically through ATMs, telephone, or your personal computer. But if you need to see a teller, it'll cost you—nearly $10 a pop at Chase Manhattan Bank in New York, according to the Bank Rate Monitor. (Other banks are less costly.)

Just the facts

- Banks typically offer more (and more sophisticated) services and products than credit unions.

- Credit unions typically offer lower interest rates on loans and credit cards than do banks.

- Credit union membership is restricted, and branch and ATM locations are often limited; by contrast, anyone who can afford the monthly fees, if any, can open a bank account and take advantage of the greater number of ATM and branch locations banks offer.

- Sometimes you can get good deals at banks if you use more than one of their products or services.

Creating and Protecting Your Wealth

GET THE SCOOP ON...
Investing in stocks, bonds, and mutual funds ▪
What risk factors are involved in investing ▪
Why buying the most home you can afford isn't
always a good investment strategy ▪
How a financial advisor can help you

PART II

Building Your Assets

Chapter 4

An important aspect of managing your personal finances is investing your money to reach your financial goals. There are many types of investment tools you can use. Each carries risks and benefits.

In this chapter, I'll tell you about the different types of risk, show you ways to evaluate your risk tolerance level, give an overview of different investment tools, and tell you about the role a professional financial planner can play if investing and directly overseeing your finances are too difficult or time-consuming for you.

Risk and your risk tolerance

All investments involve some form of risk. Even the safest type of investment, a federally insured bank account, poses a risk—the possibility that inflation will outpace your earnings from interest, leaving you with less real purchasing power than when you started. Other types of risk include:

▪ Market risk. The stock market is unpredictable because it reacts to outside forces, including

Wall Street analysts' predictions, moves in interest rates (or just anticipation of a change in rates), real and predicted company earnings, politics (both stateside and foreign), unemployment rates, and more. There is really no way to predict market fluctuations, though many people try. Market risk poses another risk to investors: The risk that you will pull out at market lows rather than stay in and buy more shares of stocks at what may be bargain prices.

- Inflation risk. Inflation affects the worth (buying power) of a dollar. With a zero inflation rate, a dollar is still worth a dollar the following year. With a 5 percent inflation rate, however, a dollar is worth only 95 cents one year later. Inflation risk also occurs when prices rise faster than your salary does. Either way, you experience a loss of purchasing power. The trick is to make sure your investment earnings keep up with or exceed the pace of inflation.

- Interest rate risk. Interest rates on investments (and loans) are linked to the Federal Reserve Board and their movements on short-term interest rates. Changing interest rates affect both equity investments (like stocks and stock-heavy mutual funds) and fixed-income investments (like bonds).

- Credit risk. This type of risk is associated with the financial stability of a company for stocks or a municipality for bonds. Generally, greater risks are associated with higher rates of return on your investments.

- Currency fluctuation risk. There is an inverse relationship between the value of a dollar and overseas investments. As the value of the dollar rises, the amount of money invested overseas declines because investors get more bang for their buck in the domestic market. The converse is also true when the value of the dollar drops overseas. Even if you don't have foreign investments, you'll probably still be affected by currency movements because many American companies have foreign subsidiaries or hold joint assets with foreign companies.

- Political turmoil. Real or perceived political distress domestically or internationally can affect the economy. Uncertainty leads to depressed share prices. During times of war, many investors scurry to invest in fixed-interest investments such as bonds.

- Portfolio risk. Are you a long-term investor or a short-term trader? If you're invested in mutual funds, the same should be asked of the portfolio managers. Timing the market rarely works. Traders must pay higher taxes on short-term investments. Portfolio risk also comes into play if your investments are concentrated among companies and industries that perform similarly during different economic cycles.

- Impulsive selling. When emotions—generally, fear—get the best of you during a dipped or slumped market, you may be selling at a low point, as noted earlier. By letting your emotions dictate your actions, you can end up with less money than what you invested initially.

Although the thought of risky behavior can put you on edge, there is a bright side. You can benefit from risk.

Investors remember it as Black Monday. On October 19, 1987, the Dow Jones Industrial Average plummeted a record 554.26 points, a steep drop of 22 percent. This drop, like others in the past, presented a great opportunity to buy stocks at lower prices. Essentially, they were on sale. Those who bought low, and those who held tight and didn't sell, ended up making a lot of money. Within 24 hours the Dow rebounded 337.17 points, setting another record. As the days went by the market had more swings, but within a week, the market peaked just 41 points shy of where it had started. Eleven years later, on October 19, 1998, the Dow Jones average was 6727.71 points higher than on that dark day.

It should also give you comfort to know that since the 1920s, fixed assets returned between 3 and 4 percent and equities returned 9 to 10 percent. The overall inflation rate averaged about 2.5 percent.

Figuring your risk tolerance

Are you a gambler, or are your fingers tightly wrapped around your cash? Gamblers will have big ups and bigger downs, more than likely. In the long run, gamblers often don't make much more than conservative investors, but they do get more of a thrill from the ride.

Answer *Yes* or *No* to the following questions:

1. Do you enjoy gambling, especially with big bets?

2. Are you glued to financial news reports all day?

3. Does daily market performance determine your mood?

4. When the market tanks, do thoughts of the 1929 stock market crash consume you?

5. Do thoughts of losing it all due to job loss or a medical emergency cross your mind when making investment decisions?

If you answered *Yes* to the first question and *No* to the rest, you probably have a high tolerance for risk. If you answered *No* to the first question and *Yes* to the others, you probably have a lower risk tolerance. But if you want a more accurate assessment, complete the risk questionnaire that follows, which was provided by T. Rowe Price. And if you want to see a sample of a portfolio mix that matches your risk tolerance level, take the asset allocation interactive quiz at Strong Funds (www.strong-funds.com/strong/Planner98/asset.htm).

Keep your risk tolerance level in mind when choosing your investments. In order to achieve your financial goals, you want to be able to stick with your financial plan. If you sell when you can no longer bear the market's downward movement, you'll lose out on later gains. By selling low you have to sell more shares than if you had sold at a higher market point to get the same amount of money.

What you can do to reduce risks
To make investing more tolerable—and probably more profitable, as a result—determine which types of risk you're willing to take. That will direct you into the different asset classes. For instance, the lowest risk class is cash. The highest risk class is an aggressive stock. Your age and knowledge of the financial market will also play a role in your selections.

The best way to reduce risk is to diversify your investments. In addition to stocks and mutual funds, you can balance your investment portfolio with

WORKSHEET 4.1—RISK QUESTIONNAIRE (SOURCE: T. ROWE PRICE)

This questionnaire is designed for investors who are at least three years from retirement and plan to keep their funds for at least five years.

1. If you have significant experience with any of the investments listed under each of the following categories, give yourself the number of points indicated for that category.

   Stability (0 points):

   Savings and checking accounts

   Certificates of Deposit

   Money market funds

   GICs

   Income (3 points):

   Individual bonds

   Bond mutual funds (corporate, government, municipal)

   High-yield bond mutual funds

   Growth (5 points):

   Individual stocks

   Growth and income mutual funds

   Aggressive growth mutual funds

   International stock mutual funds

   Other (6 points):

   Investment real estate

   Options

   Precious metals or commodities

   Limited partnerships

2. Over time, inflation can dramatically affect an investment's real return. Higher returns from some investments can help compensate for the effects of inflation but, in general, higher returns can only be achieved by accepting more risk. Which one of the following objectives has the most influence in shaping your financial strategies? (Please check only one box.)

   ☐ I want investments that are expected to keep pace with inflation. These types of investments generally have lower chances of short-term losses. (0 points)

☐ I want investments that are expected to moderately outpace inflation. These types of investments generally have a moderate chance of short-term losses. (8 points)

☐ I want investments that are expected to significantly outpace inflation. These types of investments generally have a greater chance of short-term losses. (14 points)

3. The average annual return for a hypothetical portfolio of mutual funds was 10 percent over a seven year period. The annual of the portfolio ranged from a gain of 25 percent to a 10 percent loss. Assume that you bought shares at the end of year six. It is now the end of year seven and the portfolio lost 10 percent this past year. What is your plan for the portfolio? (Please check only one box.)

☐ Sell (0 points)

☐ Hold (10 points)

☐ Invest additional money (14 points)

☐ Sell half of your investment and hold the rest (4 points)

4. Which of the following is your main concern when selecting or maintaining an investment? (Please check only one box.)

☐ The potential for loss (0 points)

☐ Mostly the potential for loss, with a minor concern for the potential for gain (4 points)

☐ An equal concern for the potential for loss and gain (6 points)

☐ Mostly the potential for gain, with a minor concern for the potential for loss (10 points)

☐ The potential for gain (14 points)

5. Suppose that one year ago you invested $20,000 in a stock mutual fund. The market has gone down during this period, and today your investment is worth $16,000. You calculate that if you had originally put the $20,000 into a relatively risk-free investment such as Treasury bills, you would have approximately $21,000 today. You decide to: (Please check only one box.)

continues

☐ Sell the fund and invest the proceeds in a much safer investment. (0 points)

☐ Sell the fund and invest the proceeds in a riskier investment in an attempt to recoup your losses faster. (8 points)

☐ Hold the fund. (6 points)

☐ Buy more shares of the fund. (13 points)

6. If your total portfolio (all of your investments combined) posted a negative return for any given year, would you be likely to sell some of your investments and invest the proceeds more conservatively?

☐ Yes (0 points)

☐ No (11 points)

7. You have $10,000 to invest and have only two investment options. Which would you be more likely to select? (Please check only one box.)

☐ Investment X: 70 percent chance of gaining $2,000, 30 percent chance of losing $500 (10 points)

☐ Investment Y: 100 percent chance of gaining $500 (0 points)

8. Would you ever purchase securities on margin (i.e., borrow money to purchase stock)?

☐ Yes (10 points)

☐ No (0 points)

Portfolios:

Score	Allocation Mix
0-7	70% Stability; 25% Income; 5% Growth
8-23	50% Stability; 35% Income; 15% Growth
24-38	35% Stability; 40% Income; 25% Growth
39-57	20% Stability; 40% Income; 40% Growth
58-73	10% Stability; 30% Income; 60% Growth
74-88	20% Income; 80% Growth
89-100	100% Growth

bonds, treasuries, money markets, Certificates of Deposit (CDs), and cash. If you invest in stocks and bonds, you should further diversify within each of those categories. For instance, with stocks you might want to balance *large-cap stocks* (stocks from large companies) with *small-cap stocks* (stocks from small companies, which often carry more risk), domestic with international, technology with pharmaceuticals, for example. (By investing in mutual funds, you are automatically reducing your risks because these funds are diversified. Each fund usually invests in somewhere between 30 and 100 stocks. For more on diversification and balancing your investment portfolio, read on.) With bonds, you should consider balancing corporate bonds with municipal bonds and short-term bonds with intermediate-term bonds. You can further diversify your portfolio by mixing stocks or stock mutual funds with bonds or bond mutual funds.

Keep your investment time horizon in mind when considering your risk tolerance. If you're a long-term investor (10 years or longer), you can consider more aggressive investments because there's more time to ride out market fluctuations. Likewise, if you're investing to reach a short-term goal, you should consider more conservative investments. While you can invest more aggressively and possibly earn more than you need to meet your short-term goals, you take the risk of losing all or most of your investment.

Developing an investment plan

Before you start investing, develop an investment plan. That plan may be as general as setting long-term mile markers ("Ten years from now I want to have $200,000") or as specific as working toward an actual goal ("In 5 years I need to have $10,000 for a down payment on a home and in 7 years I need to have another $2,000 for a down payment on a car").

When you figure out your investment goals, and the amount of money it will take to achieve them, your investing strategies become more clear-cut. After you determine your objectives, prioritize them. Then you'll see where your trade-offs are going to have to come from. Being result-oriented should make it easier to save because it will give you an incentive to pass by nonessential purchases that will interfere with reaching your goal.

In any investment plan, the major hurdles you must overcome are inflation and taxes. (To determine the return on your investment, subtract taxes and the cost of inflation (as well as any investment expenses) from your total. The difference is your return.)

Age plays a role in developing a plan. The younger you are, the more time you have to ride out market lows, thus, the more aggressive you can be in your investing strategy. In addition, you should consider your investment time horizon, risk tolerance, goals, and how much money you can afford to invest routinely or in infrequent lump sums.

Moneysaver
Don't think you must come up with large amounts of up-front money to be active in the stock market. If you only have a small amount of money to invest every month, even only $50, you can find investment tools, like mutual funds, that will allow you to invest small amounts incrementally.

Building a diversified portfolio

It's important to build a diversified portfolio to reduce your risk. The mix of securities experts say you should include in your portfolio depends on your age, risk tolerance, and investment goals. Many investment experts say that if you're young, you should consider more aggressive investments because you'll have plenty of time to ride out market volatility. In fact, if your investment time horizon is 10 years or longer, you should consider an aggressive portfolio, at least in part. An aggressive portfolio would include a mix of small- and large-cap stocks, either through building up a portfolio of stocks from different companies or through aggressive growth equity mutual funds, or a combination of both.

You can reduce investment risk further by choosing both domestic and international funds (though not necessarily in equal allotments), different market sectors (since the economy is cyclical), large and small companies, corporate and government bonds, and similar combinations.

If your tolerance for risk is low, or if you have a shorter investment time horizon, you should consider less aggressive securities or a mix of aggressive and conservative investments, such as bonds, treasuries, money markets, and CDs.

Even if you have a long-term investment horizon you can use these conservative investment tools to balance your portfolio and reduce your market risk.

Types of investments

There are many types of investment tools. Each one presents risks and potential benefits. As noted above, you shouldn't limit your portfolio to a single type of investment tool because you'll increase your risk. The only exception is if you have all or mostly mutual funds in your investment portfolio because through mutual funds you can invest in equities, both domestic and international, large- and small-cap stocks, bonds, and Treasuries.

Stocks

You can share in the profits (and losses) of both large and small publicly held companies by purchasing stocks. Some stocks, though, are very expensive, and many you can't buy directly from the company; you must go through a broker and pay fees for the privilege of buying and selling. The advantage of buying stocks in specific companies is that you know exactly what you're getting—you can research the company, its management, as well as its history, credit worthiness, and market forecasts. As a shareholder, you also get to vote on certain company issues. On the other hand, when you invest in single companies, it's hard to get a well-diversified, balanced investment portfolio. To do so, you have to have a lot of money invested. You also have to spend a lot of time researching companies. Even so, it's difficult to thoroughly research small companies and foreign companies.

For more information on investing in stocks, read *The Unofficial Guide to Investing.*

Bonds

When you invest in a bond, you're lending your money to a corporation or to the government. In return, you receive a set amount of interest over a specified period of time, at the end of which, the bond matures and you receive the face value of the bond.

Unlike stocks, where you're buying a slice of ownership in the company, with bonds you're lending money, just like your mortgage lender.

There several types of bonds:

- Government bonds (some offer tax-free earnings and are backed by the government)

- Corporate bonds (bonds issued by private corporations)

- Junk bonds (often issued for takeovers and buyouts, junk bonds are low-rated, high yield, high-risk securities offered by companies with undetermined credit and few earnings or sales records.)

Bright Idea
Like with a mortgage lender, you should be sure to investigate the credit of the bond issuers to decide how much risk they will present to your portfolio.

- Bonds in emerging markets (bonds invested in young markets)

Because some bonds, like those issued by small businesses, carry more risk, they often offer higher yields. However, if the company goes under, you've lost your investment.

Time is a risk factor, too. The shorter the time horizon (maturity date), the lower the risk. But you'll get lower interest rates for shorter maturity dates.

Bonds are rated for risk. The higher the rating, the lower the risk, and the lower the income they will produce for you.

While bonds are typically used to add a conservative balance to an aggressive portfolio, there are two main ways to profit from them:

1. Bonds have price fluctuations (in terms of their marketplace value, not face value), which generally move in the opposite direction of interest rates. These price fluctuations can produce gains or losses if you sell, in addition to the interest the bond pays.

2. Bonds typically have a long-term maturity date, 10 to 30 years from the date they're issued, and a call date, the right of the debtor to call in debt, sometimes at a 2 to 3 percent premium.

Mutual funds

Each mutual fund's portfolio varies widely, and so does the balance of its investments. As with stocks, in exchange for investing in the company, mutual fund investors receive a part of any profit through either an increase in value of the share prices or through quarterly dividends, which is similar to the interest you would receive from money in a bank account.

Watch Out!
Single bonds won't hold their value if interest rates rise in the marketplace. If you're holding a long-term $1,000 bond that pays 5 percent interest, and interest rates jump to 10 percent 8 years into it, you've lost 50 percent of your investment if you decide to sell that bond in order to invest at 10 percent. That is, if you sell a $1,000 bond that generates 5 percent interest (5% X $1000 = $50), it's worth only $500 in a market that's paying 10 percent interest (10% X $500 = $50). But if you hold the bond to maturity, assuming the government or company doesn't default, you won't lose your principal.

Equity funds, which make up the bulk of mutual fund offerings, are made up of shares of stocks in large, midsized, and small companies. They are further broken down by investment style, such as aggressive, and type, such as growth. Within each category are large-cap, midsized-cap, and small-cap stocks, which are investments in large, medium, and small companies. Usually, the size of the company equates with the level of risk. Larger companies are often associated with less risk than smaller start-ups. Equities also can be divided into sectors, such as consumer products, financial services, health care and biotechnology, precious metals, technology, transportation, and utilities. Sector funds are highly volatile because of their narrow focus.

Mutual funds are also divided into domestic, international, and world funds. Domestic funds are invested primarily in the United States. World funds are invested globally, including the United States. International funds are invested outside the United States.

Income funds invest in companies with track records of distributing dividends and/or corporate or government bonds, which, by definition, have a fixed rate of return. Income funds are an investment tool you can use to increase your current income while typically, though not always, preserving your capital.

Although this type of fund is usually a "safer" investment than stock funds, it is, nevertheless, not completely without risk because bond prices fluctuate with changing interest rates. Risk also relates to the type of investments in the portfolio. High-yield funds use lower-rated bonds with longer maturity dates to produce higher incomes. Those types of bond funds are subject to much more volatility.

If you have a hard time deciding what type of mutual fund to invest in, or simply want a variety of stocks that will reflect market performance as a whole, consider *index funds*. Index funds are made up of many of the stocks listed on one of the indices, like the S&P 500. They reflect that index's market performance. These funds have lower fees because they are not actively managed. Typically, they also have fewer realized capital gains (unless you sell shares yourself), again because they are not actively managed, that is, the manager is not trading stocks in an effort to beat the index.

Money market funds are short-term "safe" instruments—short-term papers like government Treasury bills, Treasury notes, and Fannie Maes and Ginnie Maes (both government-backed, mortgage-based investments). Or they can be in short-term corporate obligations. Shareholders receive current money market interest rates and retain asset liquidity, that is, you can access your money when you want it. Some funds offer tax-exempt money market securities.

Tax-exempt money market funds are useful to you if you would have otherwise placed your money in a money market fund, but your income is high enough that your tax bracket would more than compensate for the lower yields put out by these tax-exempt funds.

There are also *bond funds*, which invest in a collection of bonds. They come in many different product lines, like municipal bond funds (munis), which invest in local and state governments, for instance. They also come in different time horizons—short-term, intermediate-term, and long-term bond funds. However, unlike a single bond, bond funds have no single maturity date because the manager is often buying and selling them. Instead, they have an average maturity, which is used to indicate how sensitive the fund is to changes in interest rates. Long-term bond funds are more sensitive to interest rate fluctuations than short-term bond funds.

Bonds funds don't pay regular interest like their single-issue counterparts. Investors get a prorated share of the earnings, that is, dividend payments plus any capital gains.

Bond funds, in contrast to individual bonds, have greater liquidity in case you need quick access to your money.

When choosing a bond fund, look at both the yield (the interest income) and total return, which measures the total gain or loss over time and includes share-price fluctuation and any dividend or capital gains distributions that have been reinvested.

Practicality is one of the biggest benefits to investing in mutual funds. You don't have to be wealthy to be a mutual fund investor, according to Christine S. Fahlund, CFP at T. Rowe Price Associates, Inc., in Baltimore. "With your purchase of even a few shares of one fund you immediately begin diversifying. If it's a stock fund, you own an interest in perhaps hundreds of companies, and if it's a bond fund you may be lending money to 50 or more corporations or municipalities all at once," she says.

Ease is another big bonus. You can often track your fund (or stock) on the Internet, Fahlund notes. Plus, you can arrange to have your investments made automatically. All you have to do is sign up for an automated investment program, and a specified amount will be deducted from your account each

Timesaver
Use the Internet to order prospectuses and to learn more about individual companies. Start your research by visiting the Web page of companies you think might be good investments.

month and invested in your fund portfolio. It's a great way to dollar cost average, which forces you to buy at market lows as well as highs. (For more on dollar cost averaging, see Chapter 1.)

"Mutual fund investing basics are easy to learn, and by applying a simple long-term investment strategy, you, too, can reach the financial goals you desire," Fahlund says.

(For more information on investing in mutual funds, read *The Unofficial Guide to Investing in Mutual Funds.*)

Real estate as an investment

"Buy the most house you can afford" is the conventional wisdom that's been handed down for years to first-time homebuyers. Real estate agents tell prospective buyers that their salaries will increase over time, making the stretch of buying the most home they can afford more palatable. When real estate prices were escalating in the 1970s and early 1980s, this home-buying strategy made good financial sense. At that time, the baby boomers were settling into family life, resulting in a significant increase in demand for real estate, and for single-family homes in particular.

There are additional factors why that conventional wisdom may not hold true in today's real estate market. Household size has changed in the last several decades. In 1960, the average household size was 3.3 people; today it's 2.6, according to Mark Eppli, Ph.D., professor of real estate and finance at George Washington University, reducing the need for larger homes. Moreover, while single-person households are growing fairly quickly, the number of married couple households continues to decline,

Bright Idea
Even though you can get a income tax deduction on a more expensive home, if you buy a less expensive home, you can use the extra money to invest in the stock market, which historically has returned between 10 and 12 percent annually.

according to Eppli, a trend he expects to continue with couples getting married at later ages than in the past, again, decreasing the demand for larger single-family homes..

In addition, between 1980 and 1992, the median household income for married couples was about $40,000 (in 1992 dollars), Eppli says. For single parents and non-family (single person and cohabitation) households, the median household income was about $17,000. It is unlikely that these single-headed households will meet lender's requirements for large mortgages.

Furthermore, demand for housing was high during the 1970s and early 1980s because of low interest rates for mortgages and higher income tax rates for upper tax brackets. Back then, borrowers were paying 6 percent interest for their mortgages while inflation was at 8 or 9 percent. Plus, higher income taxes made it more advantageous to own because of the tax deductions.

"In short, in today's real estate marketplace, where households are shrinking and house appreciation rates are slowing, purchasing the most home you can afford may not be the best strategy," Eppli says.

Tax savings

While housing demands, and consequently appreciation, are currently lower compared with the 1970s and early 1980s, there are still plenty of financial benefits to being a homeowner. Investing in a primary residence gives you a capital gains tax shelter. The current capital gains exclusion is $500,000 ($250,000 for singles), and age is no longer a factor in qualifying for it. This exclusion is available once every two years for each home that is used as your primary residence.

Moneysaver
If you are investing for the long run, you should expect to do better in the market than the 5 to 6 percent you would be paying on after-tax basis (in the 31 percent tax bracket) on an 8 percent fixed-rate mortgage. In equities, the average return over the last 70 years has been between 10 and 12 percent.

This tax exemption may make owning a home as an investment more profitable than investing in the stock market. Here's why: If you buy a stock, and sell it 10 years later, you must pay a 20 percent capital gains tax on the increase in value. But your house can increase in value up to $500,000 ($250,000 if you're single) before you'll have to pay a capital gains tax on the profit when you sell it.

While home buyers tend to focus on the tax deductions they get from their monthly mortgage payments, these deductions aren't as valuable as they were in the 1970s, when top earners were in the 50 percent federal tax bracket. For those mortgage holders, every dollar paid in mortgage interest was worth 50 cents in federal tax savings. These days, however, those in the highest tax bracket (39.6 percent rate) are only getting 39.6 cents back on each federally taxed dollar.

Leveraging: getting the most bang for your buck

If you are including your home as part of your investment portfolio, consider this: When inflation is high, it makes sense to buy as much house as you can afford, a strategy called *leveraging*. (When a low inflationary period is expected, buy only what you need.)

Leveraging—using credit to enhance your speculative capacity—is a way to use debt to your advantage. The advantage comes from borrowing more and investing less in a high inflationary period.

If you borrow 80 percent (you put $20,000 down, or 20 percent, on a $100,000 home) from a bank, you are leveraged 5:1. Therefore, for every percent increase in inflation, the amount of increase in the value of your equity investment is multiplied by a factor of five.

For example, if you buy a house for $100,000, get an $80,000 mortgage, and put $20,000 down during a year with a 10 percent annual rate of inflation, after one year your house would be worth $110,000. You would have made $10,000 dollars off a $20,000 investment. That's a 50 percent return. Now you own a larger percentage of your home, a profit you can take with you when you sell it. Remember, though, after adjusting for the 10 percent inflation, your original equity has lost $2,000 (a 10 percent inflation reduces the buying power of a dollar by 10 percent). So your $20,000 investment has gained $10,000, lost $2,000, for a net gain of $8,000. Note, however, that when your house increases in value, you become less leveraged because your equity has increased.

While you want to have leverage, Bernie Kent, Midwest regional partner in charge of financial planning at PriceWaterhouseCoopers in Detroit, advises putting at least 20 percent down on a mortgage loan to avoid paying private mortgage insurance (PMI), which is required by the lender on most loans with down payments of less than 20 percent. The insurance costs are not tax deductible, and the premiums increase the cost of the mortgage by about 2 percent over the life of the loan, he says. This money is thrown away, in a sense, because it yields no return.

But, like with most investments, being leveraged is risky. Leveraging (the use of debt in financing your home) can mean painful losses during periods of depreciation in the real estate marketplace. Returning to our example above, if the value of your home decreases 10 percent, you've lost half your investment. (Your $100,000 home is now worth

$90,000, a $10,000 loss, a 50 percent loss on your $20,000 investment.)

You should also keep in mind that generally older homes tend to depreciate, not appreciate, as newer ones do. (This is not true where there is a shortage of supply, like in historic districts, and a high demand.) Say your $100,000 home depreciates just 1 percent. This means that it's now worth $99,000. If you had started with a $20,000 down payment, your investment would be reduced to $19,000, a 5 percent loss.

Before you get scared off, consider this: If you can borrow money at a fixed rate of 8 percent and invest it in the market at a 10 percent annual rate of return, it pays to borrow the most you can, in other words, leverage as much of your home as possible. With a 3 percent inflation rate and an 8 percent fixed loan rate, inflation is markedly less than the cost of borrowing.

The reality is that prices in today's housing market generally aren't climbing like they were in the 1980s. Salaries aren't skyrocketing as quickly, either. You have to make reasonable judgments so you won't lose money buying and selling. The most basic rule to preserving your savings is to diversify your investments.

Enlisting the aid of a financial advisor

For some people, getting their finances in order is a difficult task. It's hard to see where you're spending your money, where you can cut back without feeling too deprived, and where you should invest your money. Even once you're on track, it's often difficult to resist temptation and not dip into your savings, and it's hard not to want to protect your assets when the market tumbles.

Bright Idea
One of the best fixed-income investments you could make is paying down your mortgage, according to Bernie Kent, Midwest regional partner in charge of financial planning at Pricewaterhouse-Coopers. Even with a 7 percent fixed-rate mortgage, it's better to pay down your mortgage than to invest in fixed-income market investments, such as treasuries, which currently have about a 5 percent interest rate.

Usually people look to financial advisors to check if they're handling their finances in a way that will best meet their goals and objectives, to see what's best for their tax situation, and to get the advisor's perspective of the market, says Gary Schatsky, vice chair of the National Association of Personal Financial Advisors (NAPFA) and a fee-only financial planner in New York. Others, he says, come in with a specific question—like how should they plan for retirement, can they afford to buy a new home, and how should they fund their children's education—or with a specific problem.

If you don't have the time or desire to handle your investments, or if you think you'll be unable to resist depleting your hard-earned savings, you may want to consider enlisting the aid of a financial advisor. This person can help you refine your spending habits, invest your money, and learn to sit tight when the market becomes volatile. While they cost money, if they do their jobs well, a good financial advisor can save you money in the long run.

Finding a financial advisor is a task in and of itself. You can locate one at a bank, through referrals from friends and family members, from a list in *Worth* magazine's annual pick of advisors, or through cold calls to people you find in the phone book or on the Web. You can also check out the Internet; try for starters:

- www.napfa.org (National Association of Personal Financial Advisors)
- www.iafp.org (International Association for Financial Planning)
- www.icfp.org (Institute of Certified Financial Planners)

But you still must give thoughtful consideration as to whether this person can actually help you. An ideal relationship should last a lifetime, Schatsky says.

There are several things you should look for in a financial planner, not the least of which is competence. To evaluate competence, ask yourself the following questions:

- Does the advisor offer comprehensive financial planning, that is, will he or she examine your entire financial situation, or does this person focus only on what you have to invest?

- What's his or her educational background? Financial planners have many different educational backgrounds, including CPAs, MBAs, JDs, and CFP licensees or a combination of these. Though the majority of Certified Financial Planner (CFP) licensees have college or advanced degrees, it is not a requirement. Degrees alone should not stand as an indicator of competence in financial planning.

- Does he or she take continuing education courses?

- What professional associations does this person belong to? Do the groups to which he or she belongs have high standards for ethics, education, and admission to the group, including a review of his or her work?

- What experience does the advisor have with clients like you? This person may be good at handling physicians or middle-class income earners, but that doesn't help you if you are neither of these.

The trust factor should also be stressed in your decision-making process. The person you choose may be acting as your *fiduciary*. (Many financial planners, in addition to providing you with a comprehensive financial plan, can serve as an investment advisor.) Because of this—and the possibility that he or she will be tempted to put his or her own needs before yours (for example, by selling you commission-based mutual funds that don't really meet your needs just to earn a fee)—Schatsky suggests asking your financial advisor to sign a fiduciary oath, which states that he or she will put your interests first and that he or she is not working for anyone else (that is, they are not working as a salesperson for an insurance company or an investment house). (Note, however, that many financial planners work on commission only, which is not necessarily a negative factor. These people can be equally astute and motivated to look out for your best interests and may work out to be less expensive than a fee-only advisor if you need a lot of hand-holding. See the discussion later in this chapter.)

Another important consideration in choosing your financial advisor is your comfort level with him or her. This person is going to be asking you a lot of personal questions, like information about your household income; assets, and debts; your monthly, quarterly, and annual expenses; your expected inheritances; your insurance policies and coverages; whether you have a will and/or a trust; what medical problems are in your family; your short- and long-term financial goals; your tolerance for risk; and more. In fact, if your advisor doesn't ask you all these personal questions, don't feel relieved. This person will not come away with a full picture of your

Bright Idea
You can download a pro forma fiduciary oath free of charge from the National Association of Personal Financial Advisors' Web site at www.napfa.org, or call toll free (888) 333-6659 to have it mailed to you.

financial life or needs, and therefore will not be able to help you create a comprehensive financial plan.

The ability to listen carefully is another key factor you should consider when selecting a financial advisor. In order to gather your financial information, your advisor must hear what you're telling him or her. You can assess listening and evaluation skills during your first appointment, which is usually free. If the advisor asks you only a few questions before telling you what you need, it's likely that he or she is more of a salesperson than a professional financial advisor. It should take several sessions of careful listening before the advisor can create a plan that meets your goals and risk tolerance level.

What's it going to cost you?

Financial advisors are compensated in a variety of ways. Some financial investors work on a fee-only basis, as discussed earlier in this chapter. If you have significant assets, this form of payment might be more economical, especially if you don't need much hand-holding when the market dips.

But the fee-only payment structure may lessen the financial planner's incentive to place you in funds with the very best performance records because researching funds takes time. And, if you're worried about spending money on this service, this might not be the best payment method for you because each time you call your advisor, the clock starts ticking.

In addition to a fee-only basis, the advisor you choose may be paid a percent of your total assets, compensated on a commission-only, fee and commission, or fee-offset basis (the flat fee is offset by a commission). In any case, check to see if anyone at the advisor's firm receives additional

Watch Out!
Financial advisors who get paid by commission probably won't suggest many products to you simply because they're not compensated for buying them on your behalf. In fact, one third of all mutual funds don't offer advisors a commission, so it's likely that none of those funds will be included in your portfolio.

compensation for selling certain securities or insurance policies. This may be the case if the firm pays through loads (commissions) from the mutual funds in which the advisor invests your money, in which case his or her payment is considered transaction (commission)-based. Again, this isn't necessarily a bad approach, but you need to be aware of how your advisor is compensated to be able to spot red flags, should they appear. An advisor who is compensated by the number of transactions he or she performs has an inherent incentive to move you in and out of funds (though many don't), which would place you in the position of continually having to pay taxes on capitals gains, if there are any. And, if you haven't held your investment for at least 12 months, you'll have to pay short-term capital gains tax on it rather than long-term capital gains tax, which can be costly.

Transaction-based trading has additional consequences. For example, frequent trading forces you to pay high back loads (sales commissions triggered when you sell shares) on certain funds because many back loads phase out only after you've held your investment for a period of time, in many cases five years.

Similarly, moving in and out of front-loaded funds (those that charge a sales commission up front) also costs you in up-front commissions. Some funds have transaction costs, redemption charges, and frequent-activity fees, as well. Stock trades incur brokerage fees.

By paying extra commissions, fees, and capital gains taxes, your principal investment is reduced unnecessarily, and, as a result, your earning power is reduced.

Furthermore, this transaction-based payment structure can be used for *churning*, an unethical and, in most states, illegal practice used by some unscrupulous salespeople to increase their commissions by turning over securities (specifically to increase their sales commissions) more frequently than needed to meet the investor's goals.

Note that some firms have their own investment products and the planner may get additional compensation for selling them to you. But those investments may not best meet your needs. Your portfolio should be tailored to *your* needs, not to line your advisor's pockets or meet his or her quotas.

Asset-based commissions and fee-only compensation come with problems, too. Under an asset-based commission scheme of payment, the greater your assets, the higher your advisor's commission (which is a percentage of your total assets). While asset-based commissions give no incentive—and in fact act as a deterrent—for the advisor to move you in and out of funds, they do, inherently, encourage him or her to put you in aggressive funds because the higher the return, the more he or she profits from your investment. (For reasons discussed above, you must be careful not to allow your advisor to heavily weight your portfolio with aggressive, high-risk funds to get quick gains, unless your risk tolerance is high, and aggressive investments will help you meet your investment goals.)

Because it takes no more effort for an advisor to perform a transaction for a $5 million account than it does for an account valued at $10,000, if you have considerable assets, you might want to request a reduced commission rate. And no matter what your assets total, you may want to structure an incentive into the compensation. For example, for every $10,000 gain, the advisor gets an additional 10 percent of the profit. Likewise, you may want to protect your investment by mandating that your advisor's compensation be based on *increases* in assets, not total assets. (Be aware, however, that this sort of payment structure gives the advisor an incentive to place your assets in aggressive investments.)

You must also be cautious if you're hiring a fee-only advisor, Schatsky says. Some salespeople change the way they market what they do by calling many of the services they provide "fee-only."

In fact, he says, many of these people often sell products. Their perspective is skewed, he explains. Schatsky believes that if a person is selling a particular product for half a day, he or she will come to believe that that product is a good one, regardless of whether or not it actually is, or whether it is well-suited for his or her client's specific needs.

Be suspicious when an advisor tells you he or she works on a "fee-based" basis, Schatsky warns. Fee-based and fee-only are *not* necessarily the same thing. True fee-only advisors don't get kickbacks or referral fees. They are paid directly by you.

How much should a fee-only advisor charge? A complete financial review, according to Schatsky, should cost from $500 to a few thousand dollars, depending on the complexity of the case, geographic location, and the advisor's experience.

Planners who oversee $25 million or more in assets must be registered with the Securities and Exchange Commission (SEC). (If they oversee less than $25 million they must be registered with state securities regulators.) Being registered means that the advisor filled out an ADV form and paid a fee. It does not mean that they are competent. The SEC

Unofficially...
Performance-based fees are allowed under federal law only for institutional accounts or clients with over $1 million net worth and $500,000 under management with that advisor. Although federal law allows for this exception, most states prohibit performance-based fees.

requires advisors to give their new clients a copy of the ADV disclosure brochure, Part II. This discloses the terms of compensation, including any payments and/or commissions received by sponsors of financial products they may recommend.

Request to see Part I of the ADV, as well. It outlines security violations, among other things. You can get the ADV directly from the SEC by writing to the Securities and Exchange Commission, 450 Fifth Street NW, Washington DC 20549.

Besides the planner's fees or commissions, be sure to find out if there will be any charges for opening, maintaining, and closing an account. (For more information on fees associated with investing read *The Unofficial Guide to Investing in Mutual Funds.*)

Putting your advisor to work

Once you have chosen a financial advisor, you'll probably be required to complete certain legal paperwork. Many brokerage firms will require you to sign a new account agreement. Read this document carefully, because it can affect your legal rights.

According to the Securities and Exchange Commission (SEC), completing a new account agreement requires making three critical determinations:

1. You must choose who will make decisions regarding your account. You'll maintain control unless you decide to give discretionary authority to your financial advisor, in which case your advisor can make investment decisions "without consulting you about the price, the type of security, the amount, and when to buy or sell," according to the SEC.

2. You must agree on a payment method for your investments.

3. You must stipulate the amount of risk you'll assume by specifying your investment objectives, such as "income," "growth," or "aggressive growth."

According to the SEC, when you open a new account, "the brokerage firm may ask you to sign a legally binding contract to arbitrate any future disputes between you and the firm or your sales representative." This contract may be part of another document. "The federal securities laws do not require that you sign such an agreement," according to the SEC. If you do sign, however, you give up the right to sue your advisor and the brokerage firm in court. However, you can still arbitrate disputes for damages without going to court. Arbitration is typically faster and less expensive for all parties involved.

Whether or not you choose to sign an arbitration contract, don't *ever* rely on verbal agreements with a financial advisor. Insist that everything be placed in writing before handing over a dime.

Just the facts

- There are many types of risk, including inflation, which can eat away the value of uninvested dollars.

- Know your risk tolerance level before setting up an investment plan.

- You should make sure your investment portfolio is well diversified in order to reduce risk.

- Leveraging your home during periods of high appreciation in the real estate marketplace can be a financially sound investment strategy.

GET THE SCOOP ON...
Why good, flexible health insurance is so
important ▪ Term insurance versus other types
of life insurance ▪ What home and renter's
insurance policies cover and what they don't ▪
Why auto insurance coverage is necessary

Safeguarding Your Assets and Your Family

Chapter 5

Insurance premiums can eat up a relatively large portion of your income. But without insurance coverage, you leave your assets—all that you've worked so hard to attain—completely unprotected. Which also means you leave your family at risk. It only takes one catastrophe to put you deep in debt.

In this chapter I'll tell you about some of the different types of insurance coverages, including health insurance, long-term care insurance, life insurance, home insurance, and auto insurance.

Health insurance

It doesn't take much—a diagnosis of cancer, diabetes, a heart attack—to eat up your savings and put you in massive debt if you don't have health insurance.

Of all types of insurance, this is the most important to have. You need it to protect yourself and your family. You need it to be able to afford good doctors and hospitals even if you don't have much money.

Health insurance coverage is the great equalizer in gaining access to good medical care.

Usually, your employer will offer you health insurance. Often, you can select from a menu of different types of coverages.

There are two broad categories of health insurance coverage. The first is *fee-for-service*. The second is *managed care*. Under managed care there are *health maintenance organizations* (HMOs), *preferred provider organizations* (PPOs), and *point-of-service* (POS) plans.

Fee-for-service policies and managed care plans have distinct differences in the amount of control the policyholder has in choosing doctors and hospitals. This is an important distinction if you have or are diagnosed with a serious medical condition or disease. For instance, if you are diagnosed with cancer, you may want to seek medical treatment at a major cancer center that specializes in that specific type of cancer, rather than have only a choice of a few oncologists registered with your plan. Plans that offer that amount of choice—fee-for-service plans—are usually more expensive than managed care plans.

Fee-for-service and managed care health plans both cover an array of medical, surgical, and hospital expenses. Some policies offer prescription drug, eye care, and dental coverage, as well. Individual health insurance policies vary in terms of what they cover.

Fee-for-service

Under a fee-for-service setup, your doctor will submit a bill to your insurance provider, or, if he or she does not have a relationship with your provider, you may have to pay the bill directly and get reimbursed from your provider. Under this plan, you can see any doctor you want. There is no gatekeeper telling you that you cannot see a specialist, nor are you limited to any particular hospital.

If you are covered under a fee-for-service structure, you'll be reimbursed for a percentage of the doctor's bill. Usually, you're covered for 80 percent of the visit. So if your doctor's bill is $60, you'll be responsible for paying $12 for that visit.

Fee-for-service plans also have an annual deductible, usually starting at $100 for individuals and $500 for families, though those numbers vary among policies. Generally, the higher your deductible, the lower your premiums. Before receiving any reimbursement, you'll have to pay the deductible amount. So in the example above, you would have to visit the doctor two times before the deductible is met. For your second visit, you would be reimbursed $16 (80 percent of $20, which is the difference after the $100 deductible is met). For visits after that during the same calendar year, you would be reimbursed $48 (the full 80 percent of the $60 visit).

If your doctor charges more than is "reasonable and customary" in your area, you will be responsible for paying the difference. For instance, if doctors in your area normally charge $60 per visit and your doctor charges $80 per visit, you'll be responsible for the extra $20, plus 20 percent of the $60. However, you have the option of appealing your insurance company's denial of the extra coverage if you can prove that other doctors in the area are charging that much as well.

Under a fee-for-service plan there is usually a limit to how much you will have to pay out of pocket before the plan reimburses you at 100 percent.

Some plans also have a lifetime limit on benefits, usually at least $1 million. Though that may sound like a lot, if you develop a condition, are stricken with a disease, or are seriously injured, medical expenses can (and do) exceed that amount. It is a good idea to make sure that the lifetime limit on your policy is at least $1 million.

Managed care

There are three major types of managed care health plans: HMOs, PPOs, and POSs. Many of these plans charge a copayment, for example, $10 or $20 per visit.

If you join an HMO, you *must* use the doctors and hospitals that participate in the plan or you'll have to pay for your medical care out of your own pocket.

HMOs typically do not have annual deductibles, and the premiums are less expensive than fee-for-service policies.

HMOs often have medical facilities where patient care is delivered. There is also a subcategory of HMOs called *individual practice associations* (IPAs). In this setup, individual practitioners are grouped together to provide patient care under an HMO. These practitioners may also practice under other HMOs and PPOs, and may provide patient care under a fee-for-service structure, as well. In an IPA setting, each HMO patient visits the doctor at his or her private office.

If you decide to join an HMO, you'll be asked to choose a *primary care physician.* That doctor will be responsible for coordinating your care. If you need to see a specialist, your primary care physician must approve it, that is, you must get an authorization from him or her or you will not be covered under

Watch Out!
In some managed care plans doctors have a monetary incentive to limit the care you receive. Your physician may reduce his or her expenses by scheduling your visit with a nonphysician practitioner, like a nurse practitioner or physician assistant, who costs less, or your physician may deny your request to see a specialist.

the plan for the visit to the specialist. It has been widely reported that many primary care doctors do not want to give authorization because to do so will affect his or her bottom line since doctors in some HMO setups have to foot the bill for patient referrals. This is one of the circumstances under which patients in an HMO lose control over their own medical care.

Members of HMOs must also get an authorization for hospitalizations. (There are exceptions for emergencies, for instance, if you need to go to the emergency room or need emergency surgery.) The request goes through a utilization review where plan administrators determine if the medical or surgical service you need is appropriate and/or medically necessary.

This is another one of those circumstances where you may lose control over the administration of your health care. Many patients and their families have filed lawsuits because they could not get the care that they (and their doctors) say they needed. State insurance commissioners' files are filled with complaints against managed care plans resulting from this administrative procedure; these cases have led to a move toward making it legal to sue administrators for malpractice when patients suffer adverse medical outcomes resulting from decisions based on cost management.

PPOs and POSs (the latter usually has a primary care physician coordinating your care) are also considered managed care plans, but differ from HMOs in several ways. Like HMOs, these plans have a network of providers, but they also allow you to seek medical help from physicians outside the network. Premiums are somewhat higher than HMOs, but the patient has more control over his or her health care. If you choose a provider inside the plan, you'll have a copayment, usually $10 or $20 per visit. If you go outside of the plan, you'll typically be covered at 80 percent, like with the fee-for-service plans. You also may be responsible for annual deductibles if you choose a physician outside the network.

Under all of these managed care plans, you'll pay the same copayment regardless of the level of care you receive. For example, if you need to see a nurse to provide a urine sample, you'll be charged the same amount as if you had seen a doctor who provided a complete physical.

Coverage through work and other options

Most people get their health-care coverage through their employer. But if your employer does not offer group medical coverage, or if you do not like the policies offered, you have two other options. You can buy an individual policy, which usually has higher premiums than those you'd be paying at the office, or you can get group coverage through some professional, civic, or religious organizations or through a union. Premiums for group coverage are usually much lower than for individual policies.

There's a benefit to getting coverage at work. Usually, your employer will foot a good portion, if not all, of the bill for you, the employee. The cost of additional coverage for your family is minimal compared with individual policy premiums.

Another big bonus with group coverage is that generally you will not be asked about your health or the health of your family to qualify for coverage. (Some policies, however, do carry an exclusion of coverage, known as a preexisting condition clause, for up to 12 months for conditions or illnesses that you or your family have been treated for recently.)

Some employers, due to the high cost of group insurance, opt for self-insured benefit plans. With this type of plan, the employer reimburses employees for their medical expenses covered under the plan. Typically, the employer hires a company to process the claims.

Pre-existing conditions and the law

You may have to wait for up to 12 months to receive coverage for any preexisting condition treated or diagnosed in the previous 6 months prior to getting new coverage. However, your prior insurance coverage will be credited for the preexisting condition exclusion period if you have maintained continuous coverage for more than 62 days. There are exceptions to this rule: Newborns and adopted children are not subject to the waiting period, nor are pregnant women. Furthermore, if you've had health coverage for at least two years and then switch jobs and health plans, you won't be affected by the exclusion period. The Health Insurance Portability and Accountability Act (HIPPA) is responsible for these recent changes.

If you were fired or left a job where you had group health insurance coverage, see Chapter 14, which provides information on COBRA and the Kassebaum-Kennedy Act (HIPAA).

Working into your golden years

If you decide to work after age 65, your employer must offer you the same health coverage offered to other employees (until you turn 70 years old). However, at age 65 you must choose between Medicare or the company's plan for your primary insurer. Medicare Part A will cover hospitalization at no additional cost to you. But be sure to enroll in Medicare Part B (medical) when you turn age 65.

Unofficially...
If you have a claim or other problem with this a self-insured benefit plan, contact the U.S. Department of Labor (www.dol.gov; 202/219-8776). Problems with all other group or individual insurance coverage should be directed to your state's insurance commissioner's office.

Do so promptly: Delaying enrollment is more expensive and forces you into a waiting period for coverage.

Shopping for a policy

When comparison shopping for health insurance, read policies carefully to make sure you receive the coverage that you need. Be sure to consider the following availability of coverages:

- Pregnancy
- Well-baby care
- Vision
- Dental
- Prescription medication
- Mental health
- Home health-care visits
- Physical therapy
- Speech therapy
- Drug and alcohol abuse treatment
- Hospice care
- Alternative medicine
- Long-term care
- Preventive care (wellness programs/physical exams)

Read the policy carefully to see if there are any exclusions or other limitations that will affect your coverage.

After finding several policies that will give you the medical coverage you want, compare prices by contrasting premiums, deductibles, and copayments (or the percentage you are required to pay out of pocket) to see which policy is the least expensive. Remember that to make the most sense financially,

Watch Out!
If you have trouble getting a claim covered, you can file a complaint with your state's department of insurance. Take note, though, that the information you provide becomes public record.

your coverage must be comprehensive and flexible in case the need arises to see a specialist at a reputable hospital.

Disability insurance

Disability insurance is often overlooked, says Carrie Coghill, CFP and senior vice president/financial advisor at D. B. Root and Company in Pittsburgh, Pennsylvania. If you become disabled, however, you must consider how you'll be taken care of and how you'll provide for your family.

If you get sick or are injured and unable to work, disability insurance will provide you with income while you recover. Sometimes employers provide disability insurance coverage. But if yours doesn't, it's a good idea to buy a policy in order to protect your savings. Look for a policy that has cost-of-living adjustments. Most policies will pay you 60 percent of the income you're earning at the time you purchase the policy.

You won't have to pay income tax on disability premium payments if you're the one who pays the premiums for an individual policy. If your employer pays the premiums, however, the benefits are taxable.

When shopping for policies, compare prices and the time you must wait before benefits are paid out (usually six months). Consider whether it would be worth it to pay higher premiums for a shorter waiting period. If your income is high, do you want to risk losing all that money? If your income is low, how long can you afford to go without any pay? Generally, the longer the waiting period, the lower the premiums.

The length of time you receive disability payments varies among policies. Consider getting a

Watch Out!
Some disability policies only cover you for accidents. Make sure your policy covers you for illnesses, too.

policy that covers you until retirement, especially if you're young. Otherwise, there may be a long period of time during which you may not be covered.

You must be healthy when you apply for disability insurance. And to receive payments, you must be legitimately disabled. There are exceptions, which vary by plan.

When you shop for disability insurance, consider buying a base policy that will meet your income needs, and don't let the agent talk you into purchasing all the other bells and whistles available, suggests Michael Chasnoff, CFP and president of Advanced Capital Strategies, Inc., in Cincinnati, Ohio. Additional features, such as cost-of-living adjustments tied to the Consumer Price Index and an automatic increase in benefits after a specified period of time, can triple the premium charge because these are highly commissionable, he says.

An alternative to disability insurance is an income replacement plan, Chasnoff says. As its name implies, this plan offers coverage that replaces loss of income, but not just due to becoming disabled. Therefore, it is not a true disability insurance plan, he adds. With an income replacement plan, you can lose your job due to downsizing and still be covered. Today, most major companies write their policies this way, Chasnoff notes.

While there is a wide range of disability coverages, an income replacement plan is all you really need, Chasnoff says. This type of plan pays a percentage of your salary if you cannot work for a prolonged period of time. For example, if you are making $50,000 a year, you can get coverage to replace 60 to 70 percent of that—$30,000 to $35,000 annually. (There aren't any policies that replace 100 percent of your income because insurance companies want to give you an incentive to get back to work.) But if you're capable of working in another "qualified" field, that is, within the scope of your training and expertise, you must. If you're a surgeon, you won't be expected to flip burgers, but you would be expected to do administrative work or teach if a job is available and you are capable of doing it, Chasnoff says.(The insurance is not supposed to be treated as vacation pay, he says.)

In addition to paying benefits on 60 percent of your income, the insurance will cover 80 percent of the difference in income between your former job and your new one (if there is any difference). For example, assume you were earning $100,000 a year at your former job, and you have income replacement insurance covering you for 60 percent, or $60,000. If you make $50,000 in your new job, the policy would cover $8,000 of the $10,000 shortfall because you're insured for $60,000. (80 percent of $10,000 equals $8,000.)

If you don't want to be obligated to work in another field, there are "own occupancy" policies. These insure you if you can't perform the work in your own profession. Needless to say, these policies are priced higher.

No matter what type of coverage you choose, read the policy carefully. It determines which disabilities are covered.

Long-term care coverage

Nursing home care can be very expensive—about $40,000 a year. In-home care is cheaper, but still costly. If you need this type of care due to a chronic illness or disability, you may not be covered under your general health-care policy. Therefore, you may want to consider buying long-term care coverage as well. Long-term care plans offer several types and levels of benefits, such as nursing home care, home health care, and adult day care.

Most long-term care policies pay a fixed amount per day for nursing home care and in-home care, though there is an extreme difference in terms of reimbursement levels among them. If you buy a policy with a daily coverage that does not cover daily charges, either you will have to foot the bill for the shortfall or find a less expensive nursing home. Many policies offer an inflation adjustment feature to cover the increase in costs over time. In order to protect your assets in the future, you may want to consider getting a policy with this feature.

Medicare does *not* cover long-term care expenses. That's why many elderly people give their savings away to their children and grandchildren in order to preserve their heirs' inheritances and, at the same time, be eligible for Medicaid nursing home coverage. In some states, where there are large numbers of retired people, financial planners and attorneys have developed a specialization in this area of financial planning, that is, helping people give away their assets in order to qualify for Medicaid. This method of "saving money" has significant drawbacks. First, many older people stay healthy and don't need to live in a nursing home. At the same time, however, to qualify for Medicaid, their total worth must decrease significantly, which will reduce their standard of living. In fact, if they deplete their savings completely, they may end up living out their golden years in poverty. They may not be able to afford to travel, dine out in nice restaurants, or even buy enough groceries. Some elderly people in this position "save" money by skimping on their medications, which can result in health complications.

Long-term care coverage is offered by some health plans. Check for the duration of coverage for nursing home and in-home care. (For a more extensive discussion on long-term care coverage, including how to judge a policy, how agents spin the coverage, and ratings of insurance plans, see *Consumer Reports* Online, "Long-Term Care Coverage" (October 1997).)

Homeowner's and renter's insurance

You just need to look at the property damage left behind from the widespread forest fires in California and Florida, the floods in the Midwest, and the torrential storms that have hit this nation's coasts in the past few years to see how important it is to have your home and its contents covered by insurance. It would be devastating enough losing your home and your possessions, but it would be much worse not to have enough money to rebuild it and replace its contents.

Of course, there are other reasons to carry insurance coverage on your home. It protects you against losses due to theft, as well as damage to either the structure or contents in certain circumstances. It also protects you from lawsuits if someone other than a resident gets hurt when visiting.

According to the National Association of Insurance Commissioners (NAIC), home insurance is not required by law in most states. But if you have a mortgage, your lender will likely require you to have it.

Bright Idea
Before buying an insurance policy, make sure the issuer is in good standing with the state and check the company's business rating with Standard & Poor, Moody's, or the A. M. Best Company.

Either way, you need home insurance—as well as other kinds of insurance—to protect your assets. If you rent your home, you'll need renter's insurance to protect your furniture and other personal property. Regardless of whether you own or rent, you need to protect yourself against liability for accidents that might injure other people or damage their property. Home insurance policies cover do just that.

How much is enough?

How much home insurance do you need and what deductible should you get? In order to best protect your assets, you want the fullest coverage possible. Though comprehensive policies are more expensive than more basic ones, in the event of a disaster, your assets are better protected. Furthermore, with lawsuits almost commonplace, you need coverage to protect yourself against liability.

The amount you'll pay for your policy depends on various factors. First and foremost are the amount of commission paid and the overhead costs of the insurance company. Other factors include the age of the home (newer homes are less expensive to insure), the type of construction (brick houses are less expensive than frame houses to insure), and local fire protection (locations of fire hydrants and the performance and proximity of your local fire department determine your fire protection class).

Additional factors that affect your overall cost include the amount of coverage you buy, any discounts (for instance, if you have deadbolt locks on all your doors or insure your cars with the same company), and the deductible amount. Higher deductibles reduce premiums, but they can end up costing you if you need to make a claim.

What kind should you buy?

There are four kinds of basic coverage available:

- Property damage
- Additional living expenses
- Personal liability
- Medical payments

Property damage applies not only to your home but also to other structures, such as tool sheds, detached garages, and contents within the house, including personal property.

Property coverage generally covers your personal belongings. But some personal property, such as valuables, antiques, and jewelry, as well as computers and cash, have only limited coverage. You may need to buy additional insurance for full coverage on these items.

When you buy insurance, you can choose to insure your belongings at *replacement cost* or *actual cash value.* Replacement cost (the cost of replacing the property without a reduction for depreciation) is the amount it would cost you to buy that item new. In terms of your home, it's the amount of money it would cost to rebuild or repair damages without deducting for depreciation.

Actual cash value includes *depreciation,* which is the decrease in value of your home and property due to age and wear and tear. As a general rule, it is always advisable to carry replacement value insurance over actual cash value. That way, if you need to replace your 10-year-old VCR because it is damaged in a natural disaster or stolen, your insurance will pay what it would cost to get a comparable VCR *today*, not the actual value of *your* VCR, which could be only $50.

Upgrades and additions, as well as inflation, affect the value of your home. NAIC suggests checking once a year with your real estate agent or insurance company to make sure you have adequate coverage.

If your home is damaged by an insured event and you can't live there while repairs are being made, most policies provide additional living expense payments to cover limited lodging, restaurants, and warehouse storage costs.

In these litigious times, personal liability coverage protects you from a claim or lawsuit resulting from bodily injury or property damage to others caused by your negligence.

If someone is accidentally injured on your property, regardless of who was at fault, medical payment coverage pays for medical expenses. Note, however, that this coverage doesn't cover medical costs associated with a home-based business or injuries suffered by other family members living with you.

There are additional coverages, at additional costs, that you might want to consider buying. These additions are sometimes offered as endorsements, a provision added to the insurance contract, to your general policy. Earthquake coverage is a common endorsement to a home insurance policy. Sometimes additional coverages are added as riders to the policy. The difference between a personal property endorsement and adding a rider for specific items of value will largely depend on the underwriting policy of the insurance company. For instance, one insurance policy may cover a computer under an endorsement, while another one may make you add a rider for an extra premium.

These additional coverages include:

- Guaranteed replacement cost coverage. This is the most complete coverage for your home. Premiums for this type of insurance may not stay the same throughout the year. They may be adjusted to keep up with inflation, although the adjustment may be made on a yearly basis.

- Inflation guard endorsement. With inflation, the value of your house may rise, making it difficult for your coverage to stay at 80 percent. This endorsement allows your insurance company to automatically change your policy limit, and, generally, the higher premium isn't paid until you renew the policy. With this type of coverage it's wise to periodically check to make sure you're not overinsured, and hence, overpaying.

- Scheduled personal property endorsement, also called a "personal article floater." This additional coverage covers personal possessions of value—such as antiques, jewelry, furs, stamps, and even gold—that may exceed the normal limits of your home insurance policy. Using this floater, each personal article is itemized with a description. The good thing about this coverage is that there's no deductible.

- Increased limits on money and securities. This endorsement is used to increase coverage on deeds, cash, securities, bank notes, and more.

- Secondary residence endorsement. If you have a summer home or other secondary residence, you may need this type of coverage, because your home coverage only covers your primary residence.

Bright Idea
Check with your insurance company to see if there are exclusions or conditions that affect your coverage.

- Watercraft endorsement. If you have a small boat, consider getting this endorsement to broaden the personal liability medical payments coverage on it.

- Theft coverage protection endorsement. This type of endorsement broadens your theft protection for contents in motor vehicles, trailers, or watercraft.

- Credit card forgery and depositor's forgery coverage endorsement. With this endorsement, you can get coverage for loss, theft, or unauthorized use of your credit cards, with a few exceptions. You're also covered if your signature is forged on checks, drafts, and promissory notes, for example, again, with certain exceptions. No deductibles apply to this endorsement.

- Flood insurance. Though many people are not aware of this, standard home insurance policies don't cover flood damage. Nor do all homes qualify for flood insurance through the National Flood Insurance Program (800/638-6620). Some insurance companies, however, do offer flood insurance policies to those who qualify.

- Earthquake insurance. This type of coverage is usually issued as an endorsement to your insurance policy and is available through most insurance companies.

- Windstorm coverage. Though most insurance policies cover damage caused by windstorm and hail, in some areas—mostly coastal—this coverage is excluded. If you're in one of those areas, contact your state's insurance commissioner's office to find out where you can get coverage.

Life insurance

You'll need life insurance coverage to protect your family financially in the event of your death. There are two basic types of life insurance policies:

- Term insurance
- Cash value insurance

Term insurance generally has lower premiums while you're young. It does not build a cash value. The policy value and death benefit are the same: A $500,000 policy pays a $500,000 death benefit. Typically, it gives the largest per premium dollar coverage.

There are two types of term insurance: *Annual-renewable term* (ART) and *level-premium term.* ART is purchased annually. Premiums start low and rise as you age. The main advantage to this type of policy, according to *Consumer Reports*, is that you can renew your coverage each year without proof of good health. A problem with at least some ARTs is that when you reach a specific age you lose the right to renew.

In contrast, level-premium term typically guarantees the same premium for each year of coverage. Policies are usually written for 5, 10, 15, 20, 25, or 30 year periods. But, according to *Consumer Reports*, if you still need life insurance coverage after the term expires, you'll have to meet the insurer's health criteria to qualify for a favorable renewal rate.

Consumer Reports found that level-premium policies generally offer more value than ARTs, even in the initial years of coverage, particularly for terms of 5 or 10 years. Based on these findings, they say you're better off buying a level-premium policy, even if the term is longer than what you need, noting that you can drop the coverage early.

Watch Out!
If you buy an annual renewable term life insurance policy, make sure the policy is convertible to a cash value policy in case there is a change in your health status that might make it impossible to buy affordable term insurance when your policy expires.

Some policies allow you to convert term insurance coverage for a *cash value policy* (one that combines basic insurance protection with tax-deferred investing), but premiums for the new policy will be higher. You can also buy term insurance with the cash value of a cash value insurance policy to further protect your family during the time when you have the greatest need for life insurance, for instance, when your children are young. (In addition to a death benefit, whole life, universal life, and variable life insurance policies have a cash value account.)

Cash value coverage has higher premiums than term insurance for the same amount of coverage. The insurance company builds the cash value by investing part of the premium paid. Your investment earnings grow tax-deferred until you withdraw them. You can borrow against the cash value, but if you don't pay back the loan plus interest, that amount is subtracted from the benefits paid when you die or the cash value if you discontinue the premium payments. You can also use your cash value to pay premiums for a limited time. The cash value may be used to supplement your retirement income or pay for a child's tuition without having to cancel the policy. As noted earlier, there are several types of cash value life insurance. These include whole life, universal life, and variable life:

Unofficially...
With cash value insurance your investment earnings grow tax-deferred until you withdraw them, but often it takes 10 years or longer before the benefits of the tax-deferral outweigh the drag on growth due to the commissions charged on these investments (see www.Quicken.com).

- Whole life insurance. This type of coverage covers you for as long as you live. Usually, this type of policy has a level premium for the life of the policy. Initial premiums are high, compared with term insurance premiums, but eventually they become lower than the premiums you would pay if you keep renewing a term policy.

- Universal life insurance. With this type of coverage, which also covers you as long as you live, you can vary your premium payments and the face amount of your coverage. Most of your premium payment goes into an account, which earns interest. You may borrow against the cash value, but eventually, if the balance continues to drop, your coverage will end. To prevent that, you'd have to start making premium payments again, increase your premium payments, or lower your death benefits. Generally, your policy will state that it will pay the premiums from the cash value of your policy. (Actually, it doesn't pay the full premiums, but the portion that covers the cost of the insurance.)

- Variable life insurance. This type of coverage is highly dependent on the investment performance of your premiums, which may be invested in mutual funds or other securities. Read the prospectus. If your investments do poorly, your benefits may disappear.

Moneysaver
In many cases, the better known the insurance company, the lower the commission rates, since the policies are easier to sell. Consider shopping through an insurance broker who represents many term life insurance companies.

With universal life insurance, the company quotes a specific minimum investment return; universal life is a single-choice investment. With variable life, you pick which funds you want to invest in within the company's menu of choices. In both cases, you can borrow the money in your account tax-free. Payments are divided between the death benefit insurance premium and the investment arm. Because of the investment component (cash value account), these policies can increase in value. Whole life insurance sometimes yields a higher interest rate than universal life. On the other hand, universal life usually has higher premiums than whole life because a larger portion goes toward the cash value in universal life.

Bright Idea
Review your life
insurance policy
coverage every
year to make
sure that it still
meets your
needs.

Finding the coverage that's right for your needs

Get the necessary coverage to protect your family in the event of your death to let your family enjoy the lifestyle you would have been able to provide, Chasnoff says.

That doesn't mean you have to buy cash policies. You can buy level-premium term insurance, which is priced the same for 30 years, he says. *Consumer Reports* also recommends getting term insurance because you pay for protection only for the length of time your dependents are financially vulnerable. They and other experts recommend, in general, carrying coverage until your youngest child has completed his or her education. You also may need coverage to adequately provide for your spouse's retirement. *Consumer Reports* suggests buying insurance with guaranteed premiums so the premium price will stay the same throughout the term of the policy.

Term insurance is much less expensive than cash policies. According to Quicken.com's InsureMarket—Life Insurance Marketplace, a healthy 30 year old man could expect to get a $300,000 annual term life policy for about $300 per year. In contrast, the same amount of coverage under a cash value policy would cost at least ten times more—$3,000 or more—per year. The cost of term insurance is mostly dependent on your gender, age, and health.

By using term insurance instead of a cash policy to protect your assets, you can take the excess cash flow from the premium savings and invest it. By "investing" in term insurance instead of permanent cash policies, you'll be far, far ahead, Chasnoff says.

Consumer Reports also recommends not getting a re-entry rider, which ensures a guaranteed rate on renewal of your policy. At the time of re-entry, you must meet the good health standards of the policy. If you don't, you've paid for nothing. And, *Consumer Reports* says, don't bother getting a waiver of premium, which continues to pay your premiums in the event you become permanently disabled. *Consumer Reports* recommends buying disability insurance instead.

Learn to comparison shop

Life insurance products are not designed for consumers; they are designed for salespeople, Chasnoff says. He gives this additional warning: An insurance company can be great one day, but "get a new chairman of the board and overnight, you can take a great company down."

Insurance salespeople are some of the best-trained salespeople there are, Chasnoff adds. And with good incentive. They generally get 50 to 90 percent of the first-year premiums on the policies they sell. Life insurance salespeople will try to show you how you can pay for your grandchild's education with the policies you buy, says Coghill. Don't be swayed. The purpose of life insurance is to cover your necessities, she says. Add up all your assets to see how much coverage you'll need to purchase to provide for your family in the event of your death, then shop around.

When you go to buy life insurance, the NAIC says to consider the following:

- How much of the family income do you provide?

- How will your family pay final expenses and debts in the event of your death?

Next, see which company gives you the most for your money. Consider the following:

Timesaver
You can use Quotesmith at www.quotesmith.com, RightQuote at www.rightquote.com, or InsureMarket at www.insuremarket.com to get term life insurance quotes. You can also call AccuQuote at 800/442-9899 or Insurance Information Inc. at 800/472-5800.

- Premiums
- Structure—do premiums or benefits vary over time?
- What is guaranteed and what is not guaranteed?

Moneysaver
You can buy life insurance commission-free by contacting Ameritas and USAA life directly at 800/531-8000. Check out the Web site www.Lowload.ameritas.com, as well.

After you decide on the type of policy you want to buy, use a cost comparison index to help you compare similar policies. There are several different indices, and each works differently, according to NAIC. One index compares costs between two policies if you give up the policy and take the cash value. Another index helps compare costs if you don't give up the policy. Still another helps you with the types of questions to ask an agent about numbers used in illustrations that they give to you to show how the policy works and the contingencies involved.

Auto insurance

Automobile insurance coverage is expensive. A NAIC study found in 1990 that average annual premiums were $573.90 for each insured car.

Costs of coverage depends on the risk pool in which you've been placed. Therefore, if you can switch into a lower risk group, you may be able to lower your premiums. To change your risk pool, you can take the following action:

- Buy a car or truck loaded with safety features.
- Buy a car or truck that scores well on crash tests.
- Buy a car or truck that has low repair costs.
- Drive fewer miles by using public transportation, carpools, or walking or biking to local destinations.
- If you're in school, maintain a B grade point average or better.

A number of other factors, both in and out of your control, affect how much you'll pay for car insurance, as well. Your age and gender will affect your premium, as does geographic location. If you are an unmarried man in his twenties driving a sports car, you should expect to pay a lot for car insurance. By contrast, being married and having a steady job seem to correlate with responsible behavior and typically reduce premium payments.

When you apply for coverage, you'll generally be asked about following:

- Your driving record. Accidents and traffic violations during the previous three to five years will be included in the premium assessment.

- Your geographic location. The number of claims made in your area affect your premium. More claims are made in urban areas than in rural areas due to traffic, vandalism, and thefts.

- Your gender. Insurance companies know that males cause more accidents than females. As a result, men tend to pay higher rates for insurance, though some states prohibit insurance companies from considering gender as a factor.

- Your age. Certain age groups also have a higher number of claims than others.

- Marital status. Married people tend to have fewer claims, so their premiums are typically lower.

- Your vehicle use. How often you drive and how far you drive your car to work affects your premium price. Higher mileage generally means higher premiums because your exposure to risk is increased.

Bright Idea
If you live in a city, county, or state that levies a personal property tax, consider buying a less expensive vehicle and investing the money you'll save from paying lower taxes, not to mention making lower monthly payments.

- The make and model of the car or truck you drive. Some makes and models have higher numbers of claims or are more expensive to repair. If you have one of these vehicles, expect to pay higher premiums.

- Your claim history. If you have a history of making claims, expect to pay higher insurance premiums.

Bringing the costs down

You can reduce your auto coverage costs by taking advantage of discounts. Discounts are available to drivers who seem like better risks to insurance companies. Look for the following types of discounts:

- Insure all your vehicles with the same company. Most insurance companies offer discounts to those who insure more than one vehicle with their company. Statistically, those that insure more than one vehicle have lower claims.

- Insure your home and car with the same insurance company. Some offer discounts for multiple policies, regardless of the policy type.

- Take a driver's education course if you are young or old.

- Get good grades. Students with a B average or better may qualify for a Good Student Discount because good students tend to be more responsible drivers.

- Buy a car or truck with safety equipment like airbags, automatic seat belts, and antilock brakes.

- Invest in antitheft devices.

- Keep your mileage low, that is, don't drive much. The fewer miles you drive, the less risk you're exposed to.

- Drive safely. A good driving record usually results in lower premiums (and a poor record almost always results in higher ones).

The savings can differ from company to company. Make sure you ask about discounts and receive the ones for which you qualify. When comparison shopping, compare the savings associated with each discount.

Types of available coverage

The type of insurance you buy depends on the tort system of your state. There are basically two types of available coverage: *Liability insurance* and *no-fault insurance.*

Liability insurance contains three parts, consisting of bodily injury, property damage, and uninsured/underinsured motorist coverage.

Bodily injury liability insurance protects you against the claims of others who are injured in an accident involving your car, and covers medical expenses, lost wages, and pain and suffering. This type of coverage is not for you personally, but for your car, so anyone who drives your car with your consent is covered. Bodily injury liability insurance has coverage limits. Understand these limits because if you're sued for more, you'll have to pay out of your own pocket.

Property damage liability insurance pays for damage to other people's property, like bent fenders or damaged fences. Again, it's your auto that's covered, so if another person is driving with your consent, they're covered, too. You should consider the cost of replacing one or more vehicles when deciding on how much coverage to carry.

Uninsured motorist coverage protects you if you're injured by a hit-and-run driver or someone

Moneysaver
Some insurance companies offer discounts to people who participate in carpools. Be sure to ask for a rundown on the discounts the company offers— you may be surprised what you find.

who otherwise has no insurance. Additionally, you may want to consider buying a policy that contains coverage for underinsured drivers in case you're hurt in an accident and an insured driver does not have sufficient insurance to cover your claim. Note that this type of insurance may not cover damage caused to your vehicle.

Some states have adopted a no-fault insurance system to avoid the legal proceedings used to determine who caused an accident. In these states, no one is considered at fault. If you live in a no-fault state and are involved in an auto accident, rather then sue the driver of the other vehicle, you file a claim with your own insurance company to get compensation for damages, medical expenses, and any lost wages.

There are many variations nationwide on the no-fault system. In general, no-fault law does not eliminate your risk for being sued. However, it does place restrictions on when a suit can be brought, that is, you can be sued only under specific conditions. Likewise, it does not completely eliminate your right to sue.

The most basic no-fault benefit is personal injury protection (PIP) coverage. Typically, it covers medical expenses, rehabilitation expenses, work loss, and funeral expenses and has a survivor's loss benefit.

Though PIP benefits cover most injury claims, many states have residual bodily injury liability coverage to protect anyone who is in your auto with your permission at the time of an accident if you are sued because of injuries caused to others.

No-fault policies in most states do not cover damage that you cause to other people's property. Nor does property damage liability extend to your auto. Therefore, you should consider buying separate collision coverage. (Note, however, that if you have a vehicle worth less than $2,000, you can consider skipping this coverage because you'll probably end up paying more money in premiums than you would get as a result of a claim.) You should also consider getting comprehensive coverage that pays for damage to your vehicle from most other causes including vandalism, theft, and fire.

There are three more optional coverages you should consider:

- Medical payments coverage, which pays for medical bills and funeral expenses for the driver and his or her passengers in the event of an accident and covers you and members of your household in any accident involving an auto while on foot, on a bike, or in another auto

- Rental reimbursement coverage, which covers the expense of a rental car while your vehicle is being repaired

- Towing and labor coverage, which pays for towing expenses to a repair shop (If you are a member of an auto club, you might want to skip this coverage.)

Getting covered

It's wise to comparison shop for auto insurance. Different companies may charge different amounts for identical coverage. The lowest price may not be the best buy if the insurance company makes it difficult to collect on claims. Ask family, friends, and neighbors about their experiences with specific companies. Or check *Consumer Reports* magazine to see how readers rate their insurance companies.

Watch Out!
Insurance agents are salespeople paid on commission. Don't rely on them to tell you what type of coverage you need or what deductible you should take.

Premium quotes (given free of charge) are useful tools with which to comparison shop. Be sure to provide the same information to each company to get an accurate comparison of prices.

Insurance companies use one of three types of marketing professionals: Direct marketers, independent agents, or exclusive agents. Understanding these methods may better enable you to shop around.

1. Direct marketers. While often considered junk mail or annoying telemarketing calls, according to the NAIC, in some cases you can actually save money buying insurance through direct marketers because the insurance companies don't have to pay commissions to agents (thereby passing the savings on to you). However, you can expose yourself to scams by buying over the phone or through direct-mail marketing, so be careful, and make sure to find out all you can about the company before agreeing to anything.

2. Independent agents. These are salespeople paid on commission to represent several insurance companies. The advantage to using these agents is that you can get quotes from multiple companies at once, saving you time. But the price you end up paying might be higher than necessary because you're also paying for the agent's commission.

3. Exclusive agents. These salespeople represent only one company. Because companies don't need to give these agents incentives to sell their products over another company's products, their commissions may be lower, and therefore, the price of your insurance may be lower, too.

Protect yourself

Before signing on the dotted line, check with your state insurance department to make sure the company and the agents you're considering doing business with are licensed in your state. If the company is not licensed in your state, you won't be protected under your state's guarantee fund, which functions as a safety net to protect insurance consumers from suffering financial loss as a result of licensed companies becoming insolvent.

Read your insurance policies carefully. They are legal contracts. Keep them in a safe place. Remember to check the credit rating status of the insurance company with Standard & Poor's or Moody's.

Just the facts

- Insurance protects your family and your assets.

- There are many types of health insurance policies; fee-for-service plans provide the greatest patient control over health-care decisions while HMOs provide the least.

- Term life insurance coverage is generally the easiest and least costly way to protect your family during the periods they most need it.

- Long-term care insurance can prevent senior citizens from having to deplete their savings in order to qualify for Medicaid.

- Different auto insurance companies charge different rates for exactly the same coverage; be sure to shop around.

Buying Big-Ticket Items

GET THE SCOOP ON...
Where dealerships make their profit ▪ How to
tell which car is the best buy ▪
How leasing works and how to get the best
deal ▪ How accidents impact insurance rates ▪
When buying a used car is a smart move

PART III

Getting a Car

More than $5 trillion has been spent on new cars and trucks in the United States since Henry Ford's first Model T rolled off the assembly line and onto the road, according to the National Automobile Dealers Association (NADA). In 1997 alone, automobile dealers sold nearly 19.2 million new cars and trucks, taking in more than $508 billion, according to NADA.

While those numbers are impressive, new car and truck sales are not where most of the dealers' profits are made. Although new vehicle sales accounted for 58.6 percent of total sales dollars, typical new vehicle departments broke even, according to a NADA spokesperson. Dealers' profits were buried in used vehicles, which made up 28 percent of total profits, and service and parts, which made up the balance at 59 percent of dealer profits. (This should come as no surprise to anyone who has sat for hours waiting to get their car or truck fixed, only to get stuck with an eye-popping bill.)

This chapter will cover the true cost of owning a car (it's a lot more than just the sticker price), how to decide when to buy and when to lease, how to compare leases, how to find the best used car to buy, and more.

What's the true cost of owning a car?

You can find out the true cost of owning a car or truck, saving yourself a little of the profit, by looking down the road a bit.

Most car and truck buyers focus only on the purchase price. But by figuring out *ownership costs*, that is, what it costs to own, operate, and drive new cars and trucks over a five-year period, you'll know how much money you're going to have to take out of your wallet when all is said and done.

The sum total of the following seven areas over time gives you an idea of your vehicle's total ownership costs:

1. Depreciation
2. Insurance
3. Financing
4. Maintenance
5. Fuel
6. Fees
7. Repairs

Interestingly, purchasing a higher-priced car or truck might actually cost *less* over a five-year period than buying a less expensive vehicle. For instance, a $30,000 vehicle that has ownership costs totaling $35,000 is going to be a better value in the long run than a $20,000 vehicle that has ownership costs totaling $40,000.

Five-year ownership costs vary from vehicle to vehicle, state to state, and even county to county, but, in any event, they're a lot higher than buyers anticipate, according to IntelliChoice, a California-based research firm that evaluates vehicle ownership costs.

IntelliChoice researched five-year average ownership costs for 1999 cars and found the percentage impact that each of the ownership cost factors has. These are (in percentage order):

- Depreciation (37 percent)—Every vehicle depreciates at a different rate. IntelliChoice calculates depreciation based on the past history of the vehicle and current and projected market trends, as well as supply and demand. *Depreciation* is defined as the amount of decline in value over time of the vehicle. It may be calculated as the difference between the vehicle's purchase price and its current value.

- Insurance (25 percent)—These numbers are based on data collected by the insurance industry, but IntelliChoice makes assumptions based on the driver's age, driving experience, and other factors.

- Financing (15 percent)—The assumptions here are 20 percent down, a 60-month loan, and an annual interest rate of 8.92 percent.

- Fuel (9 percent)—IntelliChoice used the U.S. EPA's mileage figures, calculated using 60 percent highway driving and 40 percent city driving, $1.02 for a gallon of unleaded regular gas, $1.21 for premium, and $1.05 for diesel fuel.

- Maintenance (8 percent)—These numbers were based on manufacturer data, as well as additional research that included items not specifically found in the owners' guide such as tires, mufflers, and other items.

- Fees (3 percent)—IntelliChoice used a national average of a 5 percent sales tax.
- Repair (3 percent)—IntelliChoice got these numbers, in part, from companies that sell extended warranties and from tracking resources. Repair costs are based on the cost of a zero deductibility warranty.

Although the numbers may vary, IntelliChoice expects relative performance among vehicles to stay the same. For instance, if you keep detailed records of the seven factors detailed above, your numbers will probably be different from IntelliChoice's because certain factors are variable—the way you drive, for example. However, if you kept numbers on a second vehicle, you should find the order of the ownership cost factors the same as IntelliChoice's rankings.

IntelliChoice's calculations show that the real cost of owning a 1999 car is nearly $37,000; for trucks it is more than $32,000. As noted above, these numbers vary by vehicle make and model.

Even if you're a savvy negotiator, it'll pay, literally, to know how much the car or truck you want to buy will *really* cost down the road. Remember that ownership costs tell the whole story. The purchase price is merely a factor that affects depreciation and financing. Take two cars, one priced at $20,000, the second priced at $23,000. The first car has total ownership costs of $27,000 over five years and the second one has ownership costs of $26,000 over the same five-year period. In this scenario, you're probably better off buying the car with the higher purchase price. Remember that the purchase price is not a reliable indicator of the actual cost.

Finding the best overall car and truck values

If cost is the only factor on which you base your buying decision, IntelliChoice's ratings of best overall values may help you decide between similar models. Best overall value does not mean those vehicles with the overall lowest ownership costs, but those with ownership costs that are substantially lower than what would be expected. Ownership costs are listed in IntelliChoice's books, *The Complete Car Cost Guide* and *The Complete Small Truck Cost Guide,* and are too numerous to note here. (See Appendix C for more information on these books.)

Each year IntelliChoice identifies which vehicles are the best overall values in each class. It does this by comparing ownership costs and purchase price for every car and truck and calculating which vehicles offer the most bang for your buck.

IntelliChoice rated the best overall values for 1999 cars as follows:

- Best Car Value Over $20,000: Mercedes Benz E320 Wagon

- Best Car Value Under $20,000: Honda Civic DX 4-Door Sedan

IntelliChoice rated the best overall values for 1999 trucks as follows:

- Best Truck Value Over $18,000: GMC Sierra C2500 3-Door Extended Cab

- Best Truck Value Under $18,000: Nissan Frontier SE King Cab

IntelliChoice rated the best overall values for 1999 SUVs as follows:

Bright Idea
There is a lot of good information from a variety of sources available to help you sort out fact from fiction. Consult www. intellichoice.com; www.edmonds. com; www.kbb. com; www. carpoint.com; www.autobytel. com; *Consumer Reports* magazine, your insurance company, and AAA, for starters.

- Best SUV Value Over $25,000: Toyota 4Runner SR5 4WD
- Best SUV Value Under $25,000: Jeep Wrangler SE

Tips for buying a car or truck

It's easy to get a bad deal on a car or truck. But you can get a good deal by understanding how extra profits are made by dealers.

One way dealers make a profit is through rebates, incentives, holdbacks, and "profit padders." You can find out about cash rebates and incentives (typically in the form of discount financing) in *Automotive News*, which is available at your local library or on the Internet at www.edmunds.com or www.ConsumerReports.com (for a fee). You can also call the manufacturer. But don't buy a car just because it has a rebate. A large rebate tacked onto a poor value doesn't necessarily make it a good buy.

Deducting the rebates and incentives from the dealer invoice price to get to your initial offer shouldn't make you feel like you're sending your dealer home empty-handed. Domestic auto manufacturers (as well as some foreign ones) give dealers a "holdback." This is a refund of between 1 and 3 percent of the invoice price that the dealer gets, essentially, for selling the vehicle. The manufacturer gives the dealer this money to fund the financing while the car sits on the lot. But if the dealer sells the car right away, or even within a couple of months, then that money is the dealer's to keep. The same is true if the dealer orders the car for you. These and other incentives make it possible for the dealer to sell a car at "cost" and still profit.

Dealers also have "profit padders," including documentation fees, dealer preparation charges,

Unofficially...
Traditionally, the best time to buy a car or truck is at the end of the month or at the end of the year, when salespeople and dealers are trying to meet or exceed their quotas in order to earn bonuses. Summer and winter are typically the slowest seasons for sales and therefore, are better for buyers.

market value adjustments, or added dealer profits, for which you should not have to pay, though you might if the car you want is in great demand. Make a reasonable offer on the destination charge and toss out the rest.

The rest of the dealer profit comes from you. To avoid lining the dealer's pockets you need to know how the deal is being formulated—you must see each calculation the dealer makes. To do this, consider buying, financing, and trade-in calculations as three completely separate transactions.

First, determine which vehicle you want and then call around to different dealers and visit Web sites with car buying services (like www.autobytel.com and www.edmunds.com) to figure out the lowest price you can find for the vehicle *before* negotiating with your chosen dealer. This way, when you begin to negotiate, you will have some idea of what other dealers are asking for the same make and model. Remember that the more educated you appear, the more likely it is that you will get a better deal.

Watch Out!
High interest rates due to credit problems can result in extremely large monthly payments, which may add to your credit problems.

Next, negotiate the price of the vehicle, starting at the invoice price and subtracting any manufacturer's rebates, both those offered to the consumer and those offered to the dealer.

After you've agreed on a price, consider financing. Compare the interest rate the dealer offers to that offered by credit unions or banks.

Finally, mention you have a car you might want to trade in, and compare the dealer's offer for your car with the retail and wholesale prices in the *Kelly Blue Book* (found in the reference section of your local library, or visit the *Blue Book*'s Web site at www.kbb.com). Used car values are also available on the Internet at www.intellichoice.com and through

Bright Idea
While shopping around for financing, consider getting a home equity loan, for which you can write off the interest. Check out this method of financing carefully, though, because it can end up costing you more if the amount borrowed is financed over a great number of years. And, if you default, it can be even costlier—the bank can foreclose on your home.

most portal sites like Yahoo! and Excite. If you sell the car yourself, you'll probably get a better deal, though it will be more of a hassle.

Remember to make sure each one of the above transactions (buying, financing, and trade-in calculations) is complete before moving on to the next one. It's a three-step process. If you try to negotiate these three transactions simultaneously, chances are you'll get the monthly payment you want, but you may also end up paying hundreds more—either by ending up with a higher interest rate, a substantially lower trade-in value, or both—than you would have if you had negotiated for them as separate transactions. Salespeople like doing all these transactions at once because they can bury the profit in the deal. Remember, the dealership's salespeople and finance managers are experts at this stuff. The have lots of ways to structure the deal so that it looks good to you.

Another way salespeople can "get you into the car" is by extending the length of your loan to make your monthly payments affordable. Perhaps your monthly payments will be in line with your budget, but by spreading them out over a long period of time, you'll be paying less equity and more interest for years, increasing the final cost of the car. Furthermore, if you end up wanting to sell the car in a few years, you may owe more than the car is worth. (This is sometimes called being "upside down" in your car.)

And remember not to be persuaded by a salesperson's passionate pleas. He or she may try to play on your emotions by appealing to your sympathy or by trying to make you think you don't know what you're doing. Or the salesperson may use more of a hardball strategy. He or she may try to pressure you by bringing in a hard-selling manager or by trying to get you to sign on the dotted line before you leave the dealership. Sometimes, the dealer may have different players using different strategies on you. Walk into the dealership expecting this type of behavior. Don't take any nonsense from sales people, and be prepared to walk away.

Whether to lease or to buy—that is the question

As the price of buying a car or truck has skyrocketed, *leasing* has become a more popular option for many drivers. Leasing is financing a portion of the depreciation, interest, and profit of the vehicle. Leasing a car or truck rather than buying one is a great way to control your cash flow and not have to put much money down.

Simply put, leasing is really just another financial transaction. Someone else buys the car and you pay for the portion of the car you "use up" and some profit to the owner for letting you in on such a sweet deal. In reality, however, the calculations are very complex.

Deciding whether you should buy or lease depends, in part, on your financial situation (for example, how much money you have available for a down payment and monthly payments), as well as the costs of maintaining the vehicle, which you are *not* exempt from if you lease. Leasing is not, after all, the same as renting.

You should also consider the length of time you want to keep your car. Unlike buying a car, your monthly payments continue as long as you lease. Take note, too, of the *residual value* should you choose to buy it later. (The residual value is the expected value of the vehicle at the end of the lease.

Timesaver
Go to credit union car shows to see many vehicle makes, models, and dealerships all in one place. These shows are sponsored by credit unions such as Navy Federal Credit Union and bring together many dealers in one central parking lot.

It is a measure of the vehicle's expected depreciation.)

Timing is also a factor. It may be that a lease on a Ford F150 truck makes more sense this month than it will in six months because manufacturers continually change lease interest rates depending largely on how well a particular vehicle happens to be selling at any given time.

In the end, you've got to determine the interest rate of the lease and compare it with the interest rate of a loan.

If you don't keep your cars for more than a few years or if you like driving new cars, leasing may be a good option, depending on the interest rate and residual value. If you hold onto your cars until they fall apart, then buying is the right choice for you.

Added incentives sometimes make leasing a good buy

Some manufacturers' incentives make it cheaper to lease than buy, according to George Hoffer, professor of economics and automotive economist at Virginia Commonwealth University, while sometimes there's no deal at all. Each case is dependent on the incentives, which he says are key.

On leases, the manufacturer doesn't give a rebate, but sets the residual value so unrealistically high it's like a subsidy, Hoffer says. It's a back-end rebate, rather than a front-end rebate. Other lease incentives may include low interest rates and low purchase prices (because, even though you're leasing, you still have to negotiate a price).

How can you figure out if a factory rebate is involved for a particular car or truck? Check the residual value as noted by the lease. The *Automotive Leasing Guide* (which can be found at your local

Bright Idea
Compare inflation rates with interest rates to figure out if it's wiser to put a large down payment on a car or invest that money elsewhere.

library) is one of several guides that finance companies use to predict what the residual value on a car or truck will be in three years. (If you get your own leasing, the bank usually bases the residual on this guide.) If the manufacturer says the residual value is higher, you're getting a big subsidy, so it pays to lease the vehicle, Hoffer says. Another way to figure the residual value is to see what a three-year-old model of the same car is worth now and figure depreciation based on that percentage. Or, you can turn to the Internet. Special lease programs, most of which are supported by the manufacturers through subsidized leases, are listed at www.edmunds.com.

Leasing is offered by automobile manufacturers, local dealerships, financial institutions, and independent leasing companies. Captive finance company (manufacturer-owned financiers like GMAC, NMCC, TMCC, and AHFC) leases are based on factory-subsidized leases.

If you read the disclaimer, you can see where the subsidy, if any, is coming from, Hoffer remarks. For instance, many car manufacturer advertisements focus on interest rates well below market rates. But to get the deal on a sale you have to borrow the money from Ford credit, for example, because the manufacturer pays its credit arm up front the difference between the advertised interest rate and the market rate, he says. The same is true for leases. With leases, if the finance arm is giving you a super deal, rest assured that it's getting the balance from the manufacturer. (Note that credit unions and banks don't have the incentive to match interest rates. The manufacturer has the incentive.) With inflated residual values, the manufacturer pays its finance arm the difference between its inflated

Bright Idea
The Federal Reserve Board published a consumer guide to vehicle leasing at www.bog.frb.fed. us/pubs/leasing. The Web site also has sample leasing forms.

value of the vehicle and what's listed in one of the guides, Hoffer says.

Why do the manufacturers do this? They want your money *now*, even if they'll pay later, Hoffer explains. And, when sales are slow, they can't run a $6,000 rebate. By structuring the lease with the incentive hidden, it doesn't look like they're having a fire sale, he says. Hiding rebates in a lease is especially useful for selling luxury cars because it looks bad to give rebates on luxury cars, he explains.

There's no hard and fast rule on when to buy or lease; it all depends on the subsidies, Hoffer maintains, with a couple of exceptions. Certain cars that depreciate or that are being discontinued are good to lease because they'll depreciate rapidly. It's also advantageous to lease right before a style change (that is, at the end of a style cycle) because those vehicles tend to depreciate and probably have lease subsidies, he says.

Here's a good rule of thumb: If the residual value of the vehicle is set too low, you'll pay too much for depreciation. Look for a lease with a high residual value (some are inflated because of dealer subsidies) because most of what you're paying for in a lease is the depreciation (the difference between the selling price and the residual value).

It's also possible that the residual value is set artificially high. To compensate, the dealer may hike up the interest rate or the capitalized cost (the agreed upon value of the vehicle plus any amortized items like service contracts). Likewise, it's possible to have a very low base interest rate and an artificially low residual value. So don't base your decision on any of those factors independently. You always need to know the base interest rate, the residual, and the price of the vehicle in order to begin making an informed decision. You can be misled if you know only one of those numbers.

Bottom line? If the monthly payments are low, the car is probably being highly subsidized by an inflated residual, which is good for leasing. When manufacturers have trouble selling cars, they may come up with high residual values on their leases, making it less expensive to lease than to buy. In essence, they're lowering their price. But don't buy it without thoughtful consideration. Look closely at the total deal first.

Getting the best lease deal for your money

"Understand the components of the deal that you're structuring," asserts Dave Nathanson, director of retail automotive operations for PricewaterhouseCoopers Management Consulting Services in Detroit. Don't go in and talk about monthly payments, he warns.

The process of leasing a car at a fair price is much more complicated than the process of getting a good deal on a direct purchase.

It's difficult to calculate the real cost of a lease because the information you need to determine if you're getting a fair deal is not readily available. Plus, leasing terminology and requirements are confusing.

Like car and truck buying, many people look at the monthly payment as the bottom line. But this is deceptive. The monthly payment only reflects your cash flow, not how much you'll end up paying in the long run for your car or truck.

When you lease, your monthly payments cover the following:

- Depreciation

- Interest charges

- State taxes

Watch Out!
If a car or truck has a high residual value, it pays to lease it, but it may not pay to buy it after the lease expires. If you like the car, give it back at the end of the lease and buy it used.

Unofficially...
The number of leases has grown more than tenfold in less than a decade. Leasing now accounts for more than 27 percent of the 15 million-plus vehicles sold in the U.S. The surge is mainly due to changes in the tax law and a decline in the percentage of disposable savings, according to the National Vehicle Leasing Association.

These costs are calculated based on the difference between the car or truck's price and the vehicle's residual value. This is why you should negotiate the price of the car or truck first, as if you were buying it.

Note that advertised monthly rates have mileage caps, down payments, inflated buyouts, and fees. What was advertised at $199 a month can come out to $299 a month when the fine print is added into the equation. Examine all the terms and conditions of the lease before you sign on the dotted line. Also be aware that advertised deals often require exemplary credit and therefore not everyone can take advantage of the special offer.

A good way to find out the lease's *base interest rate*—that is, the interest rate before the fees, discounts, and penalties are factored in—is by asking what "money factor" is used to calculate the monthly payments. Multiply the money factor by 2,400 to get the base interest rate.

How leasing calculations work

Lease payments are based on the expected depreciated value of the leased vehicle. The lease calculation is determined primarily by the following factors:

- The cost of the vehicle
- The rate of depreciation
- The interest rate charged on the lease

Leases aren't simple. Here are some questions you can ask yourself to get on the right track:

- Is the purchase price of the vehicle set too high or too low compared to the invoice price?

- Is the residual value set too high or too low compared to the *Automotive Leasing Guide* (or one of the other guides)?

- Is the acquisition fee (also called a bank fee, administrative fee, or assignment fee) too high?

- Is the security deposit they're asking for too much?

- Is the disposition fee, assessed when you turn the vehicle in, set too high?

The answers to these questions, by equation, can be turned into a *net interest rate*—a number comparable to an APR for a loan. (The *APR* is the actual interest rate you pay after all fees are added into the loan, and these fees plus the original, or base, interest rate are amortized over the life of the loan.) The lower the net interest rate, the lower the cost of the lease.

There are two factors that are negotiable:

1. The price of the vehicle (except in cases of one-price, no-haggle dealerships, although some reportedly do negotiate. Furthermore, prices vary by dealership due to differing overhead costs.)

2. The interest rate (compare rates among finance companies)

(Note: While virtually everything is negotiable, a change in one factor often results in a change in another.)

While allowed mileage is generally not negotiable, it does factor into the residual calculation. The amount you're charged (per mile) for excess mileage is higher at the end of the lease, often by 100 percent, Nathanson says. (If you think you're going to put more mileage on than the set cap, negotiate the rate for extra miles up front.)

Neither is the residual value negotiable. The residual value is typically determined by finance companies based on the *Automotive Leasing Guide*'s projections. It's also called a residual percentage and covers a specified period of time, for example, 36 months. While the residual value is not negotiable, the numbers can change periodically to reflect current market conditions. Furthermore, the residual value can be affected by promotional programs like rebates. Or, you can get a rebate and go to your own finance company to lease, Nathanson says.

You should start the leasing process as if you were buying the car or truck, that is, by negotiating a price, starting with the invoice price and subtracting the manufacturer's rebate, if any.

Unofficially...
Dealerships often use software that identifies leases from many different sources, each with its own characteristics.

"You should compare rates [both interest and residual] with various leasing sources, such as banks, credit unions, and exclusive leasing agencies," Nathanson suggests. "Remember that the residual and interest rate for each program will be fixed. [Y]ou cannot take interest rate[s] from one source and compare them to residual [values] from another—you must look at both together," he says. (You can't, for example, take Bank of America's interest rate and put it together with Ford's residual value. This limitation makes it difficult to cook your own deal.)

"Often, manufacturer finance companies [in coordination with the manufacturer] offer incentive programs through their leasing programs that raise the residual value or reduce the interest rate," Nathanson adds.

The following is an example of a lease calculation (you can substitute your own numbers):

> You want a 36-month lease for a Chevy Suburban with a manufacturer's suggested retail price (MSRP) of $41,000.

> The acquisition fee (a fee charged by the finance company to process the lease) is $450. (This fee may vary.)

> The residual value is 66 percent (of $41,000), or $27,060.

> You negotiate a price of $39,000 and the program has an interest rate of 7.5 percent.

There are two parts to a lease payment. These are the depreciation portion of the payment and the monthly charge portion of the payment.

To figure the depreciable portion of your payment, add the acquisition fee to your net capitalization cost (NCC), that is, the dealer cost of the vehicle plus or minus any negative equity rolled over from a previous car, or your down payment or equity from a trade-in; in the above example, that totals $39,450. Take that number ($39,450) and subtract the residual value ($27,060), which leaves you with $12,390. Divide that number by the number of months in the lease (36) to get the depreciable portion of your payment—in this example, $344.17.

To figure the total monthly charge portion of your payment, take the NCC ($39,450) and add the residual value ($27,060) to it ($66,510). Figure the "money factor" by dividing the interest rate of the program (in this example it's 7.5 percent) by 24; in this case, 0.003125 (7.5 percent divided by 24). Take the sum of the NCC and the residual value ($66,510) and multiply it by the money factor

Watch Out!
While the monthly payment may remain the same if you lease a car with added options, the residual value and/or purchase price will probably change, increasing the cost.

(0.003125) to get the total monthly charge portion of your payment, which, in this case, would be $207.84.

The total monthly charge portion ($207.84), plus the depreciable portion ($344.17), equals your total monthly payment ($552.01), excluding state sales tax.

Note, however, that there may be other charges involved, such as lease termination fees, if at the end of your lease you don't buy the car or trade it in for another lease.

IntelliChoice has a different approach to lease calculations. Table 6.1 is the example IntelliChoice uses to calculate lease interest rates in its book, *The Complete Car Cost Guide.*

When considering whether it is a good idea to lease a car, make sure that you can afford the monthly payments. Lease agreements are extremely difficult, if not impossible, to get out of. And if you terminate the lease early, you still owe the payoff, or balance. This number is based on the lease termination value and is determined by the finance company, Nathanson warns. "Most lease contracts will spell out the calculation that will be utilized to determine the payoff for an early termination," he says. And unlike buying a car, with a lease you pay for damages and excess wear and tear.

On the other hand, you might have built equity if the vehicle didn't depreciate as much as anticipated. This is unlikely, however. In today's market, vehicles depreciate fast, Nathanson says.

Most consumers who lease are mostly interested in cash flow and don't really care (in part because it's hard to understand) what it means to lease. They want to know what they can drive for $199 a month

TABLE 6.1—LEASE INTEREST RATE WORKSHEET

Step	Your Figures	Example Figures	Explanation
(A) Enter your monthly payment		$299.00	This does not include tax, license, and extra options.
(B) Enter the net capitalized cost		$21,171.00	The offer price of the car minus and required dealer and manufacturer discounts down payment.
(C) Enter the residual amount		$15,035.00	The predetermined value of the car at end of lease.
(D) Enter the lease term in months		36	This is the number of payments that need to be made.
(E) Subtract C from B		$6,136.00	This is the net depreciation for the lease.
(F) Divide E by D		$170.44	This is the depreciation per month.
(G) Subtract F from A		$128.56	This is the interest per month.
(H) Add B to C		$36,206.00	This is a total cap cost and residual.

The figures used in this example were taken from the "Special Lease Incentives" section on page 50A of *The Complete Cost Car Guide* (1998), published by IntelliChoice.

continues

Step	Your Figures	Example Figures	Explanation
(I) Divide G by H		0.0035507	This is the money factor used in the lease.
(J) Multiply I by 24		8.52%	This is the base interest rate in the lease.
(K) Multiply acquisition fee:			
—by 0.000044 for 24-month lease			
—by 0.000032 for 36-month lease			
—by 0.000026 for 48-month lease		0.00%	$0.00 times 0.000032
(L) Multiply disposition fee:			
—by 0.000036 for 24-month lease			
—by 0.000022 for 36-month lease			
—by 0.000015 for 48-month lease		.33%	$150.00 times .000022
(M) Add J, K, and L		8.85%	This is the approximate net interest rate.

or they're impressed when they can drive a nice car or truck for only $249 a month. To many it looks like the lease makes things affordable—and it does, from a cash flow perspective.

But if the overall deal is important to you, you may want to know how much depreciation you're paying for, the interest rate, and the cost of the vehicle.

Protecting yourself

"Ask for a copy of a blank contract and read it thoroughly before agreeing to the terms of the lease. Often, customers do not see the contract until they are taking delivery of their vehicles, and in their excitement, they neglect to pay attention to the commitments they are making when signing the lease contract," Nathanson says. "Many times termination fees or excess mileage is not noticed until it becomes an issue, well after the lease has been signed and is in effect."

When comparing lease contracts, pay attention to:

▪ Interest rates

▪ Termination clauses (whether you can end the lease early, what the penalty is, how it is calculated)

▪ Excess mileage and wear and tear guidelines

▪ Your responsibilities at the end of the lease

Consumers may not be aware that there are laws to protect them from unscrupulous lenders. The Consumer Leasing Act, known as Regulation M, was passed in 1976 to make sure that consumers are given a written statement by the lender that fully explains the terms of the agreement before signing it.

According to the *Federal Reserve System Compliance Handbook* (revised 10/96), lenders are required to include the following information, as applicable (this list is not inclusive):

- Description of the leased property
- Amount of the initial payment due on signing (for example, security deposits, advance payments)
- Number, amount, and dates that payments are due, as well as the total number of periodic payments
- Total fees and taxes owed by the lessee (for example, registration fees, certificate of title)
- Total miscellaneous charges such as maintenance charges
- Insurance required
- Applicable warranties
- Who is responsible for maintaining and servicing the vehicle, scope of the responsibility, and standards for wear and tear set by the lender
- Security interest held by the lender
- Method of determining late payments, delinquencies, or default, and amount owed as a result
- Whether the lessee has an option to buy, when, and at what price
- Whether the lessee has the option to terminate early and any penalties

The long and the short of it? Know what you're getting into. The more informed you are at the time of signing, the less chance there is that something will go wrong throughout the term of your lease, costing you more money.

Surfing the net

The World Wide Web can be a valuable resource for finding information about vehicle leasing and buying.

At IntelliChoice's Internet site (www. intellichoice.com) you can see what your car or truck is worth, and you can get current lease cost analyses free of charge. Also at this site, you can input a set of criteria and IntelliChoice will attempt to identify which vehicle makes and models meet the criteria you've specified. Say you want a pickup truck with 4-wheel drive, manual transmission, passenger's and driver's side airbags, cup holders, and a monthly payment of $350 or less. IntelliChoice will respond with a list of vehicles that meet your specifications, including the name of the vehicle, IntelliChoice's evaluation of the vehicle, and the amount for which you can either finance that vehicle or lease it, if they're tracking the lease for that vehicle. The finance figure is based on a set of assumptions, including annual mileage of 14,000 (depreciation and maintenance costs are at least partly mileage-based).

You can also access a "Just the Facts" at Intelli-Choice's Web site. This report includes a purchasing and buying report. Invoice prices, including costs for every option and package, and ownership cost data also can be obtained. That same information, without the ownership costs, is available at www.edmunds.com and other sites, as well.

At the IntelliChoice Web site, you also can build a car with all the build rules—that is, if you want a particular engine, the site will tell you what else you must order to get it, or if you want air-conditioning and the air-conditioning package is a better value,

Bright Idea
Take a look at an article on Debt Counselors of America, Inc.'s Web site at www. GetOutOfDebt.org called "Your Next Vehicle: Should You Lease or Buy?" written by Wayne Ruckman, CFP. In the article, Ruckman offers practical information to help you decide whether you should lease or buy. For example, he suggests saving on costly repairs by leasing for a term that is within the vehicle's manufacturer's warranty.

the site will prompt you and ask if you'd like that instead. It also lets you print out the sticker price with all the codes.

Another good Web site to visit before buying a car or truck is www.nhsta.gov, the National Highway Transportation Safety Administration's site, where you can look up crash test results. Additionally, the Federal Reserve Board has information on buying versus leasing, rights and responsibilities, lease costs, leasing language, and more at www.bog.frb.fed. us/pubs/leasing.

The cost impact of accidents

Another way to minimize costs is to know how much minor accidents are going to cost to repair.

According to the Insurance Institute for Highway Safety, there's a significant difference in repair costs among different makes, models, and years. Take, for example, 1998 models of small pickup trucks. At a relatively slow 5-mph crash ("Front into Flat Barrier; Rear into Flat Barrier; Front into an Angled Barrier [the car is moving straight]; and Barrier Rear into Pole"), the total repair cost for a Chevrolet S-10 LS is only $2,246. That cost nearly doubles for the Toyota Tacoma—a whopping $4,361. The Ford Ranger came in slightly above the Chevy at $2,952. The Dodge Dakota Sport cost $3,863 to repair, while the Nissan Frontier XE racked up $3,867 in damages.

But those numbers don't tell the whole story. For example, the damage accrued from the "Rear into Flat Barrier" at 5 mph was just $30 for the Chevrolet S-10 LS, but cost much more for the others—$312 for the Ford Ranger XLT, $339 for the Nissan Frontier XE, $827 for the Toyota Tacoma, and $1,250 for the Dodge Dakota Sport.

The best way to find out about structural soundness is to look at crash tests. Both the National Highway Safety Administration and the Insurance Institute for Highway Safety conduct crash tests. They signify how well the vehicle protects its own occupants. Results are posted at their Web sites.

Moreover, insurance premiums may be more costly if your vehicle's repair rate is high, adding another few bucks to your tab.

To catch a thief: more on insurance rates

The make and model of your car or truck has an impact on your insurance premiums. The two parts of the policy that impact premium price are *collision*, which pays for damages to your vehicle, and *comprehensive*, which pays for things other than collision, such as theft. Premiums for collision coverage are dependent on make and model because some cars are more expensive to fix than others. The same goes for comprehensive because it's obviously more costly to replace an expensive vehicle that's been stolen than it is to replace a cheap one.

Collision costs and the likelihood that a particular vehicle will be stolen are scored by the Highway Loss Data Institute, which reports that the Ford F-250 series scored "substantially better than average" on injury and collision and "better than average" for theft. The Ford F-150 series scored "substantially better than average" on the first two categories and "average" on theft as did the Chevy 2500 series four-by-four, the Chevy Tahoe 4-door, and the Plymouth Voyager minivan. Scoring "substantially better than average" in all three categories are the Chevy Astro 4-wheel drive and GMC Safari

Unofficially... The National Highway Transportation Safety Administration is developing an Automated Collision Notification (ACN) System, a kind of "mayday" system, for passenger vehicles. It will detect automatically the occurrence of a crash and alert emergency medical services, police, and fire agencies by transmitting the vehicle location and crash severity data through a cell phone transmission.

Moneysaver
When shopping for a car or truck, call your insurance company and get quotes for different makes and models. Prices will differ from company to company, depending on how many of a particular model and make they insure and what they've had to pay out on it.

4-wheel drive. Results are based on 1994 to 1996 models. For more data, visit www.carsafety.org.

Some vehicles come with theft-deterrent features. For instance, Chevy's C/K Pickup, Astro Van, S-10, Blazer, Tahoe, Suburban, Chevy Van, and Chevy Express all have the Passlock theft-deterrent system. If the proper key is not used, the fuel cuts off for 10 minutes.

A stolen vehicle tracking/emergency communication system is an option that can be installed on the Suburban, Tahoe, and Venture. It can help locate a truck or car that has been stolen or one in which the driver is lost, for example, in a snowdrift in a blizzard. It works accurately within a few meters.

Should you buy a new or used car?

You never really know what you're getting when you buy a used car. Did the previous owners take good care of it or drive it into the ground? Did they maintain it? Buying a used car is risky, though it can save big bucks. One way to try to protect against getting a junker is to ask to see the current owner's maintenance records. But this still may not give you an accurate picture. What if the mechanic used did shabby work? What if the owner did all the maintenance him or herself and has no proof that repairs were made?

Buying a used car is risky, but can also save you money in the long run if the car you buy has been well maintained and is a car that was well built. (Remember, some new cars are lemons, too, and some cars weren't built to last years and years. You can check to see if the car you're considering buying is a lemon at www.edmunds.com. You'll need the vehicle identification number (VIN) to do the search.)

The traditional route of buying a used car from a private party is sometimes wise, sometimes not. It really depends on the car itself, how it has been maintained, and how gently it's been driven.

You may want to consider buying a used car or truck off a dealer's lot. If you're buying a one- or two-year-old car (and sometimes even older than that) a dealer will typically "certify" the car and provide an additional warranty through the manufacturer.

But if you're going to buy a used vehicle, buying one that has been previously leased is probably a better bet than purchasing one that has been rented or owned by an individual.

When you lease a car, dealers nickel and dime you on the slightest thing wrong, so drivers of these cars often keep the vehicle in better shape than if they owned it, according to Hoffer. Plus, because extra mileage is expensive at the end of a lease, the mileage is usually lower in these cars and trucks. They're the best buys you can get, he says.

How do you tell which cars on the lot were previously leased? Previously leased cars are always two or three years old with low mileage, Hoffer explains. Rental cars are a year old with high mileage. Hoffer says that rentals are bad buys because people ride them like they're in the rodeo.

IntelliChoice does exactly the same analysis for used cars that it does for new cars, and all the information is available free on its Web site. IntelliChoice is the only company that provides ownership cost data for used cars along with calculating a value based on the mileage and options on the car and providing a report that details specifications. IntelliChoice also annually presents the Best Overall

Bright Idea
If you want to buy a used car, look at the history of that make and model to see how the vehicle performed in the past. Also, check www. consumerreports. org to find out if there are any Technical Service Bulletins (TSBs) or recalls issued on the car. If there are recalls, make sure the work for which the vehicle was recalled for has been completed. TSBs are problems that haven't reached the recall level of importance and dealerships are required to take care of them if you ask.

Value for Pre-Owned Vehicle award. Other sources for used car information include the *Kelly Blue Book* for current valuations.

Strategies for negotiating price and extras

Car buyers are gaining more and more leverage and getting better deals as a result of the Internet. Car buyers can find dealers' invoice prices at the following Web sites:

- www.edmunds.com

- wwww.autobytel.com

- www.intellichoice.com

- www.kbb.com

- www.cars.com

- www.carpoint.com

Many major newspaper Web sites also provide this information, including the sites of *San Jose Mercury News* and *USA Today*.

You can also access one of the car buying services on the Internet, like autobytel.com (listed above), to avoid the hassles of negotiating with a salesperson and still get a decent buy. Or, you can visit shopper's warehouse clubs, like Price Club, BJ's, or Sam's Club, which offer these services to members.

If you decide you want to get a good deal face to face, it's not as difficult as it used to be. Remember to negotiate from the dealer's invoice. And, if you have a trade-in, don't mention it until the deal is already done. Otherwise the salesperson will likely hide a bigger profit by subtracting less for the trade-in, making you think you got a better deal than you did.

Moneysaver
You can earn AAdvantage miles from American Airlines if you purchase or lease a new or used vehicle using their service. You'll earn one mile for every $4 of the purchase price. For more information call 888/BUY-2FLY or visit www.aabuy2fly.com.

Just the facts

- It costs more to buy a car or truck than just the price you negotiate.

- Sometimes it's cheaper to lease than to buy a car or truck.

- Buying, financing, and trade-in calculations should be approached as three separate transactions to get the best deal.

- The make and model you drive, as well as your car or truck's estimated repair costs, can have a significant impact on the amount you pay for insurance.

- If you buy a used vehicle, try to get one that has just been returned from a lease because these vehicles are often well maintained.

GET THE SCOOP ON...
Figuring out if buying or renting is best for you
■ What you need to know before buying a home
■ How to pick an agent ■ How to get a house
"on sale"

Finding Your Home Sweet Home

Chapter 7

Owning a home is the American dream. But without a thorough understanding of what's involved in the buying process, you can end up with more debt than you can handle. Your dream can turn into a living nightmare when making the mortgage payments causes constant stress. Worse, yet, some people lose their homes to foreclosure.

This chapter will cover the issues involved in deciding whether to buy or rent a home and the home-buying process. It will also give you tips on how to get a good deal on a house. For detailed information about financing options available to you once you've found your dream home, see Chapter 8.

Should you buy or should you rent?

Choosing to buy or rent a home is a matter of personal preference—a lifestyle choice. Many people enjoy the amenities some rentals offer, like concierge service and planned social activities. Others like to rent to relieve themselves of the responsibilities of repairing and maintaining a home, freeing up more time for leisure activities. For others, financial circumstances limit their housing choices.

There are many lifestyle reasons for renting:

Moneysaver
If you decide to rent, look for specials offered by apartment complexes, like $100 off your first month's rent or free moving van service. If you decide to rent from an individual owner, and you're handy, try to negotiate a lower rent in return for making small improvements to the home.

- Renting is usually cheaper than buying, and no down payment is required (although usually an up-front deposit of two months' rent—a security deposit—is required, which is later refunded if there's no damage to the rental).

- You usually do not have to pay property taxes, homeowner's insurance (though you'd be wise to get renter's insurance), or upkeep expenses (a new roof, new air-conditioning unit, or new siding, for example, which can be costly).

- You can move at the end of your lease term, avoiding the hassle and costs of putting your house on the market.

- You have no repair costs.

- Your weekends won't be spent mowing the lawn or shoveling snow.

- If you can't pay your rent, you won't have to worry about foreclosure and loss of a hefty down payment (although you will have to worry about your credit record and losing your security deposit).

And there are many financial advantages to owning a home:

- Your monthly payments build up equity.

- The interest paid is usually tax-deductible and can save you thousands of dollars on your federal income tax bill.

- If you get a fixed-rate mortgage, your monthly payments will remain the same for the term of the loan (renters can expect annual rent hikes); when you factor in inflation, you're paying the same dollar amount each month, but with cheaper dollars as time goes on.

- Your home will typically increase in value over time, especially during high inflationary periods.

There are psychological factors to owning your own home, as well. "I am an advocate of home ownership, not only for the prospective financial benefits but because of the social and psychological benefits as well," says Lois A. Vitt, president and CEO of Money Studies, Inc. "It is no accident that some 80 percent of older Americans own their own homes free and clear. My research clearly shows that in later life, home ownership improves one's feelings of both financial and psychological security."

One of the prospective homeowner's primary financial considerations should be the inflation rate. If inflation continues at its current rate of about 2 to 3 percent per year (inflation was at 1.6 percent in 1998 and less than 2 percent in 1997, but the annual compounded rate of inflation over the past 12 years is 3.3 percent), your home will appreciate at a rate of about 1.5 percent per year, taking into consideration depreciation due to age and the cost of improvements to maintain its value. (You usually don't get a dollar-for-dollar return on improvements; sometimes you need to make improvements just to keep up, which in essence is lost money.)

Moneysaver
There is an undeniable tax benefit to owning your own home (assuming you itemize your taxes) because you can deduct the interest you pay on your mortgage and your real estate taxes from your income taxes.

In addition to depreciation and inflation, you must also factor in closing costs when purchasing the home, points (mortgage origination costs), and any brokers' commissions. Your net appreciation is about 1 percent.

Interest rates also must be considered. A couple whose gross income is $50,000 and who have $10,000 for a down payment can afford to buy a $168,997 home at an 8 percent 30-year fixed interest rate; this same couple, with a 6 percent 30-year fixed interest rate, can afford a $204,590 home. (Note: The figures in this example are the most this buyer can afford; I strongly recommend buying less than you can afford to reduce the stress caused by tight finances. Housing affordability and mortgage interest rates are discussed in detail in Chapter 8.)

No one can tell you with absolute certainty that owning is better from a financial perspective than renting, or vice versa; you really have to work it out on a case-by-case basis. You must figure out if your money would be better invested in a down payment or in the market. Of course, since there is no way to predict inflation or market performance, you must make certain assumptions to make the calculation comparisons.

Consider this scenario: You plan to pay $1,000 a month on rent or your mortgage. If you buy, you plan to put $10,000 down. If you rent, you plan to invest $10,000 in the market with an expected annual return of 10 percent. If you buy, you plan to take out a 30-year mortgage with an interest rate of 7.5 percent. You assume a long-term inflation rate of 3 percent and a long-term income tax rate of 28 percent.

The house you are considering buying costs $153,017.63. Using the calculator at Mortgagecalc. com, after 30 years the house will be worth $371,413.95, and you will have saved $60,755.06 in income taxes from interest payments totaling $216,982.37. Overall, you end up paying $156,227.31 in interest after deducting your tax savings. If you had decided to rent, and placed the $10,000 that you would have used for the down payment in an investment with an annual 10 percent rate of return, after 30 years it would grow $174,494.02. While that sounds like a hefty profit, the profit from the sale of the house is $218,396.32—$196,559.69 after accounting for 10 percent in moving expenses. Consider also that the profit on the sale of the house is tax free, whereas the gain on your $10,000 investment in the rent scenario is subject to long-term capital gains taxes at a rate of 20 percent. You can plug in your own figures at mortgagecalc.com. (Note: While the use of Web site information can be helpful, certain assumptions are usually used to determine mortgage qualification. For more information on these assumptions, see Chapter 8.)

There is another important factor to consider when deciding to rent or own, and that is length of occupancy. Owning a home makes no sense if you think that you're going to be moving in less than five years. Using the numbers in the earlier example, it will cost you 10 percent when you sell the house, and closing costs for your next purchase are likely to be 1 to 2 percent, excluding mortgage origination points. So the entire cost of the move will total between 11 and 12 percent of the purchase/sale. If the value of the house increases at only half the rate of inflation, or 1 to 1.5 percent, it will take eight to 10 years to break even on the home purchase, including the equity buildup from paying down the mortgage. The house, however, will probably increase in value a little more than one half the rate of inflation, so you should stay in the house at least five years because of the high costs involved in real estate transactions.

There are, then, four main variables to consider:

1. The anticipated increase in real estate values over the time you live in the house, which is not expected to match the impressive growth during the 1970s and 1980s (see below)

2. Occupancy costs of owning versus renting (such as standard maintenance and the cost of tools necessary to perform those tasks)

3. Inflation

4. Stock market performance

Keep in mind that even if your home appreciates in value, you will not realize that gain until you sell it. Many people view buying a home as a method for saving for retirement, but this argument fails if they plan to spend their retirement years "at home," unless they take out a reverse mortgage, which has its own drawbacks. Note, however, very few people in the U.S. have taken out reverse mortgages. (See Chapter 12.)

Getting representation

Let's say you've decided that home ownership is right for you. After figuring how much home you can afford, the first thing you need to do is get a *buyer's broker*, or *buyer's agent.*

Many home buyers operate under the misconception that real estate agents work for them. The real estate agent drives you around to see homes, points out features, and generally acts like your best friend. Meanwhile, the agent has a fiduciary responsibility to take every personal thing you disclose to them—like your salary, how much house you can afford, and how much you are willing to bid on a house—directly to the seller. That's because "your" agent actually works for the seller, even if the seller has a listing agent of his or her own.

Because of this confusion (not to mention a few lawsuits), several years ago a new type of real estate representative threw his hat into the ring, one whose fiduciary responsibility is to the *buyer*. These agents are called buyer's brokers or buyer's agents. They are financially obligated to represent the buyer's interests in the transaction, not the seller's.

While some buyer's agents insist on a retainer fee, many will waive the fee and just take the typical 3 percent real estate agent commission when the deal is closed. So the total 6 percent commission, which is common on most residential sales transactions and typically paid for by the seller, is split between the seller's listing agent and your buyer's broker.

Buy! Buy! Buy!

A buyer's agent exists to make the deal fairer for the buyer. Accordingly, he or she can help amend the contract to the benefit of the buyer. At the very least, your agent should be able to tell you the history of the neighborhood in terms of crime, housing turnover, changes in housing prices over the year, and expected changes in the neighborhood in terms of zoning and road construction. Additionally, a buyer's broker may have specific information on the house, such as structural problems, age and condition of the roof, and its occupants, such as

Watch Out!
If you visit a home without your agent, don't forget to mention to the listing (selling) agent that you have representation. If you don't and decide to buy the home, the listing agent will declare that he or she showed the home to you and will try to claim the entire 6 percent commission. Meanwhile, if you lose the battle, you'll owe an additional 3 percent to your agent for his or her commission.

marital status of the current owners and the owners' moving plans. But one thing brokers and agents seldom uncover are any liens against the property. To protect yourself against this problem, get mechanics lien insurance.

If you're looking at newly constructed homes, it's important for your buyer's agent to know which builders deliver a good product. It's your agent's job to negotiate with the builder to pay some closing costs and to try to get the builder to kick in options like hardwood floors, upgraded appliances, upgraded carpeting, and upgraded windows and doors, all of which will make your home more enjoyable and competitive when you sell the house in the future.

A buyer's agent can go the extra mile for you. For instance, on many new home contracts, once there is a Residential Use Permit issued (the county says the house is safe to live in), you must close the deal. The house is yours, regardless of its condition. Builders don't have to escrow (have funds held in a trust by a third party to be returned only when a condition is fulfilled) for sod, paint, or other similar items. A buyer's agent can try to get escrows from the builder for unfinished items, like lawns and backyards, to make sure the builder completes the job.

Here are some tips to selecting a buyer's agent:

- Choose one who will waive his or her fee. (Some charge extra to serve as your representative.) It becomes lost money if you decide to get out of the house-buying market.

- Make sure he or she will work for a 3 percent commission.

- Don't lock yourself into a long-term relationship. Select an agent who will work for you for a few days. Personalities sometimes conflict. If you like the person, you can extend the agreement.

- Choose a person you think you can trust.

- Pick a person with experience.

- Choose an agent who is easy to reach, one with a beeper and a cell phone. Sometimes getting into the home of your dreams is all about good timing. Your agent must be available to you.

- Ask for three references and call them. There's a lot of money at stake. People who weren't pleased with how their agent handled their situations will likely welcome the opportunity to tell you about it.

- Find out about the agent's training. Some construction background is a plus, especially if you're buying a home that hasn't been built yet.

Sell! Sell! Sell!

If, on the other hand, you're selling a home, you should pick a real estate agent who has experience selling in your neighborhood and who has a track record of motivating buyers. You should find one who can emphasize the features of your home—one that's a savvy marketer. Ask for your agent's marketing plans, advertising budget, and the number and dates of broker's open houses he or she plans to hold, as well as the type of appetizers or "welcome snacks" he or she plans to serve. (In some areas there are so many broker's opens to attend that menus from local caterers are what line up the agents at the door.) It is to your advantage to have as many brokers and agents as possible tour your house because each of them has buyers they can bring to show your home.

Moneysaver
If you sign a buyer agency agreement, it will say that 3 percent of the house sales price is due at closing. To save money, scratch that provision out, initial it, and write, "Commission is to be paid by the seller." Then sign it.

Watch Out!
If your buyer's agent tries to sell you one of his or her own listings or his or her company's listings, he or she must disclose his or her role to you and have you sign a dual agency agreement. Note, too, that in reality, it is difficult for an agent to fully represent the interests of both parties.

Likewise, you can skip the traditional weekend open houses used to attract home buyers. These can result in few sales and many "nosy neighbors."

Some sellers worry about competing with new homes. But the only time you'll have a real problem is if you're competing with the exact same product in the exact same location, which happens when people buy into a development that is under construction for years. Keep this possibility in mind when you buy. Know the length of time you plan to live in the development and when the builders plan to finish construction. Verify their completion dates with the county.

Not all is lost for the savvy seller who owns a home in a new community. If your home site has more value than those currently on the market, you can get a leg up on the competition.

Here are some tips for selling your home, especially if you're competing against new construction sales:

- Price your property right. New homes usually bring a higher price than resales. The cost per square foot needs to be about 10 percent below that being sought by the new construction because buyers often prefer new. The 10 percent reduction becomes an incentive to prospective buyers.

- Find out how much builders are charging for your "extras." How much does landscaping cost? A covered patio? In your marketing materials, show prospective buyers the value they are getting.

- Have a listing inspection handy to show buyers that your home is in tip-top shape, and buy an insurance policy to cover costs if major appliances, plumbing, or heating or air-conditioning units fail in the first year.

- Match the builder's financial incentives.

- Make your home look like a model. Eliminate clutter to make it look spacious. Visit model homes to see how professionals set the stage to sell a home.

- Neutralize your house's decor. Buyers like models because someone else's taste isn't being imposed on them.

- Depersonalize your home by putting away pictures and other sentimental and personal items.

- Emphasize the benefits. With a resale, the buyer can move right in. With new construction, builders can run into delays. Furthermore, builders leave wiggle room in their contracts for delivery dates (see Chapter 8). If the ground isn't broken yet, it could be six to eight months before the home is ready.

- Location is important. Convenience is an important selling point.

- Size matters. New construction tends to have fewer square feet.

- New homes often have defects that may not be apparent for some time. A resale is time-tested for defects.

- Get an appraisal and set your price based on it. Show it to prospective buyers to show you're only asking market value for your property.

- Pick a top agent—preferably from the $1 million or $5 million club. Top agents have vast networks of other agents and previous buyers from which they get leads and market exposure for their customers.

Moneysaver
Use the same agent to list your home and help you buy another. Usually agents will cut at least 1 percent off their commission for this double sale.

Using the Internet to find an agent

The Internet can be used for finding a buyer's or seller's agent.

REALTOR.COM (www.realtor.com) lists members of the National Association of Realtors. You can search by location and then further limit your inquiry by professional designation, office name, ZIP code, keyword, or the Realtor's name, which can also yield some background information.

The Residential Sales Council's Web site (www.rscouncil.com) can be searched by state or name for a Certified Residential Specialist (CRS)—agents who have completed an advanced education certification program—and the specialist's contact information. You also can search by location, areas of specialization (condominium, buyer brokerage, and/or relocation, for example), and language spoken.

Although you can pick an agent by location and corporate affiliation, it's a good idea to meet him or her in person before deciding to sign on.

The home-buying process

A home is the biggest purchase most people will ever make, and it can be even more costly than necessary if you don't know what you're doing. Most people go through the process with blinders on, assuming their real estate agent is looking out for their best interests.

A very common and costly misconception is that if you buy a home for $200,000 and sell it two years later for $200,000, you'll break even. Not only will you not break even, but you'll end up with a huge loss. Closing costs alone add up to thousands of dollars. And if you sell the house, you'll probably end up paying a good chunk, if not all, of the real estate commission. At 6 percent, that's $12,000 right there. A good rule of thumb is to figure that selling a house will cost you about 10 percent of the selling price after you have paid the real estate commission, transaction costs, and incur some minor repair and fix-up costs. (See Chapter 8 for more on this topic.)

There are also psychological stumbling blocks to buying a home. Have you ever noticed that open houses are marked by brightly colored helium balloons? Once inside, after getting a whiff of the freshly scented air, you're greeted by a warm, enthusiastic host or hostess. The party atmosphere is not just a fluke. It is intentionally orchestrated to get you into a festive mood so that you'll make a quick decision based more on whim than on reason. There's no telling how far some agents will go to get you in a buying mood. One agent gave his client a six-pack of beer and ended up talking him into buying a house at the full asking price.

Once you're firm on what you want to spend (or are able to spend)—see Chapter 8 for a discussion on financing options—consider the following key elements in choosing your home:

- Location. This includes proximity to work and the reputation of the community.

- Schools. The sale prices of homes often go hand in hand with the reputation of nearby schools. The higher the sale price, the higher the property tax and the more funds for education.

- Neighborhood upkeep. Do neighbors take care of their homes and yards? A well-kept home indicates pride of ownership and implies a sense of neighborly respect, community involvement, and a high regard for real estate as a

Bright Idea
If you can afford more than what you want to spend, get a pre-qualification letter based on that amount. Show only the prequalification letter to your representative. Your salary should remain private if you want to increase your chances of getting the best deal.

financial and emotional investment. Stronger neighborhoods lead to less crime.

- Zoning. Many quiet streets can become main arteries. A lack of community strength to fight zoning changes can result in high traffic and falling prices.

- Newness. New homes often sell for more than older homes because it's assumed they'll need fewer repairs in the near future.

- Builder reputation. Some builders have reputations for building homes that last. Others have reputations for sloppy workmanship.

- Number of homes for sale. The desirability of a neighborhood can be reflected in the number of homes for sale in a community at any one time. Generally, the more homes for sale, the less desirable the neighborhood. Where there's a sense of community, homeowners are more likely to make improvements to their homes than move because they can't easily replace a community.

- Housing amenities. Of course you then need to decide on the style of the home (colonial, ranch, duplex, for example), number of bedrooms and bathrooms, and other requirements.

Once this is done you can schedule visits to homes fitting your criteria. After you find a home that interests you, you can bid on it. While your buyer's agent will help you fill out the proposed contract and may make some suggestions as to how to amend it, it is always a good idea to have a real estate attorney review it before you sign. (For tips on the fine print, see Chapter 8.) Whatever you do, make sure the contract includes a provision stating that

Watch Out!
If a buyer's agent showed you a house, and, after your agency contract expires, you buy that same house, you still may be liable for the agent's commission.

the contract is contingent on funding by the lender, specifying the amount, the interest rate, and the number of years. For example, state that this contract is contingent on the lender's approval of a mortgage loan for X dollars at a fixed rate of interest at X percent for 30 years. Also, make certain that the contract is contingent on your acceptance of the home inspection report and the lender's appraisal. Otherwise, you could end up being forced to buy a home in need of expensive repairs or a home that's valued for less than what you've bid for it.

When you submit your offer, you must give an "earnest money" deposit, which is a good faith deposit that shows the seller you're serious. (It usually ranges from $500 to $2,000.) This money is deposited in an escrow account and is ultimately applied to your closing costs if the seller accepts your contract. If you back out of the deal, you forfeit the earnest money to the seller. However, if the seller doesn't accept your offer, you get your money back.

Once you have a ratified (accepted) contract, there are certain steps you must take. First, you must get a home inspection report. Make your contract contingent on your acceptance of this report, which will indicate any structural or mechanical deficiencies. If any problems are found, you may be able to renegotiate the contract to have the seller repair or replace these items. However, beware of the term *repair*. The seller's idea of "repair" and your idea of "repair" may not be the same. For instance, rather than replace a damaged parquet tile, the seller can simply (and legally) fill in the empty tile space with a similarly colored glue. Better to skip the term *repair* altogether and just use *replace*.

Also, it's a good idea to lock in an interest rate as soon as possible if you think interest rates will rise by your closing date, which is usually 30, 45, or 60 days after contract ratification. Make sure your lender can meet your deadline. This process will cost several hundred dollars for the application fee, which often includes an appraisal fee (about $250 to $350) to estimate the market value of the property and to cover the lender's costs. There's also a fee for about $60 for a credit report.

After you submit your application, your lender will assess the appraisal (the property itself serves as collateral for your loan). The lender will establish a loan to value (LTV) ratio. Most loans do not exceed 95 percent of the appraised property value or 95 percent of the sale price, whichever is less. If your down payment is less than 20 percent, the lender must get approval for Private Mortgage Insurance (PMI), used to protect the lender from loss if the borrower defaults on the loan.

The lender will also verify your employment and assets, and check your credit history (by reviewing the credit report and verifying rent payment or mortgage payment history).

By law, the lender must provide you with the following:

- Disclosures—the lender must disclose the terms and costs of the loan and past performance of the index to which the rate is tied, and must provide you with a copy of the *Consumer Handbook on Adjustable Rate Mortgages*, either when you receive an application form or pay a nonrefundable fee, whichever comes first.

- Annual percentage rate (APR)—this percentage includes interest and certain closing costs, and any points and other finance charges. These costs are factored over the term of the loan. Comparing APRs can be the best way to compare the real cost of similar loans. (The lender must provide the APR within three business days after receiving your loan application.)

- Good faith estimate—the lender must provide an itemized estimate of your closing costs within three days after receiving your application. Costs vary, though. Be prepared to pay more.

- Guide to settlement costs—the lender must provide you with a copy of the government publication *Settle Costs: A HUD Guide* within three business day of receiving your application.

At closing, ownership is legally transferred from the seller to the buyer. At this meeting you must review and sign the relevant documents and pay the closing costs. Closing costs include:

- Appraisal cost
- Credit report/credit score
- Title insurance
- Inspection fees
- Recording fees
- Underwriting fees
- Attorney's fees

Both real estate agents, attorneys (if hired), closing agent, and title agent are usually present. Some lenders may also attend. But only the buyer and the closing agent are *required* to attend the closing. (Some areas have no formal meeting, and collecting signatures and disbursing funds is all done by an escrow agent.) After all the documents are signed and the monies are disbursed, the closing agent

Watch Out!
The appraised value of a house can be less than the purchase price. Include this as a contingency in the contract.

officially records the mortgage and deed at the county courthouse. When the deed is recorded, the buyer becomes the official owner of record.

As the buyer, you should bring the following to the closing:

- A certified check for closing costs
- Evidence of homeowner's insurance
- A checkbook, in case the certified check is not in the correct amount

At closing you should receive the following documents:

- Affidavits—for various reasons, you may be asked to sign affidavits stating that you'll occupy the property as your principal residence. Likewise, the seller may be asked to sign one stating that certain improvements were completed before closing.
- Truth in lending statement—this document outlines the cost of your loan and is distributed by the lender.
- HUD-1 settlement sheet—this document lists the actual charges to the buyer and seller. (Ask to see this document in advance of your closing meeting and check both computations and amounts for accuracy.)
- Mortgage or promissory note—this document represents your promise to pay the lender in accordance with the terms specified in the loan agreement and details penalties for late or missing payments.
- Mortgage or deed of trust—this is a legal document that secures the note and gives your lender a legal claim against your home if you fail to make payments.

Using the Internet to find a home and get insurance

Using the Internet to find a home to buy can help you save time and money by enabling you to compare prices on homes and mortgages. As stated above, the Internet can also be used to find a real estate agent or a buyer's broker; it can help you procure homeowner's insurance, as well. Many sites, for instance, have interactive calculators to help you figure out how much house you can afford and determine expected monthly mortgage payments.

There are many Web sites that can aid you in your search for the perfect home.

REALTOR.COM (www.realtor.com)—At the National Association of Realtors Web site, you can search more than a million listings of new and resale homes from hundreds of multiple listing services (MLS) nationwide by city, county, ZIP code, or MLS number. You narrow your search by specifying the number of bedrooms, price range, square footage, home age and style—including handicap features, interior features (such as a workshop, tile floors, an in-law suite), exterior features (such as horse stalls, boat facilities, tile roof, tennis courts, and garage), lot features, and acreage and views—community amenities, financial considerations (options include "fixer-upper," "lease-option considered," and "trade considered"), and more. Once you've selected the criteria, you can read about the homes that fit your criteria and view color photographs.

HomeScout (homescout.homeshark.com)— This site has more than a million listings,

Timesaver
Have your agent send you listings that match your "wish list" and price range. Look at photos of the homes on the Internet to see if they appeal to you before heading out to see them.

Unofficially...
The Internet can
help home
sellers, as well.
At United
Homeowners
Association's
Web site
(uha.org), sellers
can get tips on
words to avoid
using in adver-
tisements. They
can get other
selling tips here,
as well. "How
Much Did They
Pay For The
House?"—sale
prices for more
than 50 metro
areas—is also
available.

from more than 350 Web sites. You can
search by city, property type, price, and minimum number of bedrooms.

Coldwell Banker Online
(www.coldwellbanker.com)—You can search
more than 190,000 listings at this site. If you
can't find a home that meets your requirements, the Personal Retriever feature notifies
you via e-mail when a home that is listed fits
your needs. In addition, "Neighborhood
Explorer" lets you get details on neighborhoods nationwide. All you have to do is enter
the street, city, state, and ZIP code to find out
about the area's school systems, average
incomes, housing prices, local climates, and
more.

Buyer's Resource (homes.inresco.com)
and The Abele Owners' Network (www.
owners.com)—These sites list homes for
sale by owners (FSBOs).

It's difficult house hunting when you're looking
for a home in a different city. The Internet can help
you find a home away from home.

Coldwell Banke (www.coldwellbanker.com)—
This site has an index to compare prices of
similar homes in different locations. The
Home Price Comparison Index is an especially useful tool if you're moving out of your
current area. It allows you to calculate how
much you can expect to pay for a similar
house in another city. You also can take a virtual tour of some homes.

Relocation Central (www.relocationcentral.com)—This site has a salary calculator, moving cost calculator, chamber of commerce information, weather advisory, Yellow Pages, and more.

Homefair.com (www.homefair.com/home)—The "Relocation Wizard" has a timeline for making a move. You can also compare the crime rates in more than 500 cities nationwide.

Relocation Online (www.relocationonline.com)—This site offers a free service that will coordinate your move by assisting in selecting your real estate professionals.

Virtual Relocation.com (www.virtualrelocation.com)—This is a comprehensive site with information specific to relocation and military moves. It also has a state and federal tax rate comparison, taxes by state, demographic information, and planning information.

REALTOR.COM (www.realtor.com)—The Resource Center at this site has a mortgage calculator, salary calculator, a change of address service, moving wizard to outline a timeline for a move, and area crime statistics.

In addition to finding a home, you can get quotes for homeowner's insurance on the Internet, but you'll have to contact the company directly to sign a policy. Note that online quotes are not 100 percent reliable because some factors might have been overlooked during the automated data collection. You can get free quotes on homeowner's (and

Timesaver
At MapQuest's Web site (www.mapquest.com) you can enter your address and the address of the house you'd like to visit, and MapQuest will give you street-by-street directions. You also can get information on what's in the neighborhood, such as restaurants, shopping, entertainment, and health care.

renter's) insurance at InsWeb's Web site (www.insweb.com). Answers to questions on homeowner's insurance also can be found at this site.

Strategies for buying a house "on sale"

Buying a home is expensive, but there are several ways you can get a good deal on a house.

The simplest way is to look for property that's already vacant. The sellers must still pay property taxes, mortgage payments, and insurance, as well as any neighborhood association or condominium fees. These sellers are usually more motivated to sell than those who are still living in the home and aren't burdened with double expenses.

Another way is to seek out sellers who are in distressed situations. Many divorcing couples are forced to sell their home in order to divide the assets. A combination of anger, a lack of sentimental attachment, and a desire to complete the sale and get out from under an unpleasant situation sometimes leads to highly motivated (and highly negotiable) sellers. This tactic isn't for everyone: Finding a "distress" sale takes a lot of time and effort, not to mention a good nose for sniffing out a troubled situation.

Yet another way to get a good deal on residential real estate is to buy foreclosed property, one where the bank or financial institution has taken ownership. In these cases, however, you'll probably have to have cash on hand to make repairs. Often the previous homeowners, who defaulted on their loans, take out their frustration on the house, leaving ripped and stained carpet, slashed wallpaper, and other damage.

In spite of a few headaches, there are definite advantages to buying foreclosed property. You can save big bucks on Fannie Mae foreclosures, depending on the specific property or borrower. In some cases you can buy a property at below the appraised value; you also may be able to obtain financing from Fannie Mae. (Properties are listed at www.fanniemae.com.) On Veterans Administration (VA) foreclosures you'll get a VA loan, which has many advantages, including qualifying for a higher loan amount, no down payment obligation, and requiring the seller to take on more of the closing cost burden, potentially saving you thousands. But don't expect to get a good deal on the selling price. The lenders holding foreclosed property want as close to market value as they can get to contain their losses.

If you're considering purchasing a foreclosed home, Fannie Mae advises keeping these cautions in mind:

- Be certain that the condition of the property is accurately represented.

- If the home needs repair, get an estimate of the costs of those repairs and find out if the condition of the property will prevent you from getting a mortgage loan to complete the sale.

- Make sure the seller will be able to close the transaction in a timely manner and will be able to provide you with clear title when you become the owner.

Another way to buy low and sell high is by buying a home at an auction. (Auctions are advertised in the real estate section of daily newspapers.) In most cases, the homes being sold at auction have been on the market for a while and are no longer attracting many potential buyers. The auction is used to reintroduce property to the buying market

Generally, a wide selection of homes, including single-family homes, condominiums, and town houses, located in a variety of neighborhoods throughout a community are available...Many of these homes are relatively new...Some homes may require repairs.
—Fannie Mae Web site.

in a different and exciting way. Both the buyer and seller get a fast, noncontingent sale. Auctioned homes usually have a 30-day settlement.

There are three types of auctions. At an *absolute auction*, the property sells regardless of price. While exciting, an absolute auction tends to generate higher prices because the bidding is more competitive. Then there is the *published minimum bid auction*. In this type of an auction, the minimum bid is a set price 20 to 40 percent off the last listed price. The minimum bid is disclosed. Finally, there is the *unpublished reserve auction*. The price is reserved for the seller's approval. Most of the properties being auctioned off will not sell if a minimum, undisclosed price is not bid.

Both new and old homes are sold at auctions. If you decide to take this route to save big bucks, visit the property in advance by scheduling an appointment with the listing agent. Properties are usually sold "as is," but you can schedule home inspections prior to the auction date to find out if you'd be facing expensive repairs after you bought it. Keep in mind you'll most likely be responsible for closing costs.

You must also contact the selling agent or auction house to find out the minimum cash deposit required to participate in the auction. Ask about the down payment requirements, as well. Failure to make the down payment if you're the winning bidder may cost you your deposit or more. In fact, if you aren't able to follow through with the purchase, you'll probably forfeit the down payment as well. Therefore, it's a good idea to visit a lender before bidding. Visit an attorney, as well.

If you buy one of the first homes in a new neighborhood, you may be able to negotiate a deal.

"When a builder says they have preconstruction prices, they do," says Carol Taylor, a buyer's agent in McLean, Virginia. "Every time they finish one section, they raise prices. But they end up reducing prices on those homes that don't sell at the end of the year or at the end of the section."

Then there are new homes that have been sitting on the market for a while, collecting dust. As the year comes to an end, many builders are closing their books and selling the last homes in newly established neighborhoods. Others are selling custom homes that weren't sold as expected. Either way, you can get a good deal and into a new home immediately.

Deals on new home construction are not just an end of the year treat. Builders actually have homes for immediate occupancy at all phases of their projects. Some builders will negotiate price, contribute to closing costs, and add options. Since options are usually marked up by up to 100 percent, that's where you can really negotiate. The more options a home has, the more negotiating room there is. Normally, there's a limited selection of models at closeouts. Because options and customizations are already there, these homes are more difficult for builders to sell, making them more willing to negotiate.

"The best deal is a house that's ready for closing and for some reason the buyer doesn't buy the house," Taylor says. This is called a *kickout*. The builder is stuck with a house that might not look like the model if it has a lot of customization. According to Taylor, most builders must carry these homes on the books until they're sold because the construction loans are not paid off. "If you're buying one of the last houses in a subdivision, sometimes you can actually save a great deal of money [anywhere from $10,000 to $40,000]," Taylor says.

Some builders are willing to pay off some of your personal debt just to get you qualified. They'll also kick in closing costs and added options. Taylor notes that sometimes builders simply want to unload the property so that they can reduce their expenses.

Yet another "good deal" option is the *lease-back*. Lease-backs are a twist on the typical immediate delivery offering. Model homes are sometimes sold and leased back from the buyer for six months to a year. This is especially appealing to buyers who come into town and buy a home six months to a year in advance of the time they will occupy it. The builder will then pay them rent to continue to use the home as a model. The buyer gets cash to pay the mortgage payment. They also get a fully appointed home, minus the furniture and accessories.

Frequent-flyer mile programs

Two airlines currently offer programs that allow you to accumulate frequent-flyer miles when you buy or sell a home.

American Airlines, through its AAdvantage Program, is now offering 1,500 miles per $10,000 of your purchase or sale price if you use a real estate agent from their network. You can earn between 2,500 and 5,000 additional miles by using one of their participating moving and storage services and 500 miles and free installation on a new home security system from ADT if you purchase it through the AAdvantage Program.

You can get airline miles for mortgages, too. American Airline's AAdvantage program allows members to earn frequent-flyer miles by financing your home using an affiliated lender. For more information call 800/852-9744.

Delta SkyMiles members are eligible for miles when they buy or sell a home using Better Homes and Gardens Real Estate Service. To register, call 800/988-5678. If you sell your home for at least $100,000, you'll earn enough SkyMiles for a round-trip airfare anywhere within and between destinations in the continental United States (including Alaska) and Canada.

You can also earn Delta SkyMiles through North American Mortgage Company's HouseMiles program, earning 1,000 miles for every $10,000 borrowed on a mortgage or when refinancing your home. For more details call 800/759-0306.

Just the facts

- For some people, renting is a better option than buying.

- Buyer's agents represent the buyer for all transactions; real estate agents represent the seller.

- Be sure to compute the "real" cost of the home you wish to buy, which can be thousands more than the sale price, when deciding what you can afford to bid; getting prequalified can help you avoid a lot of headaches.

- Buying your home at auction or foreclosure sales can be a terrific way to save money, but there are definite risks involved.

- You can use the Internet to search for a home and an agent, and to learn about neighborhoods and schools.

Buying the Home of Your Dreams

Chapter 8

Most people buy a home after just a few weeks or months of shopping. Some even buy one after only a few days of house hunting. While it might make the job easier, it makes the purchase more risky.

This chapter covers the cost of buying a home, the pitfalls to avoid, and the importance of having legal representation and of reading the fine print on contracts, categories, and types of mortgage loans. It also explains how to compare mortgage rates, and more.

For detailed information regarding the home-finding process, see Chapter 7. To see if you should buy the most home you can afford for investment purposes, see Chapter 4, and to see if you should borrow from your 401k to buy a home, see Chapter 12.

Shop for your mortgage wisely

The house you buy is probably the largest debt you'll ever incur but you may rush into the process, falling victim to real estate agents who are motivated by a quick sale. Real estate agents often show buyers how they can afford a house and qualify for a loan, regardless of whether the buyer actually should.

Buyers, excited at the prospect of owning a particular home—or any home at all—sometimes neglect to consider other expenses and lifestyle changes that may be necessary to make financial ends meet. Sometimes they mistakenly believe that the monthly mortgage payment includes only principal and interest, when in fact real estate taxes and mortgage insurance need to be considered as well. These additional expenses can add several hundred dollars a month to the payment.

Real estate agents often tell their younger clients to count on pay raises that will make their monthly bills easier to stomach down the road. While this may true for a majority of buyers, there are also those who will lose their jobs or will end up with a reduced household income due to divorce.

It costs about 10 percent of the price of the home to sell it. That means, for example, that if a person buys a home for the median Washington, D.C., price of $154,000 and sells it within a year at a projected gain of 2.8 percent for a selling price of roughly $158,000, there is on paper, a $4,000 profit. But 6 percent of the selling price, or $9,480, goes to real estate agent fees and another estimated $1,500 might go to help the buyer pay points. Add approximately $4,000 in attorneys' fees and other closing costs and what looked to be a profit is now an $8,000 loss. For more expensive properties, that loss increases.

Remember that when you buy a home, you take on massive debt. You can increase your savings prior to the purchase, thereby reducing your debt load, by taking your time and shopping around. Investigate as you would for any other investment or large purchase.

Getting professional representation

When you buy a home you deal with many different people who are experts in many different industries and disciplines. These include:

- Law
- Real estate
- Brokerage
- Mortgage finance
- Insurance (hazard, liability, title, and possibly mortgage and home warranties, to name a few)
- Real estate title issues
- Survey issues
- "Sticks and bricks" issues, which include structural, electrical, mechanical (heating, ventilating, air-conditioning, and plumbing), equipment (stove, refrigerator, and washer and dryer) roofing, foundation, soils, and water issues, among others

The surprising reality of buying a home, according to Beau Brincefield, a real estate attorney and consumer advocate based in Alexandria, Virginia, is that so many transactions are completed with relatively few disasters.

Get experienced experts in each profession who will protect your interest, Brincefield advises. Get a lawyer, a buyer's broker, and an experienced professional home inspector. They will have the tools and

Watch Out!
According to industry standards, you should spend no more than 28 percent of your net income on housing and no more than 36 percent on total indebtedness. Even using these percentages, you'll feel the financial stretch. You'd be better off borrowing less than the loan amount for which you qualify.

Bright Idea
How do you find a good real estate attorney? Look in *Best Lawyers in America,* or *Martindale-Hubbell,* a sort of telephone book of attorneys. Additionally, check out the following Web sites: www.martindale.com/locator/home.html; www.wld.com; and www.abanet.org. Many state bar associations have Web sites and referral lists of attorneys, as well.

skills to help you assess the home, community, contracts, and documents, he says.

Note, however, that "an experienced real estate lawyer is probably the only person who understands the entire home-buying process who has no interests that are adverse to the home buyer," Brincefield says. "Even a buyer's agent has an inherently conflicting interest," he says, as do all of the other players.

Although the buyer's broker has a fiduciary responsibility to represent the buyer's interests, the buyer's broker has a conflict of interest that comes from the desire to complete the transaction. The buyer's broker does not get paid if there is no sale. Therefore, the buyer's broker is motivated to complete the sale, whether or not it is a good deal for the buyer.

Conflicts of interest can also exist when an agent refers a buyer to a settlement service, title agent, appraiser, and mortgage lender. The conflict arises if the agent charges a referral fee to the service provider. In most states such a fee is illegal if it is not disclosed to the buyer. And even if the agent doesn't personally make the referral, the conflict remains because these contractors will want the agent to refer them business in the future.

Real estate agents will use appraisers, mortgage lenders, and so on with whom the agent has a good relationship. The good relationship stems from helping out the agent. The agent will use an appraiser, for example, who has a history of appraising the property's value at the same amount as the closing price. These contractors, as well as the agent, have an interest in each other and maintaining a business relationship, and this can conflict with the buyer's interests. As a result, the buyer's interest (because the relationship with the buyer is short-term) can fall by the wayside in an effort to maintain a good business relationship with the contractor (with whom the agent will maintain a long-term relationship).

Another conflict comes from the contracted service provider. These providers have incentives to not find major problems that could interfere with closing the deal, especially if the service provider wants repeat business from the agent.

It is also important to find an independent home inspector, preferably one who's a member of the American Society of Home Inspectors (ASHI)— a voluntary trade association with voluntary standards—because home inspectors are not licensed in many areas.

Brincefield warns that you shouldn't sign a contract that limits a professional home inspector's liability to a return of the fee. Find out the inspector's credentials, experience, and expertise, he says, and read the contract carefully. If the inspector is knowledgeable, he or she will take responsibility for anything that goes wrong. Doctors and lawyers simply can't return their fees and be done with it if they commit malpractice. "Why should a professional home inspector be treated any differently from any other professional?" Brincefield points out. Don't agree to hold a professional home inspector to a lesser standard than you would any other professional.

Builders' contracts: understanding the fine print

Being clear on what your contract actually says is especially important when buying from a builder.

Unofficially...
To find out about ASHI requirements or to find a professional home inspector in your area who is a member of ASHI, point your Web browser to www.ashi.com.

No matter how friendly they are, builders will probably sue you if you breach the contract, and they have the financial backing to do so easily. They're apt to sue you for breach even if they can line up another buyer the very next day. Your down payment simply becomes more profit to them.

If you aren't clear about your contract's language, you can end up paying, literally, for building delays, as well. Builders are notorious for having very one-sided contracts, Brincefield warns. If you don't seek to amend the language so that it's more favorable to you, or at least are clear about what you're getting yourself into, and the builder doesn't deliver on time for whatever reason (a heated market, bad weather), you can be left with added moving, storage, and temporary housing expenses if you've already sold your home or given notice to your landlord.

"No builder contract obligates the builder to deliver the house when promised," Brincefield notes. A verbal delivery date doesn't obligate the builder, and even if the builder puts something in writing, the actual contract date supersedes the estimate, he says.

It's not just the delivery date you need to worry about. Builder contracts typically allow for changes in the physical construction and layout of the home, Brincefield says. A builder can modify the floor plan, the grading of the lot, building materials, and even the orientation of the home on the lot.

The builder contract simply does not protect the buyer if the property isn't completed properly, Brincefield says. Although many contracts provide for a presettlement inspection, the *punch list*, which is a list of building specifications and minimum completion standards, may or may not identify everything that is defective or deficient.

While it is advisable to bring along a professional home inspector when you walk through your home, the typical builder contract prohibits the purchaser from delaying the settlement or from requiring funds to be held in escrow to complete anything deficient or lacking in the home, Brincefield explains.

When buying a home in an undeveloped or only partly finished community, be sure to question the placement of neighborhood structures, for instance, utility power poles and lines and the like, advises Steve Peddy, a partner at the law firm Berkman, Henoch, Peterson and Peddy, PC, in Long Island, New York. How will the placement of these structures affect your unit? Peddy suggests viewing the original map filed with the county in order to look for easements.

You should also know what will trigger your obligation to close. It should be based on *certificates of occupancy* (CO), Peddy says. (A CO is issued by the local zoning board and indicates that the structure complies with building codes of the municipality. A CO does not specify whether the builder built your house using the specifications to which you both agreed.) The county issues a CO after inspecting and determining that the project and construction was completed satisfactorily, in accordance with the applicable county codes and standards and the building contracts. Note, however, that the issuance of a CO by the county does *not* mean that the home is in perfect condition. It means that it has passed the county's inspection. Your insurance provider will need this certificate before issuing a home-owner's insurance policy.

Bright Idea
Before buying new construction, check out the builder's reputation with the Better Business Bureau and county consumer complaints office. The county or state consumer affairs or consumer protection office is usually in the state's Office of the Attorney General.

Peddy says you should be sure to review the plans and specifications of the home. The specs include materials and finishes. Model homes are typically furnished and upgraded, so if you want your house to look like the model, get the costs for extras up front. Extras and upgrades can be very expensive. Upgrades include hardwood floors, higher quality windows, higher quality carpeting, crown molding, and higher quality bathroom fixtures, among others.

Purchasers can choose to finish some rooms themselves, opting for a credit from the builder, Peddy says. The credits are less than what the consumer will have to pay in the marketplace to complete such work.

Peddy gives these additional tips to consider before signing a contract to buy a new home:

- While you still have some leverage, negotiate in your contract to have your attorney create an escrow account for repairing items that are defective or deficient. Some builders, once they have your money, are not so inclined to fix things.

- In certain states, property taxes are high. New construction taxes are amassed on vacant land. Find out what they will be when the home is fully assessed and who pays them prior to closing.

- Some states have a statutory warranty, a certain amount of time the builder guarantees the product. You may be able to negotiate a longer term or more comprehensive coverage in your contract.

The bottom line is that you must negotiate your contract before you sign it. Brincefield advises his clients to add the line, "This contract is subject to review and approval by an attorney for the purchaser" to every contract.

The lowdown on resale contracts

In addition to issues similar to those encountered with builders' contracts, resale contracts have some issues of their own, not the least of which is the timing of the closing date. If you get your mortgage commitment too soon, the bank may not hold the interest rate long enough for you to close, and you may have to pay to lock in the rate or extend the hold period. Lock-ins of 30 to 60 days are common, but they can be shorter—just until your loan is approved—and they can be longer, up to 4 months.

Or, if the interest rate increases, you may not qualify for the loan, or, if you do, you may have to pay a higher mortgage payment.

The following is a list of many of the issues that, according to Peddy, should be addressed in a resale contract.

> You should first make sure that the contract states that the seller shall deliver COs for all home improvements. Your lender may want to see these.

> The contract should be contingent on a home inspection meeting the purchaser's approval. Expenses should also be set in the contract, that is, who pays for what—points, a home warranty, for example—should be determined ahead of time.

> The contract should specify what personal property items are included in the sale of the home and what the seller plans to take with him or her. Personal property that conveys with the sale of the land and the home

should be clearly stated on the sales contract to protect both the buyer and seller. Personal property includes items that can be removed from the premises without damaging the premises. Some examples might include washers and dryers, dishwashers, refrigerators, stoves and ovens, lighting fixtures, and area rugs. But questions arise regarding fixtures, which are things attached to the home, such as outside air conditioner units or heating coils, dishwashers, and ceiling fans. If they're included with the home, and the presumption is that they are, the contract should state that they need to be in working order at closing.

Use in occupancy should also be addressed. Commonly referred to as a *rent-back*, the seller may close, but contract to stay in occupancy of the home for a set amount of time, paying rent to the buyer, who is legally the property's owner. Before opting for this arrangement, make sure the contract states that the seller must leave the property in the condition in which it was inspected, and have your attorney set up an escrow fund to cover any damages. (This fund should be set up even if the seller moves out right after closing. If it isn't, inspect the property on your way to the closing.)

Finally, the contract should allow for a specific remedy if there is a default by the seller. Insist on the return of your good faith deposit and for a reimbursement of all costs you incurred. Ask for the specific right "to sue the seller for

Watch Out!
It is ill advised to allow a seller to stay in occupancy of your home once you've closed, because unforeseen circumstances may force the seller to extend his or her occupancy period, which can end up costing you big (at least up front) in legal fees (if the seller refuses to evacuate) and temporary housing expenses, not to mention stress.

legal and equitable damages" and the right to require the seller to perform obligations under the contract, called the "right of specific performance."

Qualifying for a mortgage

Qualifying for a mortgage loan is the first step in the underwriting process. Having a high enough household income is not in itself enough to qualify for a loan. The lender must also have reason to believe that you're responsible enough to pay back the loan on schedule. One indication of your reliability is whether you've paid back other loans on time (your credit cards and school loans, for example). So the lender will check your credit record compiled and held by one of the three credit bureaus: Equifax (800/685-1111), Experian (800/397-3742), or Trans Union (800/888-4213). You can order a copy of your credit report to check its accuracy and to see where you might need to make repairs in your credit record before applying for the loan. While you don't have to have squeaky clean credit to get a loan, you'll end up paying for your blemishes in the form of higher interest rates, which can be expensive.

Computer-aided credit scoring

Many loan officers rely on computers when making lending decisions, using a computer-generated score when approving or denying mortgage loans. Credit scoring is a system used to rank the relative risk of default presented by groups of borrowers, that is, it is used to assess the chance of whether or not you'll live up to your debt obligations. These systems, usually based on models developed by Fair, Isaac in San Rafael, California, use statistical analysis techniques to assess the likelihood a borrower will pay back a loan based on his or her past payment performance, credit utilization patterns, and credit history. The system is not perfect: The fact is that some borrowers who are accepted by the lender will become delinquent, and some declined would have been great customers.

The score provides an index—a level of risk—based on the credit report. There is no specific "passing" grade. Nor, by itself, is the score a deal maker or breaker. Lenders develop their own lending policies including their own acceptable score ranges for particular credit and loan products. A "good" score is a number that matches the level of risk a lender is willing to accept for a particular loan (or credit card).

The categories assessed, in order of importance, include:

1. Past payment performance
2. Amount of debt
3. Length of credit history
4. Number of inquiries made on your credit record
5. Mix or types of credit

Past payment performance is the most predictive of these characteristics and carries the most weight. Late payments fall into groups including 30, 60, and 90 days or longer past due. Your score here depends on how often, if at all, you were late in making payments, how late you were, and how recent these delinquent payments were.

Amount of debt is next. People who are heavily extended tend to be higher risks than those who use credit conservatively, according to Fair, Isaac. For example, someone using 75 percent of his or her available credit represents greater risk than someone who is using only 25 percent.

"Recent research has found that unused credit capacity is very important in the credit score, along with late payment information," Mark Eppli, professor of finance at George Washington University, explains. "Unused credit capacity is the difference between the credit used on all your credit cards, less the credit available. If an applicant is constantly bumping against their credit limits, [he or she is] considered a poor credit risk in that [he or she] might not be able to appropriately handle [his or her] own financial limitations. Credit capacity is highly predictive of mortgage default."

On the plus side, the longer you have had credit established, the better you fair, according to Fair, Isaac. For example, a borrower who has had credit for less than two years represents a relatively higher risk than someone who has had credit for five years or more. But having a relatively brief credit history does not automatically mean higher risk. What carries the most weight is how people pay their bills and how extended they are on their available credit.

Note: To create the credit scoring system, Fair, Isaac has taken a stratified sample of more than one million borrowers culled from tens of millions of credit records (good and bad loans, across populations, and spanning the nation) to devise statistical models that consider many risk factors. These scores don't take into account nationality, race, national origin, gender, marital status, ethnicity, or other factors prohibited by the Equal Credit Opportunity Act and Regulation B, according to Fair, Isaac. In addition they don't use income or other loan

66

There is no mystery about how people can improve their scores. It really makes sense when you think about it. Credit scores automatically improve as one's overall credit picture gets better. That means showing an historical pattern of paying your bills on time and using credit conservatively. Maintaining good credit is a lot like maintaining a car—you want to make sure it is always in good repair, and attend to any problems right away.
—Sondra Harris, spokesperson, Fair, Isaac.

application information. The computer-generated credit score is designed to be objective. Some banks have their own systems and may use the information noted above.

There are about 35 reasons you can receive a low score. Four will be listed on each credit report to explain why you didn't receive a higher score. Some of the reasons are "Amount owed on accounts is too high," "Delinquency on accounts," "Too many accounts with balances," "Too many inquiries last 12 months," "Too few accounts currently paid as agreed," and "Account payment history too new to rate."

The Fair, Isaac credit bureau score models consist of 10 different scoring models based on groups defined by overall credit profile, such as presence of derogatory information, the age of the file, and the amount of information in the file. Predictor characteristics within each of these groups indicate if a borrower will default or pay. So if you are relatively new to this country or young and just beginning to establish a credit history, you won't necessarily get a low score based on having a relatively new credit history. You will be evaluated in comparison with those with similar new credit histories using those credit patterns found to be predictive of credit risk for that group. If you don't have a credit record, traditional underwriting methods will be used to determine if you are a good credit risk.

If you're considering buying a new home, keep in mind that no score lasts forever and no one can change your score but you. Better credit management leads to a more favorable score.

Fair, Isaac gives these three tips for improving your credit score over time:

1. Pay bills on time. Delinquent payments and collections can have a major impact on a borrower's credit risk profile.

2. Keep credit card balances low. High outstanding debt can affect your perceived risk.

3. Apply for new credit sparingly. Acquiring lots of new credit is considered a warning sign by many lenders.

For more information on credit scoring, visit Fair, Isaac's Web site at www.fairisaac.com.

How much can you borrow?

Traditional underwriting has been guided by the three "Cs":

- *Credit reputation*, which is the determination of a borrower's willingness to repay (this is the category for which the credit scores are used to provide an indication of delinquency and foreclosure risk)

- *Capacity*, which is measured by overall income and expense profiles and is confirmed, in part, by debt-to-income ratios

- *Collateral*, which is measured by a loan-to-value (LTV) ratio

Once a credible payment history is established the borrower can move on to the next step—capacity. Generally both Freddie Mac and Fannie Mae suggest, but don't require, that housing payments not exceed 28 percent of total household income, that is, your gross household income. Housing payments include the principal, interest, taxes, and insurance, commonly referred to as PITI. Principal and interest are the debt service payments on the loan. The taxes of concern here are the real

Bright Idea
Don't apply for, or open, multiple credit accounts in a short period of time. And don't try to change a score overnight by suddenly closing or opening accounts. Scores are based on complex statistical models and such actions may backfire, according to Fair, Isaac.

estate taxes on the home—make certain that the real estate taxes are based on the anticipated purchase price of the home and not some other hypothetical number. Insurance here refers to the homeowner's insurance.

These fixed housing payments should not exceed 28 percent of household income. Generally speaking, principal and interest make up 25 to 26 percent of the 28 percent, real estate taxes, 1 to 1.5 percent, and insurance is usually less than 0.5 percent of the 28 percent. (These ratios are also used in the Internet mortgage qualifier programs.) Note: Real estate taxes vary by municipality.

There is a second hurdle for capacity: Your total fixed payments should not exceed 35 percent of your total household income. Total fixed payments include housing payments, car payments, student loan payments, fixed credit card payments, and other fixed monthly expenses. All of these should be listed on your credit report. If you have a high credit score or other mitigating factors, lenders may go as high 30 percent and 38 percent, respectively. While this is great if you've found the perfect house and it's a bit more expensive than one you'd normally qualify for, don't expect to have a lot of spending money until your income increases. These high percentages will stretch your discretionary income to the limit.

The third hurdle you must clear is collateral. You must have a 20 percent down payment or pay private mortgage insurance (PMI), which is usually required by lenders on down payments of less than 20 percent. Even if you have enough cash for a down payment, you must consider whether you can afford the closing costs for the loan, discussed later in this chapter.

The best mortgage for you

Getting the best deal on a home doesn't end when your bid is accepted by the seller. The interest rate and terms of a mortgage have a significant impact on how much it will cost to occupy that home.

For example, if you have a $200,000 loan fixed at 8 percent over 30 years, you'll pay $328,310.49 in interest alone over the life of the loan. But if you lock in a 6 percent interest rate you'll pay only $231,676.38 in interest, a difference of $96,634.11.

It's obviously a good idea to understand the various types of mortgages and to shop around for the best overall rates.

Types of mortgage loans

There are three basic types of loans available to home buyers.

The first is the conforming conventional mortgage. With a current limit of $240,000 as of January 1999 (this amount changes annually), this popular form of financing is usually underwritten by banks, savings and loans, or other types of mortgage lenders. The most common types are 15- and 30-year fixed-rate mortgages. Because these mortgages aren't backed by the government, many lenders require borrowers to pay PMI if you make a down payment of less than 20 percent.

The second type is government loans. The most common of these types of loans are Federal Housing Administration (FHA) loans, which attract many first-time home buyers because they require smaller down payments than conventional loans, as is the case with Department of Veterans Affairs (VA) mortgages. Veterans can qualify for a loan up to $203,000 with no down payment. These mortgages are government-backed, so lenders do not require PMI.

The third type of loan is the subprime mortgage. This loan charges higher interest rates and/or a higher down payment than that charged on a conventional loan. It is geared toward prospective buyers with less-than-perfect credit histories.

Mortgage loan options

There are many mortgage loan options available to borrowers. There are 30-year fixed-rate mortgages and 15-year fixed-rate ones. There are one-year adjustable-rate mortgages (ARMs), as well as three-, five-, and seven-year ones. You can also choose between zero-point loans and paying discount points. (One *point* is equal to 1 percent of the total mortgage amount paid at closing. Paying points up front reduces the loan's interest rate, and may save you money if you keep the house long enough to recapture the cost of the upfront points.)

While most lenders will loan between 80 and 90 percent of the home's total value, there are some loan programs that will allow you to borrow up to 125 percent of the purchase price of your home. Although it may make sense to use the extra money to pay off credit card and other debt, Steven Schnall, president of The New York Mortgage Company LLC, warns to carefully consider the consequences if you fail to pay in a timely manner. If you default on your credit card payment, the result may be a bad credit rating. But if you default on your mortgage, you will probably lose your home. Furthermore, with a loan that's valued more than your home, you'll have negative equity. If you want to sell the house, you'll have to come up with the difference between the selling price and the amount owed on the loan.

Also, only the interest on the purchase price of your home can be deducted from your income taxes. Improvements can also be deducted from your income taxes if you make the improvements to a home office. Otherwise the improvement costs are used to figure out your net profit from the sale of your home. Note that the interest on the first $1.1 million in debt can be deducted from your income for tax purposes.

Remember that the more you borrow on a conventional loan relative to the price of your home, the more risk a lender takes, and, therefore, the higher your interest rate. A high interest rate increases the cost of owning a home for you.

There are also mortgage programs that require no income or other verification. These are called no doc or low doc loans. These programs are useful to people who are self-employed because income verification may be more difficult, but if you select this type of loan, you should be prepared to pay for the privilege of not having to prove your income in the form of a higher interest rate.

Whether or not the lender verifies the information you do provide, if you overstate your earnings to get a loan and the lender finds out beforehand, your loan will be declined, Schnall says. If the lender finds out afterward, then you've committed fraud. You'll be considered in default of the loan, he warns, and the lender can foreclose on your home and prosecute you because committing fraud is a felony. Usually, Schnall says, the lender will default you and force you to take a higher rate loan someplace else.

As you know, lenders make money from borrowers by charging interest. There are many different categories of loans from which lenders collect interest. With a fixed-rate mortgage, the interest rate is

Timesaver
Don't waste time calling various lenders to get the latest interest rates. Instead, look in your newspaper real estate section for a weekly listing or for daily updates through various Internet sites—www. amomortgage. com, for example.

Bright Idea
There are quite a few special programs available to help those who can afford monthly payments, but not a large down payment, and for those who can't really afford monthly payments at all. For information, contact a lender, Fannie Mae, and your county's housing authority. If you've spent time in the military, contact your local VA office.

fixed for the life of the loan, which is usually 15, 20, or 30 years.

Mentioned above, an adjustable-rate mortgage (ARM) starts out with a comparably low interest rate, which is tied to an index (usually U.S. Treasuries—obligations of the U.S. Federal Government—or cost of funds index). The interest rate index changes from month to month and year to year based on many economic factors. Your mortgage interest rate will therefore also change at the anniversary of your mortgage loan. Most one-year ARMs will adjust to the interest rate index plus 2.75 percent. The 2.75 percent is the premium for the risk the lender assumes in issuing the loan. For most ARMs, if the index rises in response to increases in short-term interest rates, your payments will increase by a maximum of 2 percent in any one year, and by as much as 6 percent over the life of the loan. That means your rate, over 13 years, can jump from a low of 5 percent to a high of 11 percent, raising your monthly payments considerably. ARMs are usually fixed at one and three years and are advantageous if you plan to spend a relatively short time in the home.

A variation on the standard ARM is the two-step mortgage, where the interest rate is adjusted only once at five or seven years.

Finally, balloon loans have a fixed interest rate for 7 or 10 years. At that time they mature, and a lump-sum payment of the loan balance is due.

The risk of foreclosure

It's important to take a minute and say a few words about loan default. Think twice before bidding on a home that's priced high enough to force you to use an adjustable-rate mortgage. Think again, too, if the purchase price is so exorbitant that you can't put down at least 10 percent. A high LTV coupled with an economic trigger such as a reduction of income (due to job loss or divorce, for example) seem to be the reason for most delinquent mortgage payments and foreclosures.

The fact is that a low down payment requirement makes home ownership possible for many buyers who otherwise couldn't afford to buy a home. But a low down payment makes it easier for owners to walk away from the loan because there isn't much of an initial investment there. It also can turn an owner "upside down," that is, the house ends up being worth less than the mortgage. An upside down mortgage can occur if housing prices decline over time to the point where the loan amount is greater than the value of the house. If the owner then tries to sell the home, his or her losses can be pretty great.

Another road to foreclosure begins with spending equity. Many people refinance their homes, using their equity for other purchases and expenses. People who do this count on their properties appreciating sufficiently to cover these expenditures once they sell their homes. If that doesn't happen, they'll have to pay the equity back out of their own pocket because the value of the house is insufficient to pay back the loan.

Getting the best mortgage rate

Once you've figured out what type of mortgage you want, the next step is to find the most favorable rate. Note that the lowest rates may not be the best overall rates. In fact, Schnall says, advertised rates generally aren't what you end up paying. They don't, for example, include points. The only way to

Moneysaver
Monitor your mortgage payments, especially if you have an ARM. Many are adjusted incorrectly. Furthermore, sometimes lenders distribute your payments between interest and principal inaccurately. Get a detailed payment record from your lender every six months to make sure your payments were properly applied to interest, principal, and escrow.

accurately compare loans is to figure the annual percentage rates (APRs) over 30 years. This will reflect the true loan cost over 30 years. But what if you move before then? Most people don't stay in their homes that long, Schnall observes. (See Tables 8.1, 8.2, and 8.3.)

TABLE 8.1 HOMEOWNER FOR 30 YEARS

Interest rate(%)	Points	APR(%)
7	0	7.00
7	1	7.10
7	2	7.20
7	3	7.30

TABLE 8.2 HOMEOWNER FOR 5 YEARS

Interest rate(%)	Points	APR(%)
7	0	7.00
7	1	7.25
7	2	7.49
7	3	7.74

TABLE 8.3 SAME LENDER YIELDS BUT NEW BORROWER TERMS

Rate%	Points	Lender Yield/APR%
7.00	0	7.0
6.75	1	7.0
6.50	2-1/16	7.0
6.25	3-1/8	7.0

The APR is not an accurate measure for comparison among different ARMs. The APR on adjustable rates has little value, Schnall says. The APR for ARMs includes the interest rate effective at the start of the loan, points and closing costs, and the approximation of interest rates for the remainder of the loan. This approximation is based on the index and the margin today, according to Schnall.

To compare ARMs you should find out the actual terms of each of the loans. Which loan has the higher margin, and which has the higher cap? If you don't hit the cap, the margin becomes relevant. For example, a three-year adjustable rate is 6.5 percent today with a 2 percent cap. On day one of the fourth year of the loan your rate will become the one-year Treasury interest rate plus a margin of 2.75 percent. Today the one-year Treasury interest rate is at 4.5 percent. Add that percentage amount to the margin (2.75 percent) and you've got an interest rate of 7.25 percent. It made no difference that you had a 2 percent cap because the adjustment was less than 2 percent.

Now assume instead that in three years from now the one-year Treasury interest rate is at 6 percent and your margin is 2.75 percent; your new interest rate would be 8.75 percent. Since you have a 2 percent cap, your interest rate is 8.5 percent (your original rate of 6.5 percent plus your 2 percent cap). The interest rate cap places a ceiling on how much your mortgage interest rate can change in one adjustment period. Since there is a 2 percent cap in this example, the rate can increase to a maximum of 8.5 percent.

What's negotiable in a mortgage?

Lenders are in the business of making money. They want your business, and if they have to reduce a few fees to get it, sometimes they'll do just that. A few costly items that may be scaled down, depending on the lender and other factors—such as how much business the lender, attorney, and appraiser have had that month—are the following:

- Points
- Application fees

Watch Out!
If you borrow as much as you qualify for, you are placing yourself in a risky financial situation if you lose your job or get sick and cannot make your monthly payments.

- Appraisal fees
- Attorney's fees
- Mortgage insurance
- Credit report fees
- Courier fees

To know where to start negotiations, call various lenders, attorneys, and appraisers to find out their fees. See Table 8.4 to get a general idea of the amount of fees that may be charged.

TABLE 8.4 CLOSING COSTS FOR A $150,000 HOME

Appraisal	$300
Credit check	$100
Application/underwriter	$600
Mortgage insurance	$600
Points (negotiated)	$0
Courier fees	$75
Attorney's fees	$600
Total	**$2,275**

(Taken from an actual 1997 closing in a Washington, D.C. home)

Any bank or mortgage broker can make changes to the loan agreement, Schnall says. If you're a good customer, they may be willing to forgo some of the fees. Schnall stresses that "your focus should be making sure your rate and your points are in line and making sure your closing costs are reasonable."

"Ask a lot of questions," Schnall encourages. Don't just sign on the dotted line. Like your contract for your home, your mortgage contract is negotiable. Before you even pick a mortgage broker or lender, be sure to call the Better Business Bureau and the banking department of your state. They keep a record of all consumer complaints. There are many lenders out there that will take advantage of those who are in too much of a rush to learn about the process and those with bad credit records.

Paying for convenience: buyer beware the mortgage broker

You can often save money by financing your loan directly from a bank. This involves shopping around for the best deal. On the other hand, if you don't have time to spend looking around, you can enlist the aid of a mortgage broker, who has access to hundreds of lenders and will be glad to do your shopping for you—for a price.

Mortgage brokers get what's called a yield spread premium, which is a rebate paid by the lender, Schnall says. (The yield spread premium is disclosed on the good faith estimate, which you receive three days after applying for the loan.) The broker gets a wholesale price from the lender, usually in the form of discount points, but passes a retail price on to you.

"The key . . . is to be aware that the interest rate the mortgage broker delivers to you is affected by the yield spread premium that the bank pays to the mortgage broker," Schnall says. This is going to cost you. On the other hand, brokers can pass some of the savings along, but you've got to ask for it. If the broker refuses to budge, be willing to move on to another broker. The prospect of losing business can be very motivating.

Here is how it works: If the broker offers you a 7 percent interest rate with 3 points, you also have the choice of taking, say, 7½ percent with one point or 7¾ percent with zero points. It's all the same to the broker because the difference is just a matter of when you pay the interest—either up front or over the life of the loan.

Note that, as you "buy down" the points, the total amount of the loan may not remain the same. You may end up qualifying for a larger loan with a lower interest rate. However, you will need a larger down payment at closing, which requires more savings up front. It's a tradeoff.

Remember, one point costs 1 percent of your loan. So, continuing with the above example, if you take out a loan for $150,000, the broker is receiving a $1,500 kickback from the lender. But if the mortgage broker prices the interest rate of the loan at 8 percent, he or she gets two points from the lender, or $3,000, as an added incentive for selling the loan at a higher interest rate. That is the yield spread premium, Schnall explains. "The higher the yield, the bigger the yield spread premium is," he says.

Watch Out!
Many loan officers are paid on commission and don't have much incentive to ensure that borrowers are fully informed about their choices.

According to Schnall, if you pay above two points, you're being taken. If a mortgage broker is charging more than one point, you could probably get the same loan cheaper by going to the bank directly, Schnall notes.

When to pay discount points

As mentioned above, many lenders will allow you to pay interest up front in the form of discount points. If you intend to stay in your new home for 30 years paying points will pay off. But if you stay only a few years, you'd better do some quick calculations.

It's true that if you pay a few thousand dollars up front at closing, you can reduce your monthly mortgage payment by hundreds of dollars. But those dollars spent on buying down the interest rate could be making more money if invested in the market than the reduction in your monthly bill.

On an ARM, you don't get as many benefits paying points as you do on a fixed-rate mortgage,

Schnall says. Moreover, paying points conflicts with wanting to save money at the start of your loan repayment term, which is most often why buyers choose ARMs.

On a fixed-rate mortgage each point generally reduces your interest rate by 0.25 percent over the life of your loan, according to Schnall. So, if you pay two points, your interest rate will be 0.5 percent cheaper than if you'd paid no points. On a 30-year fixed-rate mortgage, you'd save that 0.5 percent every year for 30 years and only pay 2 percent of the cost of the loan up front, Schnall says. If you're in the home for the long haul, this strategy pays off, says Schnall. But if you pay the points and stay only one year, you've wasted your money. Generally it takes at least five years to recoup the cost of your points, according to Schnall.

Home loans on the Internet

Shopping for a home loan can be a full-time job. You can speed up the process by using the Internet to make comparisons.

Many lenders will prequalify you for a loan over the Internet. Note, however, that this is not the same as preapproval where the lender checks your credit and verifies your income and assets. Full approval also necessitates an appraisal and title search be completed.

United Homeowners Association (www.uha.org) has a mortgage rate shopper that offers your profile to hundreds of lenders and allows them to make you an offer.

Liberty First Financial (www.LoanGuide.com) has an online educational tool that can help you decipher which loans are best for you. After pitching its own product, it takes you step by step

Unofficially...
Rates move up and down daily. When you do decide to lock in a specific rate, remember that it's always a guessing game. You may have gotten an even lower rate had you waited another day. Alternatively, you may get a higher rate and no longer be able to qualify for the loan.

through the loan process. It also has a rate notification program, which will send an e-mail to you if the rate you want becomes available.

Mortgage Market Information Services Inc. (www.interest.com) has a directory of mortgage rates and mortgage lenders by state and by programs for special mortgage needs, such as vacant property.

QuickenMortgage (www.quickenmortgage.com) has the average interest rate by loan type and state. The rate is updated daily, and the time of last update is posted.

Mortgage-Net (www.mortgage-net.com) has an APR calculator that will answer questions such as "which loan is cheaper, 8 percent at 1 point or 7.75 percent at 2 points?".

Bank Rate Monitor (www.bankrate.com) has national averages for interest rates and news stories on the latest trends in interest rates. The Mortgage Rate Alert will send an e-mail to you when national mortgage rates move up or down by $\frac{1}{10}$ point or more.

E-loan (www.eloan.com) allows you to search for rates and apply for a loan at its site.

HomeShark (www.homeshark.com) has a rate shopper by e-mail and a rate watcher to get today's rates. You can also apply for a loan at this site.

MicrosoftHomeAdvisor (www.homeadvisor.com) permits you to track daily mortgage rates and shop for loans.

The Lending Tree (www.lendingtree.com) allows you to fill out a questionnaire at its site and get responses from lenders within two business days.

GetSmart.com (www.getsmart.com) has a mortgage finder.

Down payment gifts

One of the biggest stumbling blocks to purchasing a home, especially as a first-time buyer, is coming up with enough cash for the down payment and closing costs. Thankfully, there are options out there for those in need of a little extra help.

PNC Mortgage, a lending institution based in Vernon Hills, Illinois, has the MatriMoney Wedding Registry Program. The program allows couples to open up a special interest-bearing money market account to pool cash wedding gifts toward a mortgage down payment and closing costs.

You also can charge up to 2 percent of the down payment on your home to your credit card. (For a discussion of credit card use pros and cons, see Chapter 2.)

Just the facts

- Comparing APRs on ARMs will not give you an accurate comparison of rates, but it will on fixed-rate mortgages.

- Appraisers and home inspectors have an inherent incentive to please the real estate agent, which can sometimes lead to inaccurate findings.

- Hire a real estate attorney who will help you fully understand all the provisions of your builder's or resale contract, and who can negotiate the best terms for you.

- Mortgage brokers are sometimes compensated by banks through yield spread premiums, which could cost you thousands of dollars.

- It generally takes five years to recoup the cost of points paid on your mortgage, so paying them is

Unofficially...
Couples engaged to be married are in luck. A survey conducted by *Modern Bride* magazine showed that in 1995, newlyweds received an average of $3,432 in cash gifts.

not a good idea if you intend to spend only a few years in your new home.

- The Web contains many sites at which you can find daily interest rates, as well as apply for loans.

Debt

GET THE SCOOP ON...
Why some people get into debt ▪ Why creditors
make it easy for you to stay in debt ▪
How to dig out of debt ▪ How to prevent
foreclosure

Digging Out of Debt

P eople often think twice about spending cash. It's real money. But the plastic stuff is deceptive. It's just a bill down the road that can be put off month after month. Max out one credit card and get another. The road to bankruptcy is paved with plastic.

Strategies often used to get out of debt can sometimes land you in more hot water. Some forms of debt consolidation can literally cost you your home. For example, if you take out a 125 percent mortgage or get a home equity loan to pay off your credit card debt and default on the payments, your lender may foreclose on your home to cut its losses.

Meanwhile, credit card issuers encourage cardholders to buy on credit by giving them incentives like frequent-flyer miles, cash-back offers, and low introductory interest rates. And there are nearly no limits to the products and services you can buy on credit, from ice cubes to gas to a new car. Although credit cards give their holders the feeling of having plenty of money to spend, the reality for many is deeper and deeper debt.

In this chapter I'll explain how consumers like you get into debt. I'll also give you tips from experts on how to set up a budget, get out of debt, and maintain a debt-free lifestyle with as little infringement on your current lifestyle as reasonably possible.

Figuring out how you got there

The Consumer Federation of America reports that more than 50 million households carry an average credit card balance of $7,000. Fifty-five percent of all households carry at least one credit card balance from month to month, 25 percent pay their balance in full, and 20 percent have no credit cards.

In 1997, U.S. consumers paid $65 billion in credit card interest. The average household with credit card debt pays more than $1,000 a year in interest, which is not tax deductible. Forty percent of households with credit cards report that they have great difficulty making their payments.

It's easy to get into debt, and it's hard to get out. People get into debt for various reasons, and not all debt is bad debt. Buying a home or going into business are common reasons to go into debt as an investment strategy. But there are many other reasons people get into debt that aren't beneficial, like a lack of planning or budgeting, poor record keeping, irresponsible spending, and gambling. Some events, like medical emergencies and job loss, are, of course, difficult to predict or prevent.

There are often psychological reasons that lead to getting into debt, as well. Some people have a sense of entitlement, regardless of income. Others want to have things immediately and are simply unable to delay their gratification until they can actually afford to pay cash. Still others mirror their parents' spending habits, or do the opposite. Some people, in an effort to impress others or belong to a certain social peer group, buy expensive gifts for others, gifts they cannot afford, or spring for expensive meals out, to "buy" friendships. No matter what the reason, bad debt is detrimental and leads to accruing more debt.

Interestingly, some people are not aware of the extent of their debt or the warning signs that their debt is getting out of hand. Delaying paying bills, finding that you don't have enough money to make it to the end of month, and charging purchases because you don't have any other choice are all signs that you're in financial trouble.

Regardless of how consumers get into debt, they are certainly not getting into it alone. Credit card issuers are lending them a helping hand. Because of the massive marketing efforts and need for corporate growth (on behalf of credit card and debt issuers), more solicitations are mailed out to grab more market share. That desire to capture more of the market share sometimes makes these issuers close their eyes to potential card holders' credit worthiness, says Howard S. Dvorkin, president and founder of Consolidated Credit Counseling Services, Inc., in Fort Lauderdale, Florida. People who shouldn't get credit are getting it—and defaulting down the road, he says. Keeping track of (let alone a handle on) 10 or 12 credit card accounts is difficult, so debt continues to accrue.

Debt has a hefty price tag of its own. If you bought a $4,000 stereo at 20 percent interest and made only the minimum payments each month, it would take you 11 years to pay it off. Furthermore, that $4,000 stereo would have ended up costing you

If you spend more than you make, you're heading for disaster.
—Howard S. Dvorkin, MBA, CPA, president and founder of Consolidated Credit Counseling Services, Inc.

$7,400, nearly twice the purchase price. It simply doesn't make good financial sense to pay this kind of money.

Minimum payments are calculated in several ways, according to Dvorkin, who is also president of the Association of Independent Consumer Credit Counseling Agencies (AICCCA), a national trade association for the consumer credit industry. One method is by a percentage of your debt, but not less than $10 per month; typically, it's 2 to 3 percent. So if you owe $1,000, 2 percent of that would be $20— that's your minimum payment. A $500 balance may be figured at 3 percent, making it a $15 minimum monthly payment. Note that the percentage drops as your balance increases. The higher your balance, the lower your payment. This is a strategy used by credit card issuers to make purchases more "afford-able." While this does make your payments lower, it extends the length of time you make those pay-ments, keeping you on the credit treadmill longer.

Dvorkin points out that the low 2 to 3 percent minimum payment per month is *not* proportionate to your balance. To find out your credit card's monthly interest rate, take the annual interest rate and divide it by 12, the number of months in a year. Now consider this: A 21 percent annual interest rate divided by 12 would give you a monthly interest rate of 1.75 percent. If you are paying only your mini-mum monthly payment toward your credit card debt, and that is calculated at 2 percent of your bal-ance, only 0.25 percent of your minimum monthly payment goes to the principal of your debt (2 per-cent minus 1.75 percent). The 1.75 percent of your minimum monthly payment is going to interest.

Now assume that you have a $1,000 balance with a 21 percent annual interest rate and a minimum monthly payment of 2 percent of the balance. The minimum monthly payment is 2 percent of $1,000, or $20. To convert the annual interest rate to a monthly interest rate (so we can see how much of the minimum monthly payment covers interest and how much covers principal), we need to divide the 21 percent annual interest rate by 12 months in a year, which is a 1.75 percent monthly interest rate. Each month, 1.75 percent of the balance goes to interest. The rest of the minimum monthly payment, 2 percent minus 1.75 percent, or 0.25 percent, goes to principal. 1.75 percent of the $1,000 balance is $17.50; this amount of the minimum monthly payment goes to interest, and the difference—$2.50—goes to principal. (Your $20 payment is only buying a $2.50 reduction of your balance. So $17.50 pays for the privilege of buying on credit. That's a pretty hefty price tag.) At this rate, you'll be out of debt in a mere 120 months—that's 10 years!

"Today's creditors are smart," says Dvorkin. "Not only will they hit you with late fees, they'll increase your interest rate to the maximum rates, which for some of the large creditors is 24 percent." Credit card issuers want you in debt, and they want you to stay in debt, Dvorkin adds. It's their business.

Don't think that a creditor won't offer you credit if you can't afford to pay it back. Some lenders often get paid bonuses for lending you money, even if the credit limit is beyond your ability to repay, according to Debt Counselors of America, a nonprofit organization in Rockville, Maryland.

Bottom line? You can't spend what you don't have and expect not to go into debt. "You can't borrow your way out of debt [either]," says Steve Rhode, co-founder of Debt Counselors of America.

Bright Idea
Ask one of the credit reporting agencies (listed in "Protecting your credit rating") for a form to remove your name from lists for unsolicited credit and insurance offers. Additionally, you can contact the Direct Marketing Association's Mail and Telephone Preference Services.

Mail Preference Service
P.O. Box 9008
Farmingdale, NY 11735

Telephone Preference Service
P.O. Box 9014
Farmingdale, NY 11735

Watch Out!
Don't engage in "credit repair." Credit repair companies charge hefty fees and can't do anything more for you than you can do for yourself for free. If there's information on your credit report that does not belong to you, contact the credit bureau and the creditor directly to get it removed.

Note: Many credit card issuers sell credit insurance. There are four basic types of credit insurance: credit property, credit life, credit disability, and involuntary loss of income insurance. *Credit property insurance* insures against damage to the property that is securing the loan. *Credit life insurance* insures that any outstanding balance on a loan will be paid in case of the debtor's death. *Credit disability insurance* insures the debtor against disabilities that result from accident or ill health—the exact disabilities included are listed in the terms. The insurance covers the periodic payments that are due while the debtor is disabled. *Involuntary loss of income insurance* insures against involuntary unemployment. For price reasons, it is generally better to get a general insurance to cover the payments rather than insurance that is tied to a particular debt.

In general, credit insurance is viewed as a rip-off because it's relatively expensive and only protects a consumer for that particular debt. There are other kinds of more general insurance that will cover payments to creditors.

Getting out of debt

While the road to debt may be paved with slick plastic, the road out of debt isn't so smooth and is a lot less fun to travel. It means going without rather than having more than you can afford. Sometimes it means deprivation. It certainly means watching every penny. But it also means gaining back self-esteem, and it means becoming disciplined and feeling more in control of your life. Getting out of debt can reduce the stress in your life as it lightens the load of the financial burden you carry on your back. Keep this in mind as you work toward financial freedom.

How, then, can you accomplish this feat? It's simple, but not easy.

Rule of thumb: "If the cash isn't in your pocket, don't buy it," Dvorkin says, "it" being that thing you can't possibly live without. Some of the people Dvorkin works with have come up with some fairly creative strategies to stop impulse buying and to give them time for thoughtful consideration before incurring more debt. The following tactics take the convenience out of credit:

- Freeze your credit cards in a block of ice.

- Give your credit cards to a trusted family member.

- Put your credit cards in a bank safe deposit box.

- Place a Band-Aid over the card's magnetic strip; this affords you an extra minute to think if you really want to go further into debt by making the intended purchase.

Many people don't even know how much they owe. They have so many credit cards that they simply lose track. Meanwhile, interest charges keep accruing. You always need to know what you owe or you won't know how to make a plan to pay the debt back, Dvorkin says. (See Table 9.1 below.) And you must develop a plan to pay back your loans. Wanting to be out of debt is not enough. You must be proactive.

Here are some suggestions that may help you get out of debt:

- Write down all your expenditures for one month—everything, including every cup of coffee, a candy bar—everything. At the end of the month, look over your expenses and see where you can cut down—by bringing a brown bag

lunch instead of going out, bringing coffee with
you, or eating out less often, for instance. The
amount you save can be used to pay off debt.

■ Don't use your credit cards—cut them up if you
have to. You can even close the account with a
balance and continue paying on the balance
(you'll still receive monthly statements). Pay
only with cash or checks.

■ Pick an amount above the minimum monthly
payments that you can afford to send every
month. Send that same amount regardless of
the current minimum monthly until the debt is
gone. Generally, it's a good idea to pay down
cards with a high balance and high interest rate
first, then move onto the others. But some people may be more comfortable getting rid of
small balances completely.

■ Shop smart: Don't shop for groceries on a
empty stomach. People generally spend more
when they are hungry. Don't give in to impulse
buying. Don't buy something just because it's on
sale. Buy in bulk when you can. Shop in discount outlets.

■ Discontinue unnecessary utilities, like cable;
discontinue newspaper and magazine
subscriptions—read them at the library—make
long-distance calls after 11 P.M. or at other off-
peak hours.

■ If you are heavily in debt and cannot pay all
your bills, prioritize your debt—usually, secured
debt should be your first priority, and unsecured should come second.

Unofficially...
A good source to
help you make a
debt payback
plan can be
found on the
Internet at
www.debtfree.
org. This site
allows the user
to type in the
name of each
creditor and the
interest rates
you're paying to
find out the date
when your debt
will be paid off.

TABLE 9.1—MONTHLY DEBT WORKSHEET

Month	Credit card #1	Credit card #2	Credit card #3	Credit card #4
Issuer:				
Interest rate:				
Current balance:				
Minimum monthly payment:				
Amount of payment this month:				
New balance:				

Month	Credit card #5	Credit card #6	Credit card #7	Credit card #8
Issuer:				
Interest rate:				
Current balance:				
Minimum monthly payment:				
Amount of payment this month:				
New balance:				

continues

Month	Credit card #9	Credit card #10	Credit card #11	Credit card #12
Issuer:				
Interest rate:				
Current balance:				
Minimum monthly payment:				
Amount of payment this month:				
New balance:				
Total combined balance this month:				

Make copies of this worksheet and fill it out each month to keep track of your credit card debt.

If you find the task of creating a plan to pay back creditors overwhelming, or if you don't have the money to make payments, contact a credit counselor at a nonprofit agency. One such agency is the Consumer Credit Counseling Service. Call 800/388-2227 to find a counselor in your area. You can also call the Debt Counselors of America (DCA) at 800/680-DEBT (3328). Or, visit their Web site at www.GetOutOfDebt.org. In addition to CPAs, they have attorneys on staff who can help you. Keep in mind, however, that DCA's attorneys can't help you if you live in Maryland, Washington, D.C., or New Jersey, where the attorneys are barred. They can try to give general information to consumers nationwide, but not legal advice, which would be violating states' laws on the "unauthorized practice of law."

If you think you got into debt as a result of trying to satisfy certain psychological needs, it may be worthwhile to try to get a better understanding of those issues. Some therapists, and even some financial planners, say they can give you advice on how to deal with those issues effectively. For instance, if you give gifts you can't afford so others will like you, they may be able to help you understand that many people wouldn't feel comfortable receiving a gift that causes you to incur more debt. If you buy expensive gifts and wear expensive clothes (both of which you can't afford) to impress others, they may be able to help you learn other ways to boost your self-esteem.

Ultimately, if you want to stay out of debt, you *must* learn to use credit wisely, if you are going to use it at all. Here are some smart ways to get started:

- Shop around for the best credit card rates and offers.

- If your current card issuer is charging an exorbitant rate, ask the issuer to lower it.

> **"**
> All of the pain, panic, and suffering that you're now feeling will be for naught unless you take a good hard look at yourself and learn from your mistakes.
> —Debt Counselors of America.
> **"**

Watch Out!
Don't apply for a lot of credit cards, even if they have low interest rates. When you apply, "inquiries" will appear on your credit report, which can harm your credit rating. (It may appear that you're trying to accumulate a lot of credit, which statistically indicates that you expect to have financial problems or otherwise will need a lot of credit.) Instead, compare credit card terms online at Web sites like www.cardweb.com, www.bankrate.com, and www.bog.frb.fed.us/pubs/shop/tablwb.pdf.

- Avoid interest charges by paying the entire balance for each credit card every month; if you can't pay your balance in full, limit interest charges by paying as much as you can.
- Avoid late fees by paying bills on time.
- Limit the number of credit cards you have, and be sure to close unneeded accounts.
- Read and understand the terms of any credit agreement you sign, and read all other terms and conditions the lender mails to you.

Dealing with creditors

If you can't pay your bills for some reason, call your creditors immediately. They often will be more open to working out a reasonable payment plan with you if you contact them before they contact you. By you contacting them first, it shows them that you're serious about your responsibilities.

"Most lenders have a hardship program," says Kathy Balzan, a credit counselor at American Credit Counselors Corporation, a nonprofit organization that offers free credit counseling services. They'll extend the length of time for repayment, reducing the amount due each month and setting up an installment payment plan. (Remember, though, that these extensions have consequences: You'll end up paying more in the long run.) The most important thing to remember is to communicate with them. "If you do not make your payments and simply ignore the correspondence from your lenders, they will assume that you do not intend to pay them, and they will take all steps necessary to get the money that you owe them," she says.

If you've waited too long and the collection agencies are knocking on your door, Dvorkin advises, don't make promises that you can't keep.

It's also important to never give collection agencies your phone number at work or they will call you there, Dvorkin says. If they do call you at work and if you're not permitted to receive personal calls there, tell them to stop. Pursuant to the Fair Debt Collection Practices Act, they must. (This is a federal law that covers collection agencies, but not creditors. Some state laws extend the Act to cover creditors, however, so consumers should refer to their state's laws for protection afforded from creditors.)

You can also write a letter requesting that the collector no longer contact you. This may provide relief from the calls, but you should know that by doing this, you will not know the collection agency's intentions and may not hear from the agency again until it sends a summons and a complaint. Therefore, it's usually a good idea to give the collection agency a time when and telephone number where the collector can reach you. You can also enlist the aid of a credit counselor at a nonprofit organization and direct creditors to the counselor. DCA has a pamphlet, reproduced in Figure 9.1, containing questions to ask a credit counseling agency to ensure it is reputable.

A reputable credit counselor can help you:

- Work out a lower payment plan—sometimes reducing your monthly payments by 30 to 50 percent
- Eliminate accrued interest or obtain a reduced rate
- Get late charges and over-the-limit fees cancelled
- "Re-age" your account if you are delinquent (this means the agency can help make your account current)

Note! ➜
"Questions to
Ask a Credit or
Debt Counseling
Agency," Debt
Counselors of
America, repro-
duced with per-
mission.

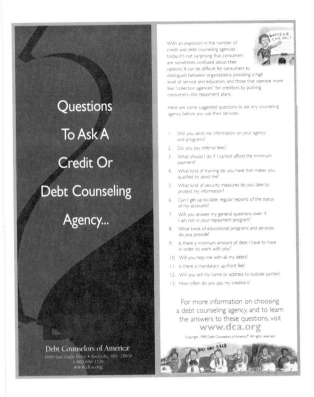

By using a credit counselor to help you get out
of debt, you'll make just one monthly payment to
the counselor, who'll then disburse it to creditors.
Typically, you'll pay off your bills in one third of the
time. Accounts are generally paid off in 3 to 4 years,
rather than the average 14 years, Dvorkin says. The
cost for such a service varies, but is typically about
$25 a month.

If don't take steps, whether directly with the
credit issuer or through a credit counselor, and continue to not make payments on a loan, you will be
considered by the credit issuer to be in default. The
usual steps taken in response to a defaulted loan are
as follows: The creditor attempts to collect the debt.

The creditor's attempts are usually limited to a particular amount of time that differs for each lender,
generally three months or so. If the creditor
does not collect the debt, it will then sell the debt to
a collection agency, which tacks on fees and penalties and continues to try to collect the debt by
calling persistently. If this tactic doesn't work, the
collector may sue you, get a judgment against you,
and enforce that judgment by garnishing your wages
and/or putting a lien on your property. This issue is
discussed in greater detail later in this chapter.

If you do settle a debt with your creditor, there
are a few things you need to know. First, you need to
be concerned about how it will be recorded on your
credit report. The settlement can appear on your
credit report as "settled" versus "paid in full." The
forgiven amount can be reported as a bad debt.
Later, if you try to get credit, a loan, or a mortgage,
those lenders will probably look negatively upon
you settling a debt rather than paying it in full.
Furthermore, if you owe $4,000, for example, and
the creditor forgives half, the creditor can show the
$2,000 written off as bad debt, Rhode warns. (In
contrast, if you entered into an agreement to pay the
debt in full by installments, the credit report will
indicate that you are paying according to an agreed
upon plan, and eventually it will read "paid in full.")

Second, the Internal Revenue Service (IRS) can
come after you for taxes on any forgiven loan
amount because the forgiven amount is viewed as
"income." If the forgiven amount is more than $600,
the creditor will report it to the IRS, and you will
receive a Form 1099 listing it as miscellaneous
income. This important information may not be disclosed to you when the settlement offer is made.

Big brother is watching...

More and more employers are accessing prospective employees' credit records before hiring decisions are made, Dvorkin says. (Your signed application for employment may include authorization giving your employer permission to access your credit record.) According to Dvorkin, employers don't want people to handle the company's money if they can't handle their own, especially if the job has fiduciary responsibilities.

It's not just employers who are interested in your spending habits. According to the Insurance Information Institute, some insurance companies are pulling credit reports when people apply for automobile insurance because there's a correlation between people who have bad credit reports and those who partake in risky behaviors.

Bad credit or significant debt can affect your ability to get *any* kind of loan, and it can affect your ability even to rent housing. Also, a large debt load can lower your credit score, which can affect *all* lending and credit opportunities. It also makes buying a home or car more expensive if you do qualify for a loan because you are considered a bigger risk, and therefore, you're socked with higher interest rates.

Protecting your credit rating

The best way to protect your credit rating is to pay your bills on time. Sometimes, however, credit reporting agencies make mistakes. Getting a copy of your credit report generally costs about $8, but you can get a free report any time you are turned down for credit. You must make the request within 60 days of receiving notice. The company that denied you credit will supply you with the name, address, and phone number of the credit reporting agency from which it received your credit report. If you are unemployed, you can obtain one free report a year if you plan to look for a job within 60 days. You also are entitled to a free report if you are on welfare or if your report is inaccurate as a result of fraud.

There are three major national credit bureaus:

- Experian (formerly TRW)—800/682-7654

- Equifax—800/685-1111

- TransUnion—800/916-8800

If your credit report contains inaccurate or incomplete information, write to the credit reporting agency and the company that provided the information to the agency. Request that your complaint be included in your file. If an error is found, the agency must correct it and notify all other credit reporting agencies.

The availability of credit also affects your credit score. Just as you should be careful of how much debt you incur, you should also keep the credit available to you to a minimum. Just because you haven't taken advantage of available credit, doesn't mean you won't. "New lenders may not want to extend you credit if they see that you already have a large amount of open credit through various creditors," says Lorri Crittenden, CFP at Dignum Financial Services in Fort Worth, Texas. (For more on credit scores, see Chapter 8.)

Debtors' and creditors' rights

If you are in debt, you still have legal rights; they are specified in the Fair Debt Collection Practices Act, which applies to collection agencies only. This law requires creditors to disclose credit terms when you're obtaining credit; it is your job, of course, to read them.

Watch Out!
Creating a new credit identity is illegal. You cannot legally remove accurate and timely negative information from your credit report. If you use the mail or phone to engage in such efforts, you will be committing federal as well as state crimes.

Once you're delinquent on your payments and you're contacted by a debt collector, you have a right to a written notice, which must be sent within five days after the initial contact. This notice must spell out the amount you owe, the name of the creditor, and what action you can take if you think you don't owe the money.

As discussed earlier, under the Fair Debt Collection Practices Act, a collection agency cannot call you very early or late in the day or at work if you tell the collector that your employer does not allow you to get personal calls at work. You also have the right to tell the collector not to contact you at all—write a letter requesting the collector to cease all communication with you. The collector must then stop communicating with you except to tell you he or she is suing you. This has good and bad consequences—good because you won't be bothered with the calls, bad because you won't know the status of the debt until you are sued.

States' laws may extend the Fair Debt Collection Practices Act's protections to creditors, but the Act itself does not include creditors. Unless your state law extends your rights under the Act to creditors, you don't have the right to tell a creditor how and when to contact you.

But creditors have rights, too, and one of those is the right to sue you for payment. Don't be fooled into believing that you can max out your cards and then not pay up. Creditors will and do sue, Dvorkin says, which he thinks is good because "people don't care what their credit looks like these days," explaining that having bad credit is not as detrimental as it was in the past.

If you are sued, and the judge rules in the creditor's favor, you *must* pay the amount of the judgment immediately or the creditor may collect it by getting a lien on your real property or personal property—like a home or car. The lien stays with the property. The judgment creditor can either execute on the lien, which means the creditor forces you to sell to liquidate the property and give the judgment creditor what you owe, or the judgment creditor can sit on the lien and wait until you try to sell the property. At that time, you will not be able to sell the property until you pay off the lien.

Additionally, the creditor will have the right to collect through *garnishment*:

1. Wage garnishment—sometimes called a writ of garnishment, the creditor can instruct your employer to withhold part of your salary, up to 25 percent.

2. Bank account garnishment—creditors can take the money in your bank account. As mentioned above, if there's not enough money in your account to pay off the debt, other property may be taken from you and sold to pay the balance owed. (There are certain "exempt" properties, which differ from state to state. You'll need to ask an attorney in your state what property is exempt.)

Be warned: If you don't have enough money in your bank account or through other assets to cover the judgment against you, or if creditors have stopped banging down your door, they haven't necessarily given up. They're waiting for you to save money. Some of them will wait for years if they must.

Once you have paid off the judgment against you, make sure to get it in writing that you're paid up.

The brink of foreclosure: how you got there and how to step back

Homeowners end up on the brink of foreclosure for many reasons, including job loss, a reduction in pay, divorce, or unforeseen medical bills not covered by insurance. Some also end up there because they pay off their credit cards and other bills before they pay their mortgage, and they run out of funds.

An increase in the interest rate of an adjustable-rate mortgage can result in you losing your home, as well. These loans start out with relatively low monthly payments with interest rates generally two points below 30-year fixed rates. But these rates can increase quickly due to inflation, often jumping 2 percent annually or biannually. When the rate increases, your monthly payments can jump several hundred dollars.

Low down payments can also lead to foreclosure. While having to come up with less money up front makes it easier for some people to buy a home, it also can turn an owner *upside down* in the house, if the value of the home depreciates, that is, if the home ends up being worth less than the mortgage. If you try to sell your home while in this circumstance, you can end up with a huge loss. If the proceeds from the sale won't cover your mortgage, you'll owe the difference. If you don't sell, but also don't have the cash and can't make mortgage payments, the lender may choose to cut its losses and foreclose.

Like low down payments, excessive loans can lead to foreclosure. There are an alarming number of home loans given that are above the value of the home, Rhode points out. If you take out one of those popular 125 percent loans and are then forced to move—for whatever reason—within a few

> **"**
> If you want to see time pass fast, get a balloon note (one that comes due in a lump sum)... the monthly payment is low so you better be saving money.
> —Steve Rhode, Debt Counselors of America.
> **"**

years, you must come up with almost 25 percent over and above the value of your home to buy your way out of it.

Spending the equity in your home can send you packing as well. Many people refinance their homes and use the equity for other purchases and expenses. When they sell their homes, these people count on appreciation to cover these added expenditures. But appreciation in real estate is highly dependent on the economy, and not all economic conditions favor real estate. Your best bet is not to expect appreciation to cover the extra debt. By borrowing against the equity in your home, you're just stringing out your debt over a longer period of time, Rhode says. You end up paying much more in the long run than you would have on your original debt—and you risk losing your home, to boot. You're also likely to rack up more debt on your credit cards, leaving yourself in a far worse place than you started.

If you're having financial troubles and your home is on the line, the first thing you should do is take action to prevent foreclosure.

Probably the easiest way to gain back your footing is to share the load. Take in boarders, or rent your house and live in the basement. If someone cosigned on your loan, contact that person immediately because his or her credit rating is also at risk. He or she may offer to help you with your payments.

If you're currently paying two points more than the current zero points/no closing costs loans, you can try to refinance your mortgage. If you can find an adjustable-rate mortgage with a low interest rate, it may also be worth refinancing, assuming the rates will remain low long enough for you to get your feet back on solid ground. Contact a mortgage broker

Watch Out!
When you get a secured debt consolidation loan or home equity loan for extra cash, or to pay off existent credit card debt, you are converting unsecured debt into secured debt. Secured debt puts the secured item—the collateral (your home in this case)—at risk if you fail to make a payment.

who has access to hundreds of loans to find the one that's best for your situation. (But see Chapter 8 first to learn about situations when consulting a mortgage broker may *not* be beneficial for you.)

There is a built-in safety net available to you if you're paying private mortgage insurance (PMI), which is insurance that lenders require borrowers putting down less than 20 percent to purchase. If you get into a jam, contact the insurer, Rhode suggests. Insurers will probably help you by lending you money or working out something else if you can't pay, he says. Insurers don't want to pay off your loan, which is what they'd have to do if you default.

Watch Out!
Making false statements on a credit or loan application, giving a fake Social Security number, and obtaining an Employer Identification Number from the Internal Revenue Service under false pretenses are all federal crimes.

If you've already missed a mortgage payment, contact the lender immediately. Try to work out a payment schedule. The lender may rewrite the loan, allow you to make interest-only payments for a while, otherwise reduce your payments, or allow you to miss a few payments, spreading them out over time, or give you an interest-free loan to get current, according to Rhode.

Most lenders will work with you. "But they won't hesitate to take your home from you if you don't make payments or if you make promises you don't keep," Rhode says.

If things still look hopeless (and you think your only option is to file for bankruptcy, discussed in the next section), Rhode suggests taking one of the following, rather extreme, actions:

1. Sell the property. When you talk to the real estate agent, find out how long it will take to sell at top dollar. If time is not on your side, price the property so it will sell quickly. But make sure the equity you've accumulated can cover the shortfall.

2. Ask your lender for a *short sale*, that is, when you sell your home for less than the value of the mortgage. Some lenders will allow you to sell low and forgive the difference, if the alternative is foreclosure. Be prepared to explain to the lender why you must sell the property. For instance, if you have medical problems, get letters from your physicians as evidence. If you lost your job, give evidence of your job search efforts. If you tried to sell your home, talk about your marketing efforts.

Be aware that there are tax ramifications for short sales, and for obtaining what's known as a *deed in lieu of foreclosure*, in which case you can get a *quit-claim deed*, that is, you quit your interest in the property and transfer ownership back to the lender, who then forgives the debt. In both cases, the lender must fill out an IRS 1099 form and report the forgiven debt as income to you. You will then owe income taxes on the portion of the debt that was forgiven (if that amount is greater than $600, which is generally the case, especially with a house), just as if the lender had given the cash to you. (If you settle any other type of debt, the same rules apply.) Before you choose this option, remember to consider this: If you don't have the money to pay your debt, where will you get the money to pay the additional taxes?

Note that while there are investors who specialize in buying homes on the verge of foreclosure, some of them are less reputable than others, according to Rhode. Don't deed your home to someone who promises to sell it for you. Although the deed will no longer be in your name once you sign it over, the mortgage will be—and you'll remain liable for its payment. If you do seek out the services of this type of investor, check him or her out with the Better Business Bureau and your state's local chapter of the National Association of Realtors first. Be sure to get all agreements in writing.

Bankruptcy

Bankruptcy is so common today that it has (almost) lost its stigma. According to the American Bankruptcy Institute, 1 in every 70 U.S. households filed for bankruptcy in 1997, for a total of 1.3 million filings.

With the economy in good shape, it would seem logical that bankruptcy filings would decrease. But the opposite is true. Consumer confidence rises in strong economies, and people feel confident they'll be able to pay their debt, so they keep spending. But increased purchases result in increased use of credit cards to supplement income, and, well, we've been down *this* road before.

A bankruptcy filing stays in your credit file for up to 10 years. Some states allow it to drop off the credit report after seven years. (The industry [credit bureaus] usually takes Chapter 13 bankruptcies off a credit report after seven years.) But it doesn't end there. Many loan applications—such as student loans and mortgages—and some job applications (if you are handling money) will ask if you have ever filed bankruptcy. Even if you filed 20 years ago, you must disclose that you have filed bankruptcy. (If you answer dishonestly, you've committed fraud. That lie can come back to haunt you if you cannot pay the debt.) Also, even though negative information drops off your credit record in 7 to 10 years, if you apply for a loan of greater than $150,000 or apply for a job with a salary of over $75,000, the lender/employer has access to your entire credit history, not just the current credit report.

There are three types of bankruptcies:

- Chapter 11
- Chapter 7
- Chapter 13

Chapter 11 is for businesses and is therefore not relevant to our discussion. Chapter 7 is a total liquidation—it discharges all debt except money owed to the IRS, student loans, child support payments, etc. The debtor must liquidate any assets he or she has, unless the property is exempt by his or her state's laws. What property is exempt differs from state to state, but may include some equity in your home and auto, property up to a certain amount, some pensions, public benefits, a certain amount of cash, and tools for work. If there are debts collateralized by your home or car, they can be foreclosed on or repossessed regardless of equity allowances. You can ask these lenders to reaffirm those debts.

Chapter 13 is designed for individuals with regular income who desire to pay their debts, but are currently unable to do so. Chapter 13 is a repayment plan executed under court supervision. Debtors are permitted to repay creditors in full or in part, usually over three years, but not to exceed five years. The creditors, bankruptcy trustee, and the bankruptcy judge must all approve the repayment plan. The debtor must pay the bankruptcy trustee, who pays the debtor's creditors all of his or her disposable income each month until the debt has been repaid.

If you're about to lose your home—and you've tried everything else—and decided to file for

Unofficially...
Many people have forgotten the original intention of bankruptcy, which was to help people get relief from enormous debt loads caused by circumstances beyond their control, like a long hospitalization.

bankruptcy to stop foreclosure, keep in mind that under a Chapter 13 filing, you remain responsible for your regular mortgage payments. This means, Rhode warns, that if you miss any payments, the lender will have the house removed from underneath the bankruptcy and foreclose on it. You might end up with both a bankruptcy and a foreclosure.

Bear in mind that you can't refile a Chapter 7 total liquidation bankruptcy if you received a discharge of your debts under Chapter 7 or Chapter 13 in a case begun in the past six years. The six years starts from the date of the filing of the first bankruptcy, not the date of discharge. You can file Chapter 13 bankruptcy at any time—there is no waiting period.

If a debtor who filed Chapter 7 in the past six years gets a mortgage or any other type of loan and stops making payments, he or she does not have the protection of bankruptcy. The lender can foreclose or repossess secured property, or if it's an unsecured loan, the lender can sue and get a judgment against the debtor.

A lender may be willing to give someone who just filed Chapter 7 bankruptcy a loan because that person presents very little risk to the lender. He or she has no debt—all was discharged—and can't discharge any debt for six years from the date he or she filed bankruptcy. If the debtor stops making payments on his or her mortgage, the mortgage lender can foreclose and sell the house, and the debtor will still be liable for any deficiency. The lender can sue on the deficiency, get a judgment, and enforce the judgment through wage attachment, liens on other property, or a lien on a bank account.

Bankruptcy should be used only as a last resort. You can get help on how to figure out the best way to pay off your debt and bear responsibility for your actions. Before filing, call a nonprofit debt counseling service. Don't go to a bankruptcy attorney first. He or she may not tell you about your other options. A nonprofit debt counseling agency, however, has little personal interest in leading you one way or the other.

Getting back on track

The first, and perhaps most obvious, thing to do to get back on track and out of debt is to stop increasing your debt. Start by tracking your cash. "Figure out where your money is actually going," Rhode says.

Just the act of recording your expenditures will help you reduce your spending because you'll be more aware of where your money is going; plus, you'll be able to pinpoint exactly where you can cut back most easily, Rhode says. This doesn't mean you have to give up everything; you'll just have to reduce the frequency of your excess spending.

Another way to get back on track is to make extra payments on your debt whenever possible. Be sure "that you specify in writing that this extra money is to be applied to the principal," Balzan says. And make sure that when you make extra payments you make them on the credit card with the highest interest rate/debt combination.

As tempting as it may seem, do *not* dip into your retirement savings to pay off your current debt load. "The worst thing you can do in most situations is borrow from your retirement plan," Rhode says. It is extremely difficult to regain that same financial position, especially if you've been saving little by little over the course of many years. It'll take years to repay yourself, and you'll lose out on potential earnings.

Bright Idea
Try taking a list to the grocery store to help you buy only what you need—this will help you keep a handle on impulse buying. And it goes without saying that, with few exceptions, if you can't pay cash for it, don't buy it.

The best thing you can do is start saving, even small amounts. Putting a little away in savings is a good idea, even when you are trying to get rid of debt. Many people who have debt problems got into trouble because they had an emergency, but no savings to handle the emergency. And if you have no savings to help you, you're out of luck. Remember that small investments in your future can build up dramatically as long as you invest consistently.

"Don't expect instant miracles," Rhode says. "You didn't get into trouble overnight. You're not going to get out overnight."

See Chapter 1 for more tips that can help you get back on track, such as setting a budget and avoiding splurges.

Just the facts

- If you only make minimum payments on your credit cards, you will pay for your purchases for years, significantly increasing your costs.

- Creditors can and do sue; call your lender immediately if you cannot make a payment because, generally, they will try to work out an easier payment schedule or make other arrangements.

- Consult a debt counselor affiliated with a non-profit debt counseling agency to figure out the best ways to handle your debt; the fee you pay him or her is small compared with the benefits gained.

- Debtors have rights; just because you owe money doesn't permit your creditors to harass you.

- Bankruptcy should be considered only as a last resort to debt management.

Counting the Beans

GET THE SCOOP ON...
How long you have to work just to pay taxes ▪
How investment earnings are taxed ▪ How to
save on capital gains taxes ▪ How to save taxes
in the event of a divorce ▪ Tax considerations
when planning for your retirement

PART V

Taxes

You learned a lot on your first job. Maybe it was how to flip a burger, work a cash register, or bag groceries. Or it may have been how to act professionally, negotiate effectively, and make a winning presentation. But no matter what field your first job was in, you learned what every working American learns when he or she gets that first, long-awaited paycheck: Taxes can be taxing on your personal finances.

In this chapter I'll tell you something you probably already know—that you work a lot just to pay taxes. I'll also show you just how much you work to foot the tax bill. Then I'll tell you about strategies financial planners use to save on capital gains taxes, tactics they use to make higher education more affordable and retirement more comfortable, and strategies they use to make divorce a little less taxing.

How much do you pay in taxes?

Every day you go to work, your earnings are being taxed. In 1998, you spent 2 hours and 50 minutes, on average, laboring just to pay taxes, according to the Tax Foundation. You spent 1 hour and 55 minutes of your workday to pay federal taxes and another 55 minutes to pay state and local taxes. The Tax Foundation notes that the total—2 hours and 50 minutes—is greater than the amount of time per day you work to pay for housing and household expenses (1 hour and 20 minutes), food and tobacco (49 minutes), and clothing (20 minutes) combined. Bottom line? You work *hard* to pay taxes.

Another way to appreciate how taxes bite into your income is to consider how many days you must work before your entire paycheck is yours to keep. The number of days was figured using a collective national effective tax rate of 35.4 percent for 1998. The Tax Foundation has created "Tax Freedom Day" to mark this day. In 1998, Tax Freedom Day was May 10. That means you had to work, on average, 129 days to pay off your total tax bill that year. Tack on another 13 days if you want to include the costs associated with complying with the tax system, like record keeping. Keep in mind, these numbers don't even include what you'll pay in the future on tax-deferred savings!

Over the years, Tax Freedom Day has been pushed to later in the year, reflecting the increased tax burden Americans carry. The Tax Foundation notes that as your income increases, the number of days you must work to pay off your tax burden also increases due to the progressive nature of the tax system.

> **"**
> The trick is to stop thinking of it as 'your' money.
> —IRS auditor.
> **"**

TABLE 11.1—TAX FREEDOM DAY THROUGHOUT THE 20TH CENTURY

Tax year	Freedom Day	Taxes as percent of NNP (Net National Product)
1902	January 31	8.5
1922	February 17	13.2
1935	February 28	16.0
1945	April 4	25.7
1955	April 7	26.5
1965	April 13	28.1
1975	April 26	31.6
1985	April 29	32.5
1995	May 4	33.8
1998	May 10	35.4

← Note!
The Tax Foundation used historical data to determine when Tax Freedom Day fell at various times throughout the twentieth century. Source: Tax Foundation

Here's another way to look at it: If you and your spouse both work, and you're earning the median income for two ($54,910), 37.6 percent of your income goes to federal, state, and local taxes, according to the Tax Foundation. If you're single, your 1997 tax burden weighs in at a whopping 35.9 percent of your income.

Those numbers are based on medians, of course. Your tax burden may be higher or lower, depending on the state where you live. This variation is due primarily to differences in per capita income among the states. Because taxes are levied as a percentage of income, states with high per capita income tend to have higher per capita federal tax burdens, according to the Tax Foundation.

This effect is further heightened by progressive income tax rates, which cause tax burdens to rise at a higher rate than what's proportional to income. The average federal tax bill for fiscal year 1998 ranged from a low of $4,481 in Mississippi to a high of $10,518 in Connecticut. See Table 11.2 for how many days you need to work to pay specific categories of taxes.

TABLE 11.2 TAX FREEDOM DAY BY TYPE OF TAX (1998)

Average number of work days to foot the tax bill	Tax type
45	Personal income taxes (37 days of which will go to federal income taxes)
38	Payroll taxes
18	Sales and excise taxes (collected primarily at the state and local levels)
12	Property taxes
13	Corporate income taxes, which is ultimately passed on to consumers, employees, and shareholders

Source: Tax Foundation

Remember, you do get something for your money: Public libraries, public schools, paved roads, lights at intersections, and much more are funded in part with your tax dollars. But taxes pose a financial burden for many, so you'd be well advised to take a careful look at the way you handle your money and assets to see where you can save on taxes. But first a word of advice: Don't ever ignore tax consequences, but don't let them drive your investment decisions, either.

Investment tax law

As noted in Chapter 4, investments are a great way to boost your income. However, keep in mind that taxes (and inflation) play an important role in determining how much you'll profit from your investments. A certain percentage of your profits will be paid as taxes. Therefore, your investment must earn enough to cover those taxes and still exceed inflation to make the investment worthwhile.

First, let's recap the types of investments you may have in your portfolio:

- Stocks: Sold in shares, these give you ownership, or equity, in a corporation, which gives you a claim on a proportionate share in the corporation's assets and profits.

- Bonds: These are debt instruments issued for the purpose of raising capital. This type of security pays a fixed amount of interest at regular intervals over a specified period of time, at which point the principal is repaid. Governments, states, cities, corporations, and other institutions issue bonds.

- Mutual funds: Open-end investment companies that invest the pooled money of many investors in a variety of securities. Mutual funds come in many forms, including value funds, growth funds, large-cap, mid-cap, and small-cap funds, income funds, specialty funds, index funds, money market funds, international funds, hybrids, fund of funds, REIT mutual funds, and funds concentrated in sectors like technology, health, and more.

  Most mutual funds invest in more than one type of investment but are heavily weighted to match their names. For instance, income funds have more bonds than stocks and index funds mirror a specific stock index. You can also buy bonds through mutual funds. These income funds are further classified. One such category is tax-exempt municipal bond funds: These mutual funds provide tax-free income to their investors

Moneysaver
To cut the tax bite on your investments, you may want to consider investing in tax-efficient mutual funds, which are funds that typically have a low turnover rate. Index funds, which mirror a stock market index like the S&P 500, are a good example of tax-efficient funds.

by investing in tax-exempt bonds issued by states, cities, and other local governments.

There are two types of federal taxes you must pay on your investment earnings: Capital gains taxes on investment gains and income taxes on dividends.

Capital gains

There are two types of capital gains—long-term gains and short-term gains—and each type is taxed at a different rate.

Long-term capital gains

When you own a mutual fund, you share in the profits that the fund makes on its own holdings, whether those holdings are stocks, bonds, or other assets. Each time the fund manager sells shares, it is a taxable event. When the fund sells its assets at a profit, it realizes a *capital gain* and passes it along to you as a capital gains distribution.

You must report these capital gains on Schedule D of your federal income tax return. Long-term capital gains only apply to assets that you've held for more than 12 months.

Long-term capital gains are taxed at a maximum rate of 20 percent. (If you're in the 15 percent income tax bracket, you'll pay 10 percent on long-term capital gains.) There are exceptions, including the taxable part of qualifying small business stock, which is subject to a 28 percent tax rate.

It's important to realize that taxation issues do not only apply to the mutual funds in your portfolio. If you hold individual stocks, you incur a taxable event whenever you sell shares. You must pay taxes on any realized gains, except when your gains are realized in a tax-deferred investment (those in your retirement plans, except Roth IRAs), certain tax-exempt money market funds, or certain tax-exempt bond funds.

Short-term capital gains

Short-term gains apply to assets held 12 months or less, and are taxed at ordinary income tax rates. (These rates will be higher than long-term capital gain tax rates.) Short-term capital gain distributions are reported to you as ordinary dividends, not as capital gain distributions.

Dividends

If you receive dividends—monies from a company's income paid to shareholders—you must pay taxes on them as ordinary income, like interest and short-term capital gains, and their distribution lowers the value of your principal investment.

Note that dividends from some tax-exempt money market funds and tax-exempt bond funds may be taxable at the state and local levels.

Taxes and timing your investments

Timing can be everything when it comes to buying shares in a mutual fund. Funds usually distribute dividends and capital gains at the end of the calendar year. Shareholders must pay income tax on dividends and capital gains tax on any gains. If you can wait until after the gains and/or dividends are distributed to buy shares, you can save on your tax bill.

For example, if you buy 1,000 shares at $10 each in December, and shortly thereafter the fund distributes a dividend of 40 cents per share, you'll have to pay taxes on $400 (1,000 shares × $10 = 10,000 shares; 10,000 × .40 = $400)—that's an immediate $112 "loss" (a 28 percent tax—assuming you're in the 28 percent tax bracket—on $400 = $112). (This doesn't include state taxes.) Even if you reinvest the

Unofficially...
Assets purchased after year 2000 and held at least five years will be taxed at a maximum rate of 18 percent. (If you're in the 15 percent tax bracket, you'll only have to pay 8 percent.)

dividend, you've just lost some of your investment dollars to taxes. The same principle applies when the fund realizes and pays out short- and long-term capital gains, though the math may differ, depending on what type of capital gain is paid out; if it's a short-term gain, the tax rate depends on your income tax bracket.

Reinvesting your shares

Every time you buy, sell, or exchange shares of mutual funds or stocks, you need to know:

1. The date of the transaction

2. The number of shares purchased or sold (this may be a fraction)

3. The price per share

4. The total price for the shares

5. Any fees or commissions paid for each transaction

Each time you reinvest capital gains distributions and dividends instead of taking the cash, you're actually buying more shares. Because share prices fluctuate daily, the prices of these shares will probably differ from the prices of the shares you purchased previously. If you automatically reinvest dividends, you need to think of it in terms of writing a check to the fund each time the transaction occurs because, as noted above, you are, in fact, purchasing more shares. By doing so, you can avoid double taxation, which can be quite costly.

Consider this: When you sell the shares you own in a fund, you pay taxes on the difference between the *cost basis*—the price paid for shares plus any commissions and fees—and the value of the shares when you sell them. For example, if you bought a fund for $10,000 and sold it at $20,000, you may

Moneysaver
Capital losses in excess of capital gains can be used to offset up to $3,000 of ordinary income—$1,500 if you're married and filing separately.

think you owe taxes on a $10,000 gain. But if $2,000 of that was from reinvested dividends, you've already paid income tax on it. If you pay tax on the entire $10,000 "gain," you'll pay tax twice on the $2,000-worth of reinvested dividends. You've increased your reported capital gains unnecessarily. This is why it is so important to keep track of reinvested dividends.

Selling your shares

When you buy shares in a mutual fund, you will receive a confirmation statement, which will show the purchase price you paid (often including any commissions). When you sell shares, the confirmation statement will show the amount of shares you sold and the selling price you received. These records will come in handy when you figure out your cost basis.

When you decide to sell shares, there are four ways to calculate your gain:

1. FIFO (first in, first out)

2. Average cost, single category

3. Average cost, double category

4. Specific shares

In order to save on taxes, you have to figure out which method works best for you when you sell shares. For different funds you may choose to use different methods.

Whichever method that you use, note that the cost basis usually includes fees and commissions, which reduce the amount on which you must pay taxes. The IRS offers this example: "You bought 100 shares of Fund A for $10 a share. You paid a $50 commission to the broker for the purchase. Your cost basis for each share is $10.50 ($1,050 divided by

The hardest thing to understand in the world is the income tax. —Albert Einstein.

100).” According to the IRS, the “amount of the distribution used to purchase each full or fractional
share is the cost basis for that share.”

FIFO

If you don't track your transactions, the IRS will
assume that the first shares you bought are the first
you sell. This selling method is referred to as FIFO
(first in, first out).

The FIFO method assumes the first shares you
sell are the first shares you purchased. This method
may not be advantageous tax-wise if the first shares
you bought have substantial unrealized gains and
ones you've bought subsequently have fewer gains
or capital losses.

Average cost, single category

In order to use either the average cost, single category or the average cost, double category method
for figuring cost basis, you must have purchased
shares at different times and at different prices. If
you decide to use this method, you must continue to
use it for as long as you're invested in that particular
fund. (Of course, if you get out of the fund completely and then get back in, you start with a clean
slate.)

Using the average cost, single category method,
each time you sell shares you must determine the
average cost of all the shares you own in that fund.
(Note: Depending on the fund and the date you
became a shareholder, the fund may provide you
with your average basis, which will save you the trouble of figuring it out.) To do this, you must add up
the total cost and divide that sum by the number of
shares you own. Then, multiply the average cost by
the number of shares sold to get your basis of the
shares sold. The shares you sell are assumed to be

the ones you bought first. This will determine your holding period, which determines whether you have short- or long-term capital gains.

The IRS gives this example for figuring the average cost, single category method: "You bought the following shares in the LJP Mutual Fund: 100 shares in 1994 at $10 per share; 100 shares in 1995 at $12 per share; and 100 shares in 1996 at $26 per share. On May 16, 1997, you sold 150 shares. The basis of shares sold is $2,400, computed as follows:

1. Total cost ($1,000 + $1,200 + $2,600) = $4,800

2. Average basis per share ($4,800 divided by 300) = $16.00

3. Basis of shares sold ($16.00 x 150) = $2,400

There are drawbacks to using this method. Say you've held some shares for 10 months and others for 5 months and you must sell some shares immediately and some in three months from now. This method of selling shares doesn't allow you to sell now the shares you bought 5 months ago so that you can hold onto the rest for two months or longer to benefit from the lower-cost, long-term capital gains taxes when you sell them. Using this method, the shares you sell are assumed to be the ones you bought first. Therefore, you must sell those you've already held for 10 months and must wait at least another seven months before selling those you've held for only five months in order to benefit from the long-term capital gains tax rate. However, if you've held all of the shares for more than 12 months, this method simplifies the math.

Average cost, double category
Using the double category method, you must divide the shares in your account into two categories:

short-term (those held 12 months and less) and long-term (those held longer than 12 months) holdings. You can choose which shares you want to sell, but you must get a written confirmation from the fund or your financial planner that the ones you specified were the ones that were actually sold. Otherwise, the IRS assumes you are selling the long-term holdings.

Specific shares

You can take advantage of tax benefits by selling shares based on the share price or on the length of time shares were held in your portfolio. This is called the specific shares method of tracking the shares you sell.

Using the specific shares method, you can sell whichever shares produce the best tax result. This method can be useful if you've held two sets of shares for differing lengths of time, for example, one for 11 months and one for only 2 months. You may want to sell those you bought two months ago to allow the others to become taxable as long-term gains in another month.

Tax savings and education

The cost of getting a college degree has outpaced the general rate of inflation for many years, making it difficult to afford a post-secondary education. But there are many ways you can save on taxes (or at least defer them) if you save for college. (There are ways to save on actual college costs, as well. See Chapter 11 for detailed information.) Some of these tax-reducing techniques can be combined for even greater tax savings.

College savings plans, which allow you to save money, tax-deferred, specifically earmarked for

Bright Idea
Visit the IRS's Web site (www.irs.gov) to find answers to your tax questions. That way, if there's a dispute later, you'll have the IRS's position in writing.

college (there are two types of qualified state tuition programs—see Chapter 11 for detailed information on each plan type), have these advantages:

- Earnings are tax-deferred.

- Earnings are taxed at the student rate when taken out and used for tuition.

- There's a distinct possibility that the funds will be entirely tax-free in the next five years. There have been bills before Congress to make proceeds tax-free.

- Contributions are not subject to standard gift tax rules. This means you can invest up to $50,000 per child at one time and avoid gift tax instead of $10,000 per child per year (the usual limit on gifts before a gift tax is due); the extra $40,000 is treated as a gift over the next four years, and is therefore exempt from gift tax. Meanwhile, the whole $50,000 is earning money for the child's tuition that much sooner.

- Contributions are exempt from federal, state, and local taxes.

The education IRA (EIRA) also provides a tax shelter, although it is small in comparison to the state tuition plans (only $500 can be contributed per year to each child's account). Furthermore, the EIRA disqualifies students from taking advantage of the Hope Scholarship and Lifetime-Learning tax credits, making this savings plan rather undesirable, says Bernie Kent, CPA and CFP at Pricewaterhouse-Coopers in Detroit, Michigan.

The Hope Scholarship tax credit allows qualified taxpayers to deduct up to $1,500 for the first two years of college for each dependent attending college. The Lifetime-Learning tax credit allows those

Timesaver
Download tax forms and publications from the Internal Revenue Service's Web site at www.irs.gov. That way you don't have to wait for them to arrive in the mail or stand in line to get the ones you need.

who qualify to claim a tax credit of 20 percent for the first $5,000 out-of-pocket qualified tuition and required fees through 2002 and for the first $10,000 thereafter. (For more information on these tax credits, see Chapter 11.)

Families with an adjusted gross income (AGI) of $100,000 or less and single-headed households with AGIs of $50,000 or less qualify for the Hope Scholarship or Lifetime-Learning Credit. Phaseouts begin at $80,000 for joint filers and $40,000 for single filers.

Families who qualify can claim Hope Scholarship credits for some family members and the Lifetime-Learning tax credit for others during the same year. These tax credits also can be used by adults attending school part-time to earn a certification or who are enrolled in the first two years of a degreed program.

For more information on the Hope Scholarship and Lifetime-Learning tax credits, see Chapter 11 and IRS Publication 970.

There are still other ways to reduce taxes if you're investing in a higher education. Education-related loan interest payments may be tax deductible (provided certain requirements are met). Parents or graduates can deduct up to $1,500 in 1999 and $2,000 in 2000 on loan interest payments over the first five years payments are owed, though there is talk of repealing this first 60-month rule. The tax-deductible amount will increase to $2,500 in 2001. You can take the deduction even if you don't itemize other deductions. To qualify, your family's AGI must be below $75,000 ($55,000 for single filers). Phaseouts begin at $60,000 for joint filers and $40,000 for single filers. (Married individuals filing separately are ineligible.) You can use the deduction for all educational loans.

Taxes and retirement

Saving for your retirement using a traditional IRA, Roth IRA, or 401(k) gives you a significant tax advantage: Your earnings grow tax-deferred in the case of traditional IRAs and 401(k)s, and tax-free in the case of the Roth IRA. (For more information on traditional and Roth IRAs and on 401(k) plans, see Chapter 12.)

401(k) plans

401(k) plans often have a unique advantage. You can make your contributions with pretax dollars, which increases your potential earning power while decreasing your taxable income. Plus, many companies match your investment dollar for dollar or 50 cents on the dollar, up to a certain percentage of your income. Because of this perk, despite how the market performs, you get an immediate return on your investment. (For this reason alone, if you can only afford one retirement account, consider investing in a 401(k) if you are eligible.)

Traditional IRAs

The traditional deductible IRA allows you to deduct your after-tax contribution from your gross earnings, reducing your taxable income by the amount you contribute each year. Plus, when you make a withdrawal during retirement, you'll pay taxes at your retirement income tax rate, which will likely be lower than the rate you were at during your peak earning years.

Roth IRAs

The Roth IRA "represent[s] a very, very attractive opportunity," says Michael Chasnoff, CFP and

"
Taxation *with*
representation
ain't so hot
either.
—Gerald Barzan.

"

president of Advanced Capital Strategies, Inc., in Cincinnati, Ohio. "The money that is invested in a Roth account goes in on a nondeductible basis, but all the earnings grow tax-free, not tax-deferred," Chasnoff explains. "That's a big difference, particularly for people who have a long time to wait before they're going to need [to draw on it]," he says. (See Chapter 12 for more information on the tax treatment of Roth IRAs.)

The Roth IRA is a good retirement tool for those who expect to accumulate a lot of savings by retirement. With traditional IRAs, you are required to take minimum distributions by the April 1 after you turn 70½. But you don't have to make mandatory withdrawals on a Roth IRA, so you can let your investment continue to grow tax-free. Those who have other investment sources "will probably only need a small portion of their assets during retirement," Chasnoff says, adding that perhaps they won't need to tap into the Roth IRA at all.

Keep in mind that the Roth IRA is not suitable for everyone. "The ideal Roth investor should be someone who will not need to tap their Roth IRA assets until they retire," Chasnoff says, because the longer the assets remain in a tax-free environment, the more opportunity there is for tax-free compounding. (See Chapter 1 for a discussion on compounded growth.)

Which IRA is best for you?

There is debate on whether it's better to place your retirement funds in a traditional IRA or Roth IRA. On one hand, if you invest pretax dollars as you do with traditional IRAs (some restrictions do apply; see Chapter 12 for details or consult your tax advisor), you'll have that much more money working for you. But if you retire at a higher tax bracket, the Roth IRA will benefit you more because withdrawals are tax-free after the waiting period requirements are satisfied. The problem is that you probably can't predict what income tax bracket you'll be in at retirement, nor can you know whether income tax rates will be the same then as they are now. Historically, taxes have ranged from 15 percent to as high as 70 percent.

One of the big advantages of the Roth IRA is that it allows your retirement assets to grow income tax-free over a long period of time. Most people have the bulk of their assets in retirement plans. If you're one of those people, then there's good reason to convert your traditional IRAs to Roth IRAs, Chasnoff says.

As discussed in Chapter 12, you can convert a traditional IRA to a Roth IRA if your modified AGI is not more than $100,000 and you are not a married individual filing a separate return. (For more information, see IRS Publication 590.) Make sure you have the cash to pay the taxes required to convert to a Roth IRA, however; if you must use retirement funds to pay these taxes, you've eliminated the benefits of conversion, Chasnoff says. It's also not useful to convert if you know you'll need to use the money in your account in the next five years because you won't have enough time to benefit from tax-free compounding.

The number of years you'll need to keep your money in a converted Roth IRA to make it worthwhile depends on the rate of return your investment is getting and your tax bracket at retirement. Generally, it takes about 10 to 15 years of tax-free compounding to make conversion worthwhile,

Chasnoff notes. If you're an older person, say, age 65 or above, you might want to convert only a portion of your retirement assets, he suggests.

Bottom line? If you can't pay the tax for the conversion without using part of your IRA funds, then you probably shouldn't convert to a Roth IRA. Under this circumstance, it is not likely that any tax savings you get from the Roth IRA will offset the reduction in potential growth you would probably experience in your current IRA savings.

If you can afford to pay the taxes from your present earnings, you may want to consider conversion. When deciding whether to convert your retirement savings plan to a Roth IRA, consider the following factors:

- The amount of time you have before you retire—generally, the longer the period before you begin taking withdrawals, the more advantageous it is to convert.

- The rate of return you expect to earn on your Roth IRA investment—the higher the expected rate of return, the more advantageous a Roth IRA becomes because the earnings are tax-free.

- Your current tax and projected tax bracket during retirement. If you expect to be in a higher tax bracket during retirement, a Roth IRA is more advantageous than other IRAs because of the tax-free withdrawals. Likewise, if you expect to be in a lower tax bracket, you may be better off with a traditional IRA. If you expect to remain in the same tax bracket, consult your tax advisor for a comparison.

If you convert to a Roth IRA, the amount you convert will be added to your current taxable income. If this increase pushes you into a higher income tax bracket, your income tax burden will increase, which may result in other tax consequences. Ask yourself these questions:

- If you're currently collecting Social Security, will converting make those benefits taxable?

- Will you miss out on the new child tax credit? This $400 tax credit per child under age 17 begins to phase out at an AGI of $75,000 for single filers and $110,000 for couples filing jointly.

- Will you still qualify for the education tax credits? Eligibility for the Hope Scholarship and Lifetime-Learning tax credits begin to phase out for single filers when their AGI reaches $40,000 and for joint filers when their AGI reaches $80,000. Phaseouts for EIRA contributions begin at $95,000 for single filers and $150,000 for joint filers.

- Will you lose out on the new deduction for interest paid on higher education loans?

- Will it affect your ability to deduct miscellaneous expenses such as investment advice and tax preparation expenses, unreimbursed business expenses, and union dues? These items are tax deductible only when they add up to more than 2 percent of your AGI.

- Will it affect your personal exemptions and itemized deductions? Personal exemptions begin to phase out once your AGI reaches a certain threshold ($124,500 for single filers and $186,800 for those married filing jointly); itemized deductions begin to phase out when your AGI reaches $124,500 for both single and married filers.

Bright Idea
If you're worried about placing money in a retirement account because you might need it before retirement age, open up a Roth IRA. Since your contributions are taxed up front, you can withdraw them whenever you want (starting five years after you open it) without paying a penalty. In addition, if you find you don't need the money in retirement, your heirs can inherit it tax-free.

Bright Idea
If you're tempted to spend your savings, put it in your retirement plan. The penalties for early withdrawal will help you keep your hands in your pockets.

- Will it affect your medical expense deductions? These expenses can be deducted once they total 7.5 percent of your AGI.

Aggressive mutual funds: In your taxable accounts or retirement portfolio?

There's some debate as to whether you should place your aggressive mutual funds in your retirement portfolio or in your taxable accounts. Long-term capital gains in your taxable accounts are taxed at 20 percent (unless you're in the 15 percent tax bracket; see discussion above) and dividends and short-term capital gains are taxed at your current income tax rate, which can be as high as 39.6 percent.

If you keep your aggressive funds in your tax-deferred retirement accounts, when you make withdrawals after age 59½, you'll pay tax at your then income tax rate, which may be higher or lower than 20 percent or your income tax rate now for ordinary income. The problem is that you don't know what the tax rates will be in the future, and you can't predict with any certainty what tax bracket you'll be in.

Regardless, you can bank on this: While it's clearly beneficial to place aggressive funds in a Roth IRA (where no taxes will be owed on earnings), whether the same is true for tax-deferred accounts (traditional IRAs) depends on what you think your income tax rate will be at retirement.

It's also a good idea to use your IRA for mutual funds that have high turnover rates in order to save on short-term capital gains taxes that are not in your control. (The fund manager controls the portfolio turnover rate.)

Divorce and taxes

In addition to emotional and financial consequences, divorce has tax consequences. You must consider them carefully when dividing assets. Here are some divorce tax tips. (See Chapter 15 for more information on divorce.)

Property transfers

The transfer of property between spouses is not considered a taxable event. Remember, though, that the spouse who receives the property receives the transferring spouse's basis. (The *basis* is the cost of the property when first acquired.)

For example, if in your divorce settlement you received a second residence appraised for $150,000 in lieu of $150,000 in cash, it wouldn't represent an equal distribution of property. "An appreciated dwelling valued at $150,000, but purchased for $50,000 [for example] is not the same as $150,000 in the bank," says Linda Lubitz, a CFP in Miami, Florida. "After the building is sold and the 20 percent capital gains tax is paid on the gain of $100,000 [$150,000 present value less $50,000 basis], the building is worth $130,000 [to you], not $150,000."

Alimony versus child support

"Alimony is a payment to or for a spouse or former spouse under a divorce or separation instrument," according to the IRS.

If one spouse is in a high tax bracket and the other is in a low tax bracket, there are some simple strategies you can consider to save tax dollars, says Jim Bruyette, partner with Sullivan, Bruyette, Speros and Blayney in McLean, Virginia.

Bruyette recommends that you both decide how much financial support should be considered alimony and how much should be considered child support. Alimony is tax deductible for the payer and taxable as income to the receiver. Child support, on the other hand, is neither tax deductible nor taxable as income. The person in the higher tax bracket will probably want to pay all support as alimony (and thus derive the benefit of the tax deduction). The receiver may not be so receptive to this idea, however, for obvious reasons. Look at your mutual tax situation, Bruyette says. "In many cases [in spite of the tax consequences to the receiver], it makes sense to classify the ongoing support payments as alimony," he says.

For example, let's assume that the husband is in a 40 percent tax bracket (rounded up from 39.6 percent) and the wife is not working. If he pays her $100,000, he could save $40,000 (40 percent of $100,000 equals $40,000) if the support is considered alimony because he'd be able to deduct those payments from his taxes. The wife's taxable income is now $100,000 at the end of the year, on which she would have to pay about $23,000 in income taxes. Together, the couple could save about $17,000 in taxes ($40,000 less $23,000) if the support is considered alimony, and not child support (from which the couple would derive zero in tax savings).

In many cases, the wife doesn't want to pay taxes on any of it, so the husband ends up paying large amounts of child support, Bruyette says. If the divorce is amicable, however, perhaps the couple can reach an agreement whereby the husband pays the wife a bit more in total alimony support to compensate for the tax loss she's realizing (and in recognition of the tax savings to him by not having to pay as much in child support).

Is such an arrangement legal? "The courts don't even have to get involved," Bruyette says. Two people can agree to anything they want, he notes, adding that once the courts are involved, there are state limitations to consider. The agreement must be put in writing or there must be a court decree.

To find out about state laws and limitations on all financial aspects of divorce, consult with a divorce attorney and financial planner.

Alimony recapture

Avoid triggering *alimony recapture*, which could add substantially to your tax bill. The alimony recapture rule forces you to pay taxes on the third year of alimony payments that you previously had deducted. To avoid doing so, make sure the alimony payments you make are not significantly decreased or eliminated during the first three years after your divorce decree is final. The recapture rule is triggered if the alimony you pay in either the second or third year decreases from the prior year by more than $15,000. (Certain exceptions apply. See IRS Publication 504, available online at www.irs.gov.) The alimony recapture rule protects against payers disguising a property settlement as deductible alimony.

Exemptions

Bruyette suggests placing the dependent exemptions with the person in the higher tax bracket, unless, of course, the phaseout applies. The person in the higher tax bracket can take better advantage of the exemptions. Your settlement agreement can provide for this. (The exemption is phased out if your income is over a certain amount, depending on your filing status. See IRS Publication 504, "Phaseout of Exemptions.")

Qualified domestic relations orders (QDROs)

To be eligible to receive a portion of a qualified retirement plan from a former spouse, a QDRO

Moneysaver
If your spouse is subject to the alimony recapture rule, you as the payee can deduct the third year's payments previously included as income to you.

must be issued by the court. (See Chapter 15 for
more on QDROs.) The state domestic relations
court will divide the account and specify the details
in the QDRO. An improperly drafted divorce decree
or QDRO could result in the immediate taxation of
the retirement plan, Lubitz warns.

A QDRO is a judgment, decree, or court order
issued in part to protect your rights to receive benefits from a qualified retirement plan (such as most
pension and profit-sharing plans) or a tax-sheltered
annuity. It can specify the amount or portion of the
participant's benefits to be paid to a child or former
spouse. Benefits paid under a QDRO to a spouse are
generally included in the spouse's or former
spouse's income for taxation purposes. If you
receive an eligible rollover distribution, as the ex-
spouse, you may be able to roll it over tax-free into
an IRA or another qualified retirement plan.
QDROs also can specify the amount or portion of
the participant's benefits to be paid to a child or former spouse and can address payment of child support, alimony, or marital property rights. (Refer to
IRS Publication 575 for more information; you can
download it from the IRS's Web site at www.irs.gov
or request it be mailed to you by calling the IRS at
800/829-1040.) "If a QDRO is entered into the
courts, a divorced wife or husband can spend any
amount [as specified in the QDRO] from the former spouse's qualified retirement plan before age
$59\frac{1}{2}$ without incurring the 10 percent premature
distribution penalty," Lubitz says. "Income taxes are
due, of course."

Once the money is rolled over into an IRA, however, the usual rules for IRA withdrawals take over,"
she says. "Any distributions before age $59\frac{1}{2}$ (except

the annuitization rules) are subject to the 10 percent penalty tax." (See a financial advisor for more information.)

Health insurance

Instead of receiving a continuation of health insurance benefits through your former spouse's policy under COBRA for 36 months, Lubitz says to consider asking for the amount in cash your ex-spouse would otherwise pay for the coverage. (See Chapter 14 for details on COBRA.) "Then [you] can purchase [your] own policy," she says.

The strategy Lubitz suggests is intended to allow the spouse without insurance to get permanent coverage. If you are in this situation and are self-employed, you can buy your own policy and deduct a percentage of the premiums from your income taxes. (You don't need to be divorced to take advantage of this tax-saving strategy if you're self-employed.)

How to handle assets with potential capital gains

Financial portfolios and retirement plans have tax implications. If you realize any gains, you'll have to pay taxes on them. Determine under whose ownership the tax rate of these gains would be most favorable, Bruyette advises.

Working together, a divorcing couple can structure a much better tax situation, Bruyette says. Most of these tax-saving strategies work only if the couple can agree to set aside their differences. "When personalities get involved, sometimes it gets expensive," he adds.

More tax-saving strategies

Financial planners and CPAs are savvy when it comes to structuring your finances to lighten your

Bright Idea
Make sure that your divorce decree has an indemnification clause that guarantees no responsibility for any deficiencies reported in an IRS audit due to your former spouse's actions.

tax burden. Here's a couple of their money-saving schemes.

Placing investments in your children's names

Placing investments in your children's names will save you up to $300 to $400 per child per year, and more than that after they turn 14, Bruyette says. Each child can receive up to $20,000 ($10,000 from each parent) a year without incurring a gift tax. If the child is under 14 at the end of the year, up to $1,400 of the child's investment income per year is taxed at the child's rate (anything above that is taxed at the parent's income tax rate); after age 14, everything is taxed at the child's rate. (Note: that the $1,400 "kiddie" tax threshold could increase after 1999.)

Bruyette explains: If you take $1,400 per year and move it from your tax return to your child's, your taxes will be reduced by $300 to $400 dollars. The goal should be to generate that $1,400 per year based on asset appreciation from stocks that don't pay dividends, so the child won't have to pay a 15 percent income tax (which is higher than a child's long-term capital gains tax rate of 10 percent). When the child turns 14, sell the investment. At that point, the capital gains will be taxed at the child's rate of 10 percent rather than your rate of 20 percent. Or, keep the investment: At age 14, the $1,400 ceiling is lifted, increasing the tax-savings potential. Be aware that this strategy may backfire if your child would otherwise qualify for financial aid for college. See Chapter 11 for more information.

Charitable contributions

If you give appreciated, long-term capital gains property (stocks) to charity, you don't have to pay the income tax on the gain, and you get to take advantage of the charitable contribution deduction, according to Kent. Many people give stocks, land, or other highly appreciable assets to charity to avoid paying the capital gains tax, he says.

Property other than land or intangible assets, that is, personal property, can be deducted only at its fair market value if it's given to a charity in connection with a tax-exempt function of the charity. For example, if you give a work of art to an art museum, it's deductible, but if you give the same piece of art to the United Way, only the cost (or basis) would be deductible, not the fair market value, Kent notes.

Moneysaver
Remember to deduct charitable contributions taken from your paycheck. Many people forget to do this because they didn't actually write a check. A good way to track these contributions? Look at your pay stub!

Just the facts

- Keep careful records of your investments to avoid double taxation.

- You can combine education tax credits with tax-deferred investing and save thousands in taxes when you pay college tuition bills.

- By taking advantage of traditional deductible IRAs and 401(k)s, you can save not only income taxes now but capital gains taxes on investment earnings until you begin making withdrawals.

- Divorce can be taxing, but, assuming you and your ex can agree, you can reduce your burden with tax-saving strategies.

Your Financial Future

PART VI

GET THE SCOOP ON...
Why it's so important to get a college degree ▪
How much more college graduates earn on aver-
age than those with high school diplomas ▪
What types of financial assistance are available
▪ What schools offer free or reduced tuition

Investing in Your Future and Your Children's Future Education

E ven with six-figure household incomes, many families find it difficult to make ends meet. Homes prices have appreciated so much in recent decades that it's hard to buy one without two incomes, and considerable incomes at that. Then there are car payments, daycare, braces for the kids...the list goes on and on.

Now imagine trying to pay for all that while working for minimum wage. It's not easy, but that's all many people with only high school diplomas earn. While four years of college is a big expense, that cost, considered as an investment, can produce an impressive rate of return.

In this chapter I'll tell you about the difference in lifetime earning power for men and women with college degrees compared with those with high school diplomas. I'll tell you where you can get financial aid and fill you in on some of the best-kept secrets to getting a good education without incurring enormous debt.

Benefits of a college degree

College education is an investment that pays off. There is a $700,000 increased lifetime income for a male who graduates college versus one who didn't, according to Tom Mortenson, a higher education policy analyst in Oskaloosa, Iowa, and senior scholar at the Center for the Study for Opportunity in Higher Education in Washington, D.C. The earnings differential for women is $400,000. Furthermore, college-educated men and women tend to marry each other as do those with high school diplomas, making the income differential for families between $1.2 million to $1.3 million over a 40-year working lifetime, he says.

Here's another way to look at it: For every $1 spent on college tuition, fees, room, and board, the eventual return is $30 in increased income for men, Mortenson says. For women it's less (because the careers they have traditionally chosen have paid less), about $18 for every $1 spent. But returns are growing, largely because women are changing fields. Either way, 30:1 or 18:1, you're getting significant returns on your investment, Mortenson says.

"[Whether or not to go to college] is not a complicated decision," Mortenson notes, adding that economists have a way of making it seem that way. "You can always patch together financial aid," he says.

Many people have learned this investment lesson the hard way and as adults are returning to school to obtain upper-level degrees. This population has typically been out in the working world for 10 years, earning minimum wage and finding out they can't buy a car or a home or support a family on their income. Community college is a good alternative for an older population, those who tried to enter the job market with only a high-school education and found out they couldn't make ends meet, says Mortenson.

A generation ago families could live fairly comfortably on blue-collar incomes. But these jobs are disappearing in this country. Now many families must find a different way to provide for their children, which more often includes higher education, Mortenson says. "I don't know any other alternative," he says. Median family incomes are the same as they were in 1973, which means that some families are doing much better and some are doing much worse. Families headed by high school dropouts have household incomes 35 percent lower than the median. This stark contrast in family incomes is due to real growth from post-baccalaureate income, he says. There's a shortage of highly trained individuals and a surplus of unskilled workers. Where you have a surplus, the value of labor goes down. Where there's a shortage, salaries are higher, Mortenson says. It's simple economics: Supply and demand.

For those people from low-income families, higher education is the only way to get out and move up. "They are increasingly competing with third-world workers for employment," Mortenson says.

But first things first. Before you spend your hard-earned money (or your parents' hard-earned money) or take out a big loan to finance your

> "
> The only thing more expensive than going to college is not going to college.
> —Tom Mortenson, a higher education policy analyst in Oskaloosa, Iowa, and senior scholar at the Center for the Study for Opportunity in Higher Education in Washington, D.C.
> "

higher education, it might be worthwhile to ask yourself if it's likely your dream career will pay you enough to earn a decent living. Many graduates find themselves struggling in careers they thought would make them happy only to find out some of the appeal wore off when they found they couldn't make ends meet. (Hence the term *starving artist.*) You might also consider asking yourself if the degree you are getting is really a useful one. For instance, majoring in psychology may not be useful unless you plan to go to graduate school because practicing psychologists all have upper-level (graduate) degrees.

Finding the right college or university

How do you find a college for yourself or help your children find one that will provide a good education at an affordable price? Consider the following criteria:

- The school's admissions requirements: preparation begins in high school.

- The curriculum: does the school offer the program that you want?

- Accreditation: make sure your degree is worth something.

- Comparison shop: does this school offer a good education at a reasonable price, or do others have equal or better programs with lower tuitions?

- Financial aid: check on the availability of and qualifications for federal and state student aid and any scholarships you qualify for.

- Student safety: what precautions does the school have in place?

- Social atmosphere: does it match your personality?

- Dropout rate: is it above or below the median?

Preparation

Preparation is the key to acceptance. Colleges have different admissions criteria. Admission may be based on:

- High school grades

- Admission test scores (SATs, ACTs, or other standardized testing)

- Class rank

- Alumni relationship (if other members of your family are graduates)

- Race/ethnicity

- Application questions and essays

- State of residence

- Extracurricular activities

- Major or college applied to within the university

- Ability to pay

Strategies for saving for a college education

College tuition and fees in the United States experienced an average annual inflation rate of 8.7 percent from 1978 to 1997, according to Department of Labor (DOL) statistics. That's 3.8 percent more than the general average annual inflation rate of 4.9 percent during that same period.

Annual tuition and fee increases continue to outpace inflation. The College Board reported that the average increase in college tuition and fees for the 1998–1999 school year at four-year public institutions was approximately 4 percent over the

Bright Idea
Many people try to increase their chances of getting accepted into the college of their choice by taking prep courses to help them prepare for the admissions test.

previous year. At private four-year institutions the hike was about 5 percent. Students at two-year schools had to pay 4 percent more. Translated into dollars, students paid from $66 to $723 more than the previous year, depending on the type of institution. Room and board increased 3 to 5 percent.

Despite the increasing price tag, college educations are still affordable. College Board President Donald M. Stewart notes that the majority of all students at four-year colleges and universities spend less than $4,000 a year on tuition and fees. Plus, the availability of financial aid was at a record level of more than $60 billion in the 1997–1998 school year, a 6 percent increase over the previous year after adjusting for inflation (though a shift from grants to loans continues). This increase was mostly in the form of loans, and few loans were subsidized, that is, the government did not foot the bill for interest while the student was in school.

Unofficially...
If cost is your determining factor, consider this: According to the College Board, half of all students enrolled in post-secondary education receive some financial aid.

Investing in and for college

College should be considered a lifetime investment rather than just a four-year expense. It requires financial planning and personal sacrifices. The earlier you start saving and investing, the less money you'll have to save and invest later. Furthermore, the earlier you start saving, the less risk you'll have to take in your investment choices because long-term investing generally carries less risk. If you know the interest rate for your investment or want to take a guess at it, you can use the following formula (or Table 11.1) to see how long you must be in the market to double your investment: Divide 72 by the number of years invested to figure out what interest rate will double your investment. For example, if you have $10,000 and you want to double it in 10 years, the equation should look like this: 72 ÷ 10 = 7.2 percent interest rate. (This is known as the Rule of 72; see Chapter 1 for more information.)

TABLE 11.1 RULE OF 72

Rate of return	Number of years to double your investment
1%	72.0
2%	36.0
3%	24.0
4%	18.0
5%	14.4
6%	12.0
7%	10.3
8%	9.0
9%	8.0
10%	7.2
11%	6.5
12%	6.0
13%	5.5
14%	5.1
15%	4.8
16%	4.5
17%	4.2
18%	4.0
19%	3.8
20%	3.6
21%	3.4
22%	3.3
23%	3.1
24%	3.0
25%	2.9

← Note!
Use this table to see how many years it will take your investment to double at a specified rate of return. Or, you can use it to see what rate of return you'll need to double your money in a specified number of years.

Even at $4,000 a year, college is expensive. But it's a worthwhile investment in your future and your children's future. You can stretch your dollars by investing. Certainly, the earlier you start, the less you'll likely have to save. This is because of two reasons: The market's historical performance is upward (the Dow Jones industrial average has returned an average of 10 percent historically) and the power of compounding. Your principal grows from the increase in the value of the investment and the interest earned grows as a result of the increased principal, compounding the worth of the investment.

You should invest by setting financial goals and benchmarks. Use the college calculator at www.collegeboard.org or *Money Magazine*'s college savings calculator at www.moneymag.com to figure out how much you'll need.

Investing in the future will force you to make some hard choices about what you can and cannot live with right now. Decide what you're willing to give up to reach your goals and stick to your decision. It will be worthwhile in the long run.

Investment strategies

Unless you've already stashed away all the cash you'll need, placing it in bank savings accounts or in Certificates of Deposit (CDs) isn't going to allow it to grow enough to cover future college costs. In fact, these investment tools barely keep up with general inflation. As you know, college costs have soared past average inflation rates. As a result, you must consider more aggressive investment strategies. For instance, stocks have averaged a historical rate of return between 10 and 12 percent. But it's hard to select a stock portfolio if you're not a professional; unless you have tens of thousands of dollars to invest, it's difficult to get a balanced portfolio (one that spreads risk among market sectors, company size, and nations). These are important factors because market sectors have different performance records depending on economic cycles, and it's hard to predict the beginning of an economic cycle to be in the right sector at the right time.

Company size is an important factor in stock selection. Small companies tend to outperform large companies, but are much riskier. There is also significantly less information available on each small company, making it difficult for you to research the company and assess its current worth and future potential.

Domestic and foreign stock markets sometimes perform in opposite directions, again, making for a good balance. But foreign stocks are often considered more volatile by industry experts because they are more subject to fluctuations as a result of political turmoil, weather, and other factors than are domestic stocks.

Investing in stocks is a balancing act. Most investors would probably be better off investing in mutual funds. By definition they are diversified, and all you need is a few of them to have a well-balanced portfolio: A couple growth funds in a few sectors (for example, technology and health), and perhaps a relatively small investment in an international fund to round out your portfolio—assuming you have a long-term investment horizon of 10 years or longer. Another benefit to investing in mutual funds is that many have low investment minimums and offer automatic monthly investments.

If your investment horizon is less than 10 years, you'll probably need a different investment strategy. Tim Kochis and Kacy Gott, investment advisors at Kochis Fitz in San Francisco, California, suggest the following plan as an example of a college investment strategy:

Bright Idea
Invest in no-load funds so that your entire sum is invested. But if you're going to have trouble sitting tight during market volatility, enlist the aid of a financial advisor who will calm your fears during these times and remind you of your goals.

Say your child is 15 years old. You expect her post-secondary education to span five to six years. So you have about eight years to let at least some of your investments grow; you want to keep every dollar invested until the last college bill is paid.

Presuming you're starting with $10,000, Kochis and Gott advise putting $2,000 into equities for her master's degree. It will have eight years to grow and ride out market downturns.

For her senior year of college, which is now six years away, they advise putting $2,000 into an S&P 500 index fund. Her junior year is five years away, so Kochis and Gott suggest putting $2,000 in a balanced fund, one which has 60 percent equities and 40 percent bonds, to reduce the risk somewhat. Her sophomore year is four years away. For that year, they suggest placing $2,000 in an intermediate-term bond fund for added safety. For her freshman year, which is only three years away, they advise putting $2,000 in a CD that matures close to that date.

CollegeSure CDs, another way to save for college, are FDIC-insured CDs guaranteed to yield a fixed rate of interest to match average college costs at maturity. At maturity, the principal and interest can be used at any school. It is offered by the College Savings Bank in Princeton, New Jersey. You can reach them at 800/888-2723, or visit their Web site at www.collegesavings.com (e-mail: info@ collegesavings.com).

Moneysaver
Check out books on seeking financial aid for college at your local library or bookstore for interesting and creative tips.

Tax packages

Tax incentives can help ease educational expense burdens, but one student can't take advantage of all of them during the same year.

Money from these funds and tax credits *must* be used to pay for tuition and required fees, less grants, scholarships, and other tax-free educational assistance. Books, equipment, and eligible room and board expenses also qualify.

Traditional IRAs

You can pay for qualified educational expenses (tuition, fees, books, supplies, and equipment, and room and board if the student attends school at least half-time) using traditional IRA distributions without incurring the 10 percent withdrawal penalty, though you will have to pay income tax on at least part of the withdrawal. Distributions from Roth IRAs and SIMPLE IRAs are not qualified. Note, however, that by using your IRA in this manner, you will miss out on the tax-deferred earnings retirement funds permit.

To qualify, the education must be for you, your spouse, or the children or grandchildren of you or your spouse.

Education IRAs (EIRAs)

Parents, grandparents, other family members, and friends can stash away up to $500 per year into an Education IRA (EIRA) for each child under age 18. Even children can contribute to the funds. The principal grows tax-free until distributed. The student won't owe tax on withdrawals if his or her qualified educational expenses for the year equal or exceed the amount of the withdrawal.

If the child doesn't use the money for education, the money can be rolled over to another family member's EIRA. Some withdrawals (for reasons other than to pay for education expenses) may be subject to income tax and to an additional tax of 10 percent.

If there are funds left over after your child has finished his or her education, there are two options:

Watch Out!
If you wait to apply for financial aid until you've been accepted into the college of your choice, that institution's grant and scholarship funds may already have been depleted.

The remaining amount can be withdrawn and given to the designated beneficiary (there are tax consequences for this), or the remaining amount can be rolled over to another EIRA for the benefit of a member of the designated beneficiary's family, in which case there are no tax consequences.

Bernie Kent, a CPA and investment advisor with PricewaterhouseCoopers in Detroit, rarely recommends this type of savings method because it carries some big disadvantages. Total annual contributions are limited to $500. Students making tax-free withdrawals cannot claim credits from the Hope Scholarship credit or Lifetime-Learning tax credit (both discussed later in this chapter) in the same taxable year. Additionally, participation in an EIRA precludes you from participating in a state savings plan or prepaid tuition plan (also discussed later in this chapter). Currently, the state program savings and prepaid plans don't interfere with the Hope Scholarship and Lifetime-Learning tax credits. If these earnings from states savings program do become tax-exempt, then these plans would make you ineligible for the Hope and Lifetime-Learning credits, he says.

Furthermore, once the EIRA account holder reaches age 30, his or her account must be closed or transferred to a younger member of the family.

You can qualify to contribute to an EIRA if you have an adjusted gross income (AGI) between $150,000 and $160,000 if you're filing jointly or between $95,000 and $110,000 if you're filing singly.

Hope Scholarship credit

Using this tax credit, you can deduct up to $1,500 for the first two years of college. Students get a 100 percent tax credit for the first $1,000 of tuition and

fees and another 50 percent credit on the next
$1,000. Families with an AGI of $100,000 or less and
single-headed households with AGIs of $50,000 or
less qualify, though phase-outs begin at $80,000 for
joint filers and $40,000 for single filers. This
scholarship can be claimed for each dependent
attending college. For more information, consult
with a tax advisor.

Lifetime-Learning tax credit

Families earning up to $100,000 ($50,000 for single
filers) and supporting a college student can claim a
tax credit of 20 percent of the first $5,000 of out-of-
pocket qualified tuition and required fees through
2002 and for the first $10,000 thereafter. Therefore,
the maximum credit in any tax year through 2002 is
$1,000 and $2,000 thereafter. Income phase-outs
are the same as those for the Hope Scholarship tax
credit.

Note that families will be able to claim the Hope
Scholarship credit for some members and the
Lifetime-Learning tax credit for others during the
same year, if they qualify. Students need not be full-
time to take the Lifetime-Learning credit, so it can
be used by adults taking a class or two to brush up
on skills or learn new ones.

Student loan interest payment deductions

Parents or graduates can deduct up to $1,500 in
1999 and $2,000 in 2000 on loan interest payments
over the first five years payments are owed. The tax-
deductible amount will increase to $2,500 in 2001.
You can take the deduction even if you don't itemize other deductions. To qualify, the family AGI
must be below $75,000 ($55,000 for single filers).
Phase-outs begin at $60,000 for joint filers and

$40,000 for single filers. You can use the deduction for all loans made for higher education.

State tuition plans

Use a state-sponsored tuition plan to save for college and your principal will grow tax-deferred until the time of withdrawal. Students who are attending school at least part-time can use money in this plan for tuition and qualifying room and board expenses. Better yet, if you pay tuition and required fees with withdrawals from a state tuition plan, you may still qualify for the Hope Scholarship tax credit and Lifetime-Learning tax credit. These types of state plans are discussed in detail later in this chapter.

Working while you go to school

If you're employed while you're taking undergraduate courses, you can exclude up to $5,250 of employer-provided education benefits (where the employer picks up all or part of the tuition tab) from your income. You must begin taking courses prior to June 1, 2000, to take advantage of this federal government offer.

Community service loan forgiveness

If your student loan has been forgiven by a nonprofit, tax-exempt charitable or educational institution for taking a community service job that addresses unmet community needs, you won't incur additional taxes. For more information, contact the IRS at 800/829-1040.

Qualified state tuition programs

There are two types of qualified state tuition programs. One kind allows you to contribute to a predetermined mutual fund account, designated by the state, that has been established to pay for invested students' qualified higher education expenses ("529 Savings Plan," referred to as "savings plan" in this chapter). The second is a prepaid tuition state program that allows you to pay for future tuition at current rates ("prepaid tuition plan"). You can take advantage of only one of these programs at a time; however, you still may be eligible to claim either the Hope Scholarship credit or the Lifetime-Learning credit. (These programs are discussed in greater detail in the next two sections.)

Both plans have advantages. Earnings are tax-deferred and are taxed at the student's rate when withdrawn to pay for tuition and other approved expenses. You can contribute $50,000 per child, which is considerably more than the $10,000 tax–free gift per child, per year allowed. While the extra $40,000 is treated as a gift over the next four years, you get the entire $50,000 earning for your child that much sooner, Kent points out.

This is a great way for grandparents to help pay for their grandchild's education without having to worry about the child using the money for something else, he says. You don't have to set up a trust. And if the child doesn't go to college, the funds can go to the child's sibling.

With prepaid tuition plans, you're buying tomorrow's tuition at today's prices. While your money may be better invested in the stock market, you're getting peace of mind that the college tuition bills are paid in full ahead of time.

Savings plans are a bit riskier. You may or may not end up covering tuition costs, and you may not get your full principal back, depending on stock market performance. You also have no control over where the money is invested.

Be aware that if you don't use these plans for the purpose of paying qualified education expenses, then, according to Kent, a penalty will be imposed.

Kent notes that for some people, it makes sense to use both plans—a prepaid plan for tuition and a savings plan for room and board. If your child may be eligible for financial aid, however, you should be cautious about using these programs, Kent says. Under current law, they could interfere with your child's eligibility for aid.

Currently, the state savings and prepaid plans don't interfere with the tax credits. If the earnings from state savings or prepaid plans do become tax-exempt, then these plans would make you ineligible for the Hope Scholarship and Lifetime-Learning credits, he says.

State education savings plans

As stated above, college savings plans are state-run investment programs that allow money ear-marked for college expenses to grow tax-deferred. The contributions to these plans are sometimes free from state and local income tax, which adds up to big savings in high-tax areas like New York and Iowa, Kent says. Assets grow free from state taxes. Federal income tax kicks in when the student begins making withdrawals, but the money is taxed at the student's income tax bracket percent. Taxes, however, may not be paid from money in this savings plan. (Savings from the plan used to pay taxes are subject to a 10 percent penalty.)

With this plan, you're getting a tax deduction for saving money, Kent explains, but you're losing control of the investment.

These plans are essentially predetermined mutual fund investment portfolios. The investment strategy—the balance of aggressive and conservative securities—changes as the child ages.

Contributions can be conveniently made with automatic monthly electronic investing. Minimum required annual contributions are about $250. Contributions are unlimited, though that is expected to change. If the child for which the plan was established decides not to attend college, the assets can usually be used by another member of the family. Usually, the money can be used to foot the bills of state, private, and out-of-state colleges and universities.

Almost half the states have a college savings plan program, and many others have one on the drawing board. If your state doesn't have one, or you know you or your family member plans to go out of state to attend college, some states will allow nonresidents to invest in their program, though you won't qualify for the state tax exemption.

As with all of these programs, there are drawbacks: Assets in this program are not guaranteed—you can lose money on your investment just as with any other investment. You have no control over where assets are invested, and the investment style may be more conservative than you might prefer. If you want to get out of a poorly performing investment, you'll be hit with taxes and be subject to a 10 percent penalty because you'll have to leave the savings plan. Students must use the funds only for qualified educational expenses or they'll be hit with the same penalty. Investments per child can't exceed $100,000 (though that won't be an issue for most people).

For more information on state college savings programs, contact the College Savings Plans

Watch Out!
If you default on a student loan, it may hinder your ability to find a job.

Network, an affiliate of the National Association of State Treasurers, at www.collegesavings.org, or write to them at 2760 Research Park Drive, Lexington, KY 40511; 606/244-8175.

Prepaid tuition programs

If you invest in a prepaid state tuition program, the return on your investment is guaranteed to equal the rate of tuition inflation (typically between 6 and 8 percent) at state universities. These programs also offer a tax benefit: Contributions are often exempt from state and local taxes, and federal taxes are deferred until the money is withdrawn (depending on when you start, this could be many years).

You can invest in this plan monthly or annually, depending on the options the state provides. Some states allow lump-sum investments. Most states offer the options of payroll deductions and electronic funds transfers from savings and checking accounts. About half the states currently have this type of program.

There are primarily two types of prepaid tuition plans:

1. Prepaid unit plans—units, representing a fixed percentage of tuition, are sold. Unit prices increase annually.

2. Contract plans—the buyer agrees to purchase a specific number of years of tuition. Prices vary according to the purchase method— installments or lump sum—and the child's current age.

Some states offer prepaid unit plans; others offer contract plans.

A prepaid tuition plan has the following benefits:

- It forces discipline—it's a savings tool earmarked for education.

- It offers safety—the investment is not subject to market volatility.

- The money deposited in these plans is generally exempt from state and local taxes.

- Federal taxes are deferred until the student enrolls in school, and even then the money is taxed at the student's rate.

- It's a simple investment device for those who are not savvy investors and who do not want to hire a financial planner.

  But there are some drawbacks:

- It restricts your choice of college.

- The potential return on your investment is limited.

- Eligibility for federal student financial aid is reduced by 100 percent, whereas other investment vehicles do not reduce eligibility so dramatically (parents' savings reduce financial aid eligibility by 5.6 percent, tops, and the student's assets reduce eligibility by 35 percent; state aid has no affect in some states).

- There may be an enrollment fee.

- There may be a load, that is, a sales commission, on deposits.

- If the student selects a school not qualified under this program, the value of your investment is reduced.

- You can only get back the principal if your child decides not to attend college; you also may have to pay a cancellation fee (note that most plans allow a sibling to take advantage of the prepaid tuition in the original student's place).

- If you move out of state, you may incur out-of-state tuition hikes, even if the student attends the school in the state where you've invested.

Watch Out!
Be sure to report contributions to prepaid tuition plans as a resource on applications for federal student aid. Failure to do so constitutes fraud.

Whether this type of plan is a good idea depends on inflation and how important the guarantee is to you, Kent says. If you want peace of mind, this is a useful investment tool. But if future inflation stays low, say, at about 3 percent, and college tuition continues to grow at a rate of 2 percent above actual inflation, college inflation will be at 5 percent, which doesn't translate to a good return on your investment. However, because you can't predict inflation, this type of plan offers a good insurance policy, a virtual guarantee that you'll be able to afford your kids' college educations. This assurance is invaluable for many.

Government financial aid

The U.S. Department of Education also offers financial aid in the form of grants, work-study, and loans.

Federal Pell grants are awarded to every eligible undergraduate. The maximum varies year to year according to funding. For the 1997–98 school year, the maximum grant amount was $2,700. The amount awarded depends on financial need, school costs, student status (full-time or part-time), and the number of semesters or quarters you enroll for that year.

Stafford loans are given out either directly from the U.S. Department of Education through the Direct Loan Program (for participating schools) or a bank, credit union, or other Federal Family Education Loan (FFEL) Program participating lender.

After other financial aid is subtracted from education-related expenses, you can use the Stafford loan to cover all or a portion of your remaining need. Because this is a subsidized loan, the government pays the interest while you're in school and for the first six months after you leave school as well as when you qualify to have your payments deferred. (The loan has a variable interest rate, adjusted annually, but which will not exceed 8.25 percent.) Unsubsidized Stafford loans are available to those who don't have a financial need remaining. If this is your circumstance, you can borrow for the amount of your expected family contribution (EFC) or the annual Stafford loan borrowing limit for your grade level, whichever is less, but you must pay interest on the loan from the time it's disbursed until it is paid in full, though you can defer payment of the interest while you qualify. Bear in mind that the interest will be capitalized, that is, added to the principal, for as long as you defer. Some students can qualify for both a subsidized and unsubsidized Stafford loan. There is a six-month grace period before repayment begins after you graduate, leave school, or drop below half-time enrollment.

PLUS loans (Parent loans) are available through both the FFEL and Direct Loan programs. Parents can use this money to pay the education expenses of a dependent child enrolled at least half-time at an eligible school. A credit check is required. Both the student and parents must meet other eligibility requirements for federal student financial aid. The annual loan limit is equal to the cost of attendance minus any other financial aid received. This loan has a variable interest rate, which will not exceed 9 percent. Interest is charged from the date of the first disbursement. There is no grace period for repayment.

Timesaver
Utilize the Internet to search for financial aid. Type in the keywords "scholarships," "financial aid," or "student aid" using any search engine.

For the Stafford and PLUS loans there is an origination fee of up to 4 percent. Late payments are subject to late fees and collection costs.

The Federal Work-Study (FWS) program provides part-time jobs for undergraduate and graduate students with financial need. Wages equal or exceed minimum wage. This award is need-dependent. Other factors in obtaining this award depend on when you apply and the funding level at your school. The amount you earn cannot exceed the amount you are awarded. Not all schools participate in this program.

The federal Perkins loan is a low-interest (5 percent) loan made through the school's financial aid office to qualified undergraduates and graduates with exceptional financial need. Undergraduates can borrow $3,000 per year, up to a maximum of $15,000.

The Federal Supplemental Educational Opportunity Grants (FSEOGs) are for undergraduates with exceptional financial need. Grants range from $100 to $4,000. First to qualify are Pell grant recipients with the lowest EFCs. In addition to financial need, funding depends on several factors, including when you apply and the funding level at the school to which you're applying.

You must begin paying back this loan nine months after you graduate, leave school, or drop below half-time status. You may have up to 10 years to repay the loan in full, with permitted extensions for special circumstances. Otherwise, missed payments incur penalties. The loan is administered through the school's financial aid office, though not all schools participate in this program.

For more information call the Federal Student Aid Information Center at 800/4-FED-AID or visit their Web site at www.ed.gov.

You can also use a home equity loan for educational purposes. The interest may be tax-deductible for borrowers who itemize deductions on their tax return. But defaulting on loan payments can result in foreclosure on your home.

Privately sponsored and insured loans are not backed by the government. These loans have lower interest rates than other consumer loans, and borrowers don't have to demonstrate financial need to qualify, though they do have to show credit-worthiness. Shop around—terms and conditions vary widely.

Finding private loans and scholarships

How do you find out about private loans and scholarships? You can start with your high school counselor and move on to the college financial aid office. Many corporations offer college tuition aid or reimbursement to their employees and some offer scholarships to their employees' children; many religious organizations offer scholarships as well. Review college financial aid books at your library. Some of them have extensive listings of sources that you can't find elsewhere. Contact both the U.S. Department of Education and your state department of education.

Finally, search the Internet. There are many Web sites that have college savings calculators and information on financial aid. Start with the Web site of the college or university you want to attend, as well as local and national banks. Here are some actual Web site addresses to get you started:

Unofficially...
According to the U.S. Department of Education, financial aid administrators have the authority to change your status from dependent to independent if there's a justifiable reason for doing so.

- U.S. Department of Education: www.ed.gov
- The College Board: www.collegeboard.org
- Nellie Mae: www.nelliemae.org
- Sallie Mae: www.salliemae.com
- FinAid: www.finaid.org
- fastWEB: www.fastweb.com

Best-kept secrets

Savvy students can reduce the cost of education by implementing some of the following strategies:

- Spend the first two years at a community college. Community colleges are usually less expensive than four-year schools.

- Save dorm and food expenses; live at home and commute if possible.

- Work part-time.

- Join AmeriCorps and earn education awards in return for national service. (Contact the Corporation for National and Community Service, 1201 New York Avenue, N.W., Washington, D.C. 20525; 800/94-ACORPS; www.cns.gov.)

- Attend a tuition-free military academy. You will receive a commission in the military after graduation.

- Join the Reserve Officers Training Corps (ROTC); it will pay for tuition, fees, and books and also provides a monthly allowance. You'll have to serve four years as an officer in the military after graduation.

- Delay college, join the Armed Forces; after you've served, take advantage of the Montgomery GI Bill.

- Earn college credit for certain qualified military training, which may reduce the number of classes you'll need to take to graduate.

- Work full-time at a company that offers tuition reimbursement.

- Take advanced placement courses in high school; convert them into college course credits by scoring sufficiently well on advanced placement exams (by reducing your required course load, you can possibly graduate early).

Many colleges and universities have exceptionally valuable programs. Some of these programs are discussed in the sections that follow. The lists of schools under each section were compiled by *Consumer Reports* (August 1998) and updated here; while not exhaustive, they give you a good idea of what desirable programs are out there if you search hard enough.

Graduation date guarantee

Save money by getting out of school on schedule. (Generally, you must stick to your major and keep your grades up.) To give you an idea of what you can save if you graduate on time (or early), check out these price tags:

- DePaul University: Greencastle, Indiana; 765/658-4006; tuition: $19,420 (for freshman and new students 1999-2000 academic year)

- Dominican College: San Rafael, California; 415/485-3204; tuition: $16,500 (1999-2000 academic year)

- Lebanon Valley College: Annville, Pennsylvania; 717/867-6181; tuition: $16,730 (1999-2000 academic year)

Watch Out!
If you want to qualify for financial aid, don't put your money in your child's name. While it may save on taxes, financial aid formulas often require that a child contribute 35 percent of his or her assets toward college costs. Parents generally need only contribute no more than 5.6 percent of savings.

Joint degrees

Almost the equivalent to a buy one degree, get one free. Some schools allow students to spend an extra year on their undergraduate education and receive a master's degree in addition to the bachelor's degree, often without incurring additional costs.

- Clark University: Worcester, Massachusetts; 508/793-7431; "Fifth year for free" program; tuition: $22,150 (1998-1999 academic year)

- State University of New York at Albany: Albany, New York; 518/442-5435; Earn a B.A. and J.D. degree in six years; tuition (in-state undergraduate): $3,400 (1998-1999 academic year)

- University of California–Riverside: Riverside, California; 909/787-3411; In conjunction with UCLA, the Biomedical Sciences Program cuts one year off the time it takes to earn a B.S. and M.D. degree; tuition for in-state undergraduate: $4,161 (1998-1999 academic year)

- University of Charleston: Charleston, West Virginia; 304/357-4750; Earn a B.A. and M.B.A. in five years in the "Plus One" program; tuition: $12,600 (1999-2000 academic year)

- University of Rochester: Rochester, New York; 716/275-3221; "Take Five" program allows students an extra year, tuition-free, to pursue a nondegree academic interest; tuition: $21,485 (1998-1999 academic year)

Low-cost loans

- Lehigh University: Bethlehem, Pennsylvania; 610/758-3100; Offers loans—up to $3,000 per year—interest-free while a student; tuition: $23,150 (for new students for the 1999-2000 academic year)

- Loyola Marymount University: Los Angeles, California; 310/338-2750; If you're a high school student in California and offered a merit scholarship, you also may qualify for the interest-free loan program; tuition: $17,932 (1999-2000 academic year)

Free tuition

The ultimate rock bottom price—nothing! Students typically must pay for room and board, though.

- Berea College: Berea, Kentucky; 606/986-9341, ext. 5083; Work 10 to 15 hours a week, receive a four-year, full-tuition scholarship worth $60,000

- The Cooper Union for the Advancement of Science and Art: New York, New York; 212/353-4120; Students admitted into the schools of arts, engineering, or architecture get a full-tuition scholarship for four years, worth $99,600

Other school tuition programs

There are scores of financial aid packages available. At www.FINAID.org you can find out about aid for disabled students, female students, older students, minority students, Jewish students, gay and lesbian students, and international students, as well as aid for medical students, law students, and business school students. There is also information on sports/athletic aid, scholarships and awards for students with specific majors or courses of study, as well as contests and much more. If you're looking for financial aid, this site is a must see.

Just the facts

- There is a $700,000 increased lifetime income for a male who graduates college versus one who didn't.

Unofficially...
Your school's financial aid administrator can adjust the cost of attendance, or some of the information that is used to calculate expected family contributions, if your family has unusual financial hardships, like high medical expenses, according to the U.S. Department of Education.

- Annual tuition and fee increases continue to outpace inflation.
- Students can pay less than $4,000 a year for tuition and fees, making college affordable for many.
- There are many ways to save for college, including Education IRAs and qualified state tuition programs.
- There are tax credits, grants, loans, and special programs available to help you pay for college, even if you can afford it on your own.

GET THE SCOOP ON...
Why it's so important to invest for your retirement ▪ How your golden years can be tarnished
if you don't consider the added expenses often
incurred as people age ▪ The different types of
retirement plans, and which ones you may qualify for ▪ Whether or not it's a good idea to borrow from your 401(k) plan

Investing for Retirement

Chapter 12

Most people picture retirement as a time to take that long-awaited cruise, to lounge around a swimming pool on sun-filled days, and to spoil long-awaited-for grandchildren with trips to the toy store. Those plans all have big price tags.

Although many senior citizens have the benefit of pensions and Social Security to help foot the retirement bill, they are often finding that they're still short of cash, and some have had to take jobs in fast food restaurants and the like to supplement their incomes. Others find they simply can't afford to live in the manner to which they had become accustomed; rather than enjoying cruises, they are battening down the hatches just to stay afloat.

Planning for your retirement is important, regardless of age. In this chapter I'll tell you about different retirement plans and their benefits and drawbacks, as well as pass along a few more tidbits of interest.

Why you should save for retirement

While you may *think* that you have saved enough for your golden years if you're nearing retirement, or that you've set your financial goals accordingly if you're young, you may be surprised. Life expectancies are longer, and a dollar just doesn't stretch as far as it used to.

For instance, while $500,000 is a large sum of money, assuming a 3.5 percent inflation rate, a 6 percent average annual interest rate, and a 28 percent tax bracket, you would receive only $22,202 a year after taxes from that large sum if you withdrew principal and interest for 25 years, according to Fidelity Investments. Even if you had $1 million, you would receive only $44,403 after taxes each year for those 25 years.

Many people bank on Social Security, but by itself, it's simply not enough to support a comfortable lifestyle for many people. It should be thought of as more of an income supplement. If you choose to, or are forced to, stay in the work force after becoming eligible for Social Security, earning a paycheck may cut into that slice of your retirement pie.

Consider this: In 1998, you could earn up to $9,120 and not lose any of your benefits if you are under age 65. (Currently, eligibility for Social Security begins at age 62.) But every $2 earned above that threshold will cut your Social Security check by a buck. As you age, however, you can earn more money without losing benefits. In 1998, Social Security recipients between the age of 65 and 69 could earn as much as $14,500 without incurring a reduction of benefits. Above that amount, every $3 earned resulted in a $1 reduction of benefits.

Bright Idea
Make a quick call to the Social Security benefits office 800/ 772-1213 to get an estimate on future benefits and eliminate guesswork. (You can also find out how much you've paid in so far.)

To add salt to your wound, Uncle Sam will still take out FICA taxes from your paycheck. Plus, you may have to pay additional income taxes if your Social Security benefits and paycheck, added to your income, capital gains, interest, and dividends from your investments bump you into a higher tax bracket. (Being aware of these potential additional tax burdens can help you better prepare for your financial future.)

But by the time you reach age 70, at least the Social Security "penalizations" end. If you play your cards right—presuming there are no legal changes affecting Social Security benefits in the coming years—you can increase your benefits; simply postpone taking them until you're over age 65.

But the forecast may be gloomier for Generation Xers and those following their footsteps into retirement, because the high number of baby boomers who will be eligible to collect Social Security benefits in the next decade is threatening to collapse the system. Currently, there are an estimated 35 million Americans age 65 and older, and by 2030, that number is expected to double, according to the Social Security Administration. And, as the baby boomers retire, there will be fewer workers paying into the system. Looking back, in the 1960s, there were about five workers paying into the system per beneficiary; in 1998 the ratio dropped to 3:1, and in 2030, projections are estimated at two workers per beneficiary.

If changes are not made to the Social Security system, trust funds will be exhausted in 2032, according to the Social Security Administration. Tax revenues will cover only three-fourths of benefit payments then.

Unofficially...
According to the Social Security Administration, in 1999, the average monthly Social Security benefit for retirees increased $10 from the previous year, to $780. That's just $9,360 a year—before taxes.

In an effort to save the system, in May 1998 the National Commission on Retirement Policy (NCRP) recommended extending the age to receive full Social Security benefits to 70 by the year 2029. The NCRP legislation is scheduled to be implemented starting in 2000. So even if today's twentysomethings and the younger crowd get Social Security benefits, which presumably they will, they will have to wait longer to receive them.

The costs of retirement

You may think that when you retire you won't need the extra boost a Social Security check provides because you won't have as many expenses, like a mortgage or your children's college tuition. While some expenses may diminish over time, you'll probably still have many of the same expenses you had before retirement, like car payments, repair and maintenance fees, utility bills, and grocery expenses. You also may have a rent payment (which will continue to rise each year) if you sell your home.

Add to these expenses that will increase as you age, such as health and car insurance premiums. If you own your home, you may have added repair and replacement expenses that also come with age. Roofs will need to be repaired and washers, dryers, dishwashers, and refrigerators will need to be replaced. Plumbing, air conditioning, and heating systems get old and eventually fail. For that matter, so do cars. And, as you age, you'll probably visit the doctor more often—perhaps even spending time in the hospital. The fact is that growing older can be expensive.

Besides Social Security and your pension—or the lack thereof—there are other factors that will affect

Timesaver
Have your Social Security check directly deposited into your bank account, saving you a trip each month and eliminating the chance of your check getting lost in the mail.

how much money you'll need to retire comfortably. For instance, are you planning to move closer to your children or to a more temperate climate? Living expenses differ significantly from city to city.

Of course, you can stretch your retirement savings by moving from an area with a high cost of living to one with a comparatively lower cost of living. For instance, by moving from New York City to almost anywhere in Florida or Texas, you'll save big bucks. (Plus, neither Florida nor Texas has a state income tax, in case you plan to continue working past retirement age.)

By contrast, if your kids have taken high-powered jobs in a more expensive area like Washington, D.C., and you want to move there from Austin, Texas, your purchasing power will be cut significantly.

Bottom line? Plan ahead.

How to plan what for what you'll need

How do you figure out what you'll need to retire comfortably?

A common tool used by financial advisors is the three-legged stool:

1. Social Security (currently, this serves as the basic income)

2. Employee pension and/or your retirement plan

3. Savings

Social Security will pay only a portion of what the average American will need to live on in retirement. This means that your investment portfolio must provide the rest.

There are four main factors that will affect the size of your retirement nest egg:

Watch Out!
Many people on fixed incomes rent condos and lease cars. This may be a poor financial choice because anything rented or leased will increase in cost over time, but fixed incomes, by definition, stay fixed, only rising with cost of living increases.

Bright Idea
As you plan
your retirement
investment
goals, keep in
mind the cost of
living of the city
in which you
think you might
want to retire—
the costs of liv-
ing varies dra-
matically among
cities, states,
and regions.
Calculate cost of
living differences
between cities
using cost-of-
living comparator
calculators such
as the one at
Money Magazine's
Web site, www.
moneymag.com.

1. The number of dollars you invest

2. The amount of time you leave your money invested

3. The annual rate of return on your investments

4. The rate of inflation

Some of the best tools you can use to save for your retirement are the Roth IRA (individual retire-ment account), which allows taxed contributions to grow tax-free, and the traditional IRA and 401(k) plan, which allow pretax contributions to grow tax-deferred. (Contributions to other IRAs are made with after-tax dollars, but grow tax-deferred; these plans are all discussed below.)

The tax advantages these plans offer when you're in your twenties cannot be recaptured later on. The longer you wait to invest in retirement plans, the fewer benefits you'll reap through the advantages of compounding and tax deferment. (The tax you will eventually pay to the government will be earning income for you until you retire.)

For example, if you invest $2,000 a year for the first eight years of a 40-year period with annual com-pounding at 10 percent, you will earn more than someone who invests $2,000 a year from years nine through 40 due to the power of compounding.

So if you invest $2,000 a year for the first eight years, a total of $16,000, you'd end up earning $515,201 after the fortieth year. By waiting and investing $2,000 a year for 32 years (years 9 through 40 of a 40-year period), you would have invested $64,000 and reaped only $378,503 in earnings, about 25 percent less than what you would have earned by starting earlier, despite having invested four times as much.

Rates of return also have a big impact on your investments, as does the rate of inflation. (See Chapter 4 for a discussion on the topic.)

The best strategy for making your retirement funds grow rapidly is to invest as much in your retirement plans each year as the government permits. This dollar amount will vary depending on the type of retirement plan.

Roth IRAs, traditional IRAs, and SEP IRAs

There are several types of IRAs. Each has its own tax advantages. Roth IRAs allow you to withdraw money tax-free during your retirement (after age 59½). With the other IRAs, earnings grow tax-deferred. None are entirely tax-exempt—it's just a matter of *when* you pay the taxes. With the exception of the Roth IRA, how much you end up paying in taxes depends on what income tax bracket you're in once you reach retirement.

Roth IRAs

In contrast to traditional IRAs where taxpayers who qualify receive a tax deduction up front and earnings grow tax-deferred, contributions to a Roth IRA are made from after-tax funds and aren't tax deductible. But earnings do grow tax-free, as long as you wait until age 59½ to make withdrawals—unless you have a severe disability, want to use the funds to buy your first home, or want to contribute to your or your children's first home purchase (up to $10,000 total for all home contributions). Early withdrawals on principal are tax-free, although you'll pay a 10 percent penalty on nonqualified distributions. (See IRS Publication 590.)

Each type of retirement plan has advantages and disadvantages. The advantages to having a Roth IRA include the following:

- Because taxes are paid up front, you won't have to pay taxes if you leave the money in the Roth IRA for five years before withdrawing it after age 59½—what you take out after that is all yours.

- There is no mandatory withdrawal requirement for the Roth IRA; you can let your money grow as long as you'd like. (With traditional IRAs, you *must* start taking distributions at age 70½.)

- Your earnings grow tax-free (as opposed to tax-deferred) if you leave the money in for at least five years and don't take it out until you reach age 59½.

- If you retire in a higher tax bracket than you are currently in, you'll have substantial tax savings. This is what makes Roth IRAs particularly attractive to those who are now in a relatively low tax bracket, but who anticipate high future income earning potential.

Roth IRAs have some disadvantages, too:

- Because you have to pay tax up front on your contribution, your principal investment is smaller than it would be for a traditional IRA (assuming the same contribution), weakening its earning power. (On the other hand, you can take out less during retirement because the withdrawals are tax-free, so you won't need as much.)

- If you retire to a lower tax bracket, you'll lose some of the tax benefits you wanted to gain.

- Contributions are at a maximum of $2,000 annually, or 100 percent of adjusted gross income (AGI), whichever is less, and are not tax-deductible. Note: The total of the traditional IRA contribution plus the Roth IRA contribution cannot exceed these limits.

■ Not everyone qualifies. You'll qualify if you're married and your earned AGI is below $160,000. If you're single, you'll qualify if your AGI is below $110,000. However, the amount you can contribute begins to phase out at $150,000 for couples filing their income taxes jointly and at $95,000 for individuals. (The traditional IRA doesn't have an earned income maximum, though it does for deductibility purposes, but it does have an age limit of 70½ for making contributions.)

If you already have a traditional IRA set up and want to convert it to a Roth IRA, you may do so, provided your AGI is $100,000 or less and you are not a married individual filing separately.

Tax experts say that for many investors it makes sense to contribute to a Roth IRA because very few people qualify for traditional deductible IRAs, discussed in the next section.

Traditional deductible IRAs

With traditional IRAs, taxpayers who qualify receive a tax deduction up front and funds grow tax-deferred. When you retire and withdraw money, you have to pay tax on the earnings in your current income tax bracket. For many, this bracket will be lower than when they were making contributions, making this type of IRA a good choice. But if you remain in (or are bumped into) a higher tax bracket because of the added income the IRA or another investment provides (or because of continued employment), choosing a traditional IRA

Watch Out!
The traditional IRA is considered a *tax-deferred* investment while the Roth IRA is considered a *tax-free* investment (provided the account is open for five years or longer).

(over a Roth IRA) could turn out to be a costly mistake.

To figure out which is best for you—the Roth IRA or the traditional IRA—you must consider the benefits and drawbacks of paying taxes now versus later. To do this, though, you must predict which tax bracket you'll be in at the time you'll be taking distributions, and that's not easy. The trouble is that it's hard to predict what your investment earning power will be during retirement, which, if you start saving early, could be several decades from now. You'll also have to predict tax rates at the time you retire, another stumbling block.

You can make tax-deductible contributions of up to $2,000 to a traditional IRA if you are younger than 70½ and you are working for an employer without, or are ineligible to participate in, a company retirement plan. (Your spouse does not have to work for an employer without a company retirement plan for you to participate in a traditional IRA, subject to income limitations.) You can still take a deduction if you are an active participant under an employer plan under these circumstances:

■ You are single and your AGI is less than $40,000 (for 1998)

■ You are married and you and your spouse's combined AGI is less than $60,000 (for 1998)

If you are not an active participant under an employer plan but your spouse is, you may deduct contributions up to $2,000 to your IRA if your combined AGI is less than $160,000 (for 1998).

As noted above, a traditional IRA is a good retirement savings plan choice if you end up retiring at a lower tax bracket than you're in now. (There are obviously exceptions. Check with your tax advisor.)

With this type of plan, you can roll over your investment to other traditional IRAs and can convert it to a Roth IRA (if your AGI is less than $100,000).

Early withdrawals are permitted, but only under the following circumstances:

- If made by your beneficiaries after your death

- If you become severely disabled

- To pay medical expenses in excess of 7.5 percent of your gross income

- To pay health insurance premiums if you become unemployed (restrictions apply; consult your tax advisor)

- If you take out equal installments intended to last the rest of your life

- To pay for higher education for your immediate family and your grandchildren

- To buy your first home or a first home for a family member (you can contribute up to $10,000 total for real estate from this plan during your lifetime)

If you withdraw funds for any other reason before the age of 59½, you'll be hit with a hefty 10 percent penalty in addition to the ordinary income taxes due.

Unlike the Roth IRA, with the traditional IRA you must begin withdrawing money by April 1 of the year after you turn 70½. The minimum payout is based on your life expectancy or the joint life expectancy of you and your beneficiary, as determined by IRS computations. (See IRS Publication 590 available at www.irs.gov or by calling 800/829-1040.)

Nondeductible IRAs

If you don't qualify for a traditional IRA or Roth IRA and you're working, earning income, and under age 70½, you can qualify for this plan. Just set up an account and make contributions by April 15 for the previous tax year. You can make an annual contribution of up to $2,000 if you're single, and up to a total of $4,000 if you're married filing jointly, split evenly under each spouse's name.

While your earnings grow tax-deferred in this plan (as in the traditional IRA), your contributions are not tax-deductible, so you can't deduct them from your gross earnings on your income taxes. But withdrawals after age 59½ are partially tax-free because you've already paid tax on the contributions (but not earnings). Earnings are taxed at your ordinary income tax rate at the time of withdrawal. (Note: If you take money out before you're 59½, you'll have to pay a 10 percent penalty.)

This type of IRA requires an investment of time as well as money. Because withdrawals will be a combination of earnings and principal in this plan, you'll need to keep detailed records of earnings, which are taxable, and principal, which is not taxable.

Early withdrawal rules and minimum distribution rules are the same as those for the traditional deductible IRA. Also of note: You can convert this plan into a Roth IRA, too.

SIMPLE IRAs

Do you own your own business? The savings incentive match plan (SIMPLE), a salary reduction arrangement, allows small businesses to make contributions on behalf of each eligible employee. You can set up a SIMPLE using IRAs (SIMPLE IRA plans) or as part of a 401(k) plan.

You can also have a SIMPLE IRA if you're self-employed, or own an S-corporation or a C-corporation, just set it up by October 31 and contribute to it by December 31. If you have employees, you have to make matching contributions by your business tax deadline. But if you have a "day job" that offers a 401(k) plan, you may not be able to take advantage of a SIMPLE IRA.

If you *are* eligible, you can contribute up to $6,000 annually and can make dollar-for-dollar matching contributions not to exceed 3 percent of your income. These contributions grow tax-deferred.

You can roll over a SIMPLE IRA to other SIMPLE IRAs and, after two years, other traditional IRAs. Except for rollovers, all withdrawals are taxed at your ordinary income tax rate. Note, however, that if you withdraw money within the first two years after making the first contribution, you'll be hit with a whopping 25 percent penalty. That penalty is reduced to 10 percent on anything withdrawn after those first two years and before age 59½. Exceptions to the early withdrawal rules are the same as for the SEP (discussed in the next section), traditional, and nondeductible IRAs.

SEP IRAs

If you're self-employed you can have a simplified employee pension, or SEP for short. Furthermore, you can make contributions to your employees' plan if you are the owner of a sole proprietorship, S-corporation, or C-corporation.

This type of IRA allows you to make annual contributions of up to 15 percent of your net income or $24,000, whichever is less. To do so, you must set it up and make contributions by your business tax filing deadline.

You can roll over your SEP IRA investments to a traditional IRA. Except for rollovers, withdrawals are taxed at your income tax rate at the time of the withdrawal. Other exceptions to the early withdrawal rules are the same as for the SIMPLE, traditional, and nondeductible IRAs.

With the SEP IRA you must begin withdrawing money by April 1 of the year after you turn 70½. The minimum withdrawal is based on your life expectancy or the joint life expectancies of you and your beneficiary, as determined by IRS calculations. (For details, see IRS Publication 590.)

Additionally, with this plan your contributions grow tax-deferred, and you may contribute to other plans, as well. But if you have employees, you must contribute on their behalf, as well.

The SEP IRA is simpler than the Keogh plan (see below), although it doesn't have all of the same advantages.

401(k) plans

If you're eligible for a 401(k) plan at work, you can save up to $10,000 tax deferred annually (in 1998) or the maximum permitted by your plan. The biggest benefit to this kind of retirement plan is that many employers match your contributions up to a certain level. Some match dollar for dollar while others match 50 cents to the dollar. If your employer matches dollar for dollar, that's a guaranteed 100 percent immediate return on your investment. Where else can you get a return like that? It is for this reason that financial experts advise contributing at least as much as your employer matches. Note, however, that you may have to stay with the company a certain number of years in order to become fully vested in your employer's contributions. Note, too, that some employers do not begin matching until you've been with the company for at least a year, although you may be eligible to make contributions to the plan sooner.

Another benefit of a 401(k) plan is that your contributions are subtracted before you even get your paycheck, reducing your taxable income. (A traditional, tax-deferred IRA works similarly—each dollar you put into it reduces your taxable income by the same amount that year.)

You can roll over a 401(k) into other qualified investment plans, if allowed by your new employer or allowed by law. For instance, legally you cannot roll over a 401(k) into a 403b plan when you terminate employment. Withdrawals of tax-deferred contributions and earnings are taxed at your income tax rate at the time withdrawals are made. There's no tax on withdrawals on after-tax contributions, rollovers to an IRA or a new employer's 401(k) plan, or loans from your account.

Note: If you change jobs, your new employer may have a plan that accepts some or none of these benefits, in which case you may have to leave any loans in the plan they are in or roll them over into an IRA. In cases where your old employer will not let you keep the loans in the plan and your new employer will not accept them, the loan amount must be paid off or declared as a distribution from the plan, which is usually what happens. If this is the case, you'll owe income taxes on the balance of the loan, plus a 10 percent penalty for early distribution if you are younger than age 59½.

There are penalties for early withdrawals—an additional 10 percent tax on withdrawals made before age 59½, except under the following circumstances:

Unofficially...
The average 401(k) account balance was more than $95,000 in 1997, up from $75,000 in 1996 and $33,000 in 1991, according to the Profit Sharing/401(k) Council of America.

- On withdrawals made by your beneficiaries after your death
- If you become severely disabled
- To pay medical expenses in excess of 7.5 percent of your gross income
- If you leave your job after you reach age 55
- If you take out equal installments intended to last the rest of your life

As long as you continue to work, you can continue contributing to the plan. If you retire, you must begin making withdrawals by April 1 the year after you turn 70½.

Minimum withdrawals depend on your life expectancy or the joint life expectancies of you and your beneficiary according to IRS calculations.

You can borrow against your account if your employer offers loans. (The question is, should you? To weigh the pros and cons of borrowing from your retirement plan, see below.)

Keogh plans

You can set up a Keogh if you're self-employed or have a partnership business. You can set it up as either a profit-sharing or a money purchase pension plan, or a combination.

If you want to share profits with your employees, set up a profit-sharing plan. As an employer you don't have to make contributions out of net profits to have a profit-sharing plan, nor does the plan have to provide a formula for figuring the profits to be shared. There are, however, a lot of exceptions to these general rules. (See IRS Publication 560 for a complete description.)

If you set up a money purchase pension plan, your contributions are fixed and are not based on profits. (Contributions to a profit-sharing plan are used to share profits with employees and are not necessarily distributed at a fixed rate.)

Whichever plan you choose, to get started, you have to set up the plan by the end of the calendar or fiscal year and contribute to it by April 15. If you set it up as a profit-sharing Keogh, you can contribute up to 15 percent of your net income or $24,000, whichever is less. If you set it up as a money purchase pension plan, you can contribute up to 25 percent of your net income, or $30,000, whichever is less. Contributions are tax-deferred.

The nice thing about a Keogh profit-sharing plan is that you can benefit from tax-deferred investing even if you have another retirement plan. But if you have employees, it will cost you; you have to make contributions for them, as well. The same holds true if you have a Keogh money purchase pension plan, except that, once you set up that type of plan, you must fund it.

If you decide to close a Keogh plan, rollovers into IRAs and other qualified plans maybe permitted as noted earlier in the discussion on 401(k) rollovers. Withdrawals are taxed at ordinary income tax rates, except if you make withdrawals before age 59½, in which case you'll have to pay an additional 10 percent penalty. Minimum distribution rules and exceptions to the early withdrawal penalties are the same as for 401(k) plans.

Should you borrow from your 401(k)?

Many prospective homebuyers have the money to make monthly mortgage payments, but haven't saved enough for a down payment. Under this circumstance, tapping into their 401(k) retirement investment may be tempting.

While borrowing from your 401(k) can provide extra cash to pay for settlement costs, moving and decorating expenses, and commissions for the mortgage lender and real estate agents, not to mention the down payment itself, such a loan has drawbacks.

If you borrow from your 401(k), you're putting your retirement at risk. If you default on the loan, you've lost part of your retirement savings—and you'll have to pay a pricey penalty, as well. A typical 401(k) loan has a maximum 30-year term if you use the money toward the purchase of your primary residence. (For other purposes, like to pay for tuition bills, it has a maximum five-year term.) But if you change jobs or your company goes under, you'll probably have only 30 to 90 days to pay it all back. If you neglect to repay the loan, you'll owe income tax on the amount borrowed, plus a 10 percent penalty for early withdrawal.

Borrowing from your 401(k) plan doesn't come cheap. For one thing, you lose out on any potential market gains and the tax-free compounding of the money you withdraw. But that's not all it'll cost you. When you repay the loan, you'll be replacing pretax dollars with money that's already been taxed. Right away that hikes the cost up 28 percent, assuming you're in the 28 percent tax bracket. In simpler terms, for every dollar you take out, you must put back in $1.28, excluding interest, which is usually the prime rate plus 1 percent—not exactly bargain basement prices.

Furthermore, the interest you pay on your 401(k) loan is not tax-deductible, as it is on home mortgage loans. (Note: The interest you pay goes back into your account.) You'll probably also have to pay a loan origination fee.

Note, too, that not all employers even allow you to borrow from your 401(k). If you are permitted, you can't borrow more than 50 percent of your account balance or more than $50,000, whichever is less. Be aware that this is a general summary of the rules that apply. The details are far too complex to discuss fully here. For more information on the specifics, please consult your tax advisor.

Although borrowing from your 401(k) may not be the most savings-efficient move, just having a 401(k) will help you qualify for a mortgage; you can borrow as much as you need from your relatives as long as you have enough money in your retirement plan to cover the loan. (Note: You must disclose the fact that you're borrowing money to your lender.)

Reverse mortgages

If you own your home and need funds to supplement your retirement, these are two of your choices:

1. You can stay in your house and obtain a *reverse mortgage* (provided you're age 62 or older). A reverse mortgage will produce income for as long as you use your house as your primary residence.

2. You can move and use your tax-free capital gains (up to $250,000 for singles and up to $500,000 for couples who have lived in their homes as a primary residence for two of the previous five years) from the profit on the sale of your home to invest in securities, thus generating income.

Reverse mortgages convert accumulated equity into cash. This tool enables qualified homeowners to draw equity through a loan that can be taken out in a lump sum, monthly payments, or a line of

Watch Out!
If you borrow from your 401(k) plan to buy a home, you'll essentially end up with two mortgage payments.

credit. This income, because it is a loan, is generally tax-free, but can affect Medicaid payments, depending on how it's set up.

The amount of cash you can borrow depends on your age, home value and location, the cost of the loan (the fee and such associated with borrowing money), and the specific loan product. (You can compare products by comparing total annual loan cost rates.) You don't have to repay the loan (plus interest and fees) until the last borrower dies, you sell the home, or move away permanently.

To qualify, all owners must be borrowers, that is, if both you and your spouse own the home, you both have to sign your names on the dotted line to get the loan. You both must be at least 62 years old for most loans, and the home must be your primary residence. To learn more about reverse mortgages, visit The National Center for Home Equity Conversion's Web site at www.reverse.org.

If you have no other source of income and otherwise could not stay in your home, a reverse mortgage may be a useful tool for you. You can live in your home indefinitely, even if the amount of money you receive from the loan exceeds the value of your home in the long run. But if you have sufficient retirement funds, a reverse mortgage could be costly. You must pay fees and interest.

Bright Idea
To find a loan counselor or lender contact The National Center for Home Equity Conversion at www.reverse.org. (If you're strapped for cash and a reverse mortgage is not an option for you, contact Elder Care at 800/677-1116.)

Just the facts

- You should think of Social Security as supplemental to the income generated from your retirement investments and pension.

- If your employer matches any part of your 401(k) contribution, you get an immediate return on your investment.

- Roth IRAs grow tax-free because you pay the tax up front, while other IRA and 401(k) earnings grow tax-deferred.

- If you borrow from your 401(k) plan, you will miss out on tax-deferred growth and you'll have to repay yourself with after-tax income.

GET THE SCOOP ON...
Why it's so important to have a will if you have
minor children ▪ What living trusts can and
cannot do ▪ How you can protect your property
from estate taxes ▪ Why you should choose an
attorney who specializes in estate planning

Estate Planning

Chapter 13

E state planning—what will happen to your property in the event of your death—is a difficult topic to even broach, let alone deal with. But avoidance could be costly to your children, especially if they are minors. Did you know that if both parents die without a will, their children will be in complete control of any money left to them— large sums through life insurance policies, or if there is a liability associated with the deaths, for example—at the age of majority? Did you know that if you die without a will, the courts will pick their guardians? Although you may have made it clear to your relatives who you would like to appoint to watch over your kids in the event of your death, if you don't do it legally through a will, a judge can decide otherwise, based on state law.

Did you know that if your estate goes through probate, it becomes a matter of public record, in which case anyone can gain access to your personal finances. They can find out about your business practices (if you own one), and who inherited what.

Furthermore, if you avoid estate planning, the government may get more of your estate than your heirs do. Currently, estates can be taxed up to 55 percent of their value. Additionally, if you don't plan ahead, you may lose control over your assets if you become mentally disabled or otherwise incapacitated and have not designated a custodian and given him or her specific directions. Or, you can lose your residence in the event of the death of your spouse or divorce if it's not jointly titled.

While it may be uncomfortable and unpleasant to deal with these issues, it's important that you do, even if it's just to let your heirs know your intentions. In this chapter, I'll tell you about the different ways you can title your assets so you can choose the method that will best protect you in your current situation. I'll also tell you what experts say your will should include, give you their opinions on the benefits and drawbacks of some of the available trusts, and provide you with tips on how to protect some of your assets from estate taxes. I'll also tell you how you can avoid probate.

Common estate planning terms

Discussing and explaining basic estate planning can be very complicated. To ease the way somewhat (and to help get you started), here are definitions of some common estate planning terms:

Charitable remainder trust—A trust that names a charity as the beneficiary of income or principle.

Conservator—Person or institution designated by the court to protect the interests of an incompetent and act on his or her behalf.

Durable Power of Attorney—A legal document that enables you to designate another person, called the "attorney in fact," to act on your behalf, even if you become disabled or incapacitated.

Estate plan—Written directions of how to distribute your assets when you die. It addresses two primary issues: Who you want to benefit from your assets and the methods used to pass those assets to your beneficiaries. The plan is supposed to minimize estate tax consequences so your heirs inherit as much as legally possible.

Estate planning—The preparation of a plan to administer and distribute your property before or after death. Tools include a will, trusts, gifts, power of attorney, and more. These tools/strategies are used to minimize estate tax liability. The goal of estate planning is to pass the greatest amount of your assets permitted by law to your heirs.

Estate—The assets and liabilities left by a decedent.

Executor—A person or institution named in your will and appointed by the court to distribute the assets as directed and pay creditors and taxes.

Family Limited Partnership—A legal partnership between members of a family for the management and control of property; used for estate planning purposes, it's set up to minimize transfer taxes.

Health Care Power of Attorney—A type of power of attorney that permits the person you designate to make medical decisions for you if you become incapacitated.

Heir—A person that will inherit assets.

Intestate—Dying without a legal will.

Irrevocable trust—A trust that cannot be changed or cancelled without the consent of the beneficiary.

Joint tenancy—A way to title (own) property where each person (tenant) owns an undivided whole. When one tenant dies, his or her interest passes to the survivor.

Martial exemption—A tax provision that allows an unlimited amount of property of one spouse to transfer to the other upon death without incurring estate or gift tax.

Power of Attorney—A legal document that allows you to appoint a representative, an "attorney in fact," to act on your behalf as long as you do not become incapacitated or disabled.

Probate court—Reviews the authenticity of a will.

Probate—The court process of reviewing the authenticity of a will; the process by which an executor or court-appointed administrator distributes the property.

Revocable trust—A legal document that may be changed or cancelled that allows you to maintain control of and use your assets. It is used to avoid probate court.

Testate—Having a legal will.

Will—A legal document that directs distribution of assets upon death.

Your taxable estate

Estate planning begins with a *will,* a legal document that states where and to whom you want your property to go; if you have children, it specifies who will be their personal and financial guardians. If you and your spouse die *intestate*, that is, without a will, a judge will make those important decisions for you.

"Everybody should have a will, [especially if you have children]," says Mark Watson, partner in the

Washington National tax practice of KPMG Personal Financial Planning Practice.

For most people, estate planning is as simple as writing a will. But with inflated home prices and life insurance, you can find yourself in an estate tax situation, Watson says. These days, most people don't qualify, but, in time, more people will, he notes. Often, it doesn't take much more than a home, a life insurance policy, and a pension or 401(k) plan to get a taxable estate.

If your estate (including insurance policies) totals less than $650,000 in 1999, you will be able to pass it to your heirs without incurring an estate tax. Currently, the estate tax starts at a hefty 37 percent and rises to an exorbitant 55 percent if your taxable estate is worth more than a combined $3 million if you're married or $1.5 million if you're single.

With these high tax rates, you can see why it's so important to try to avoid or minimize estate taxes. To determine how best to approach estate planning, you must project the potential size of your estate, which might not be apparent at first glance. Many people simply think of just their savings. Your estate will probably include much more, including one or more of the following:

- Group insurance

- Life insurance death benefits

- Real estate (primary residence and any vacation or rental properties)

- Retirement plans and annuities

- Savings and checking accounts, Certificates of Deposits (CDs), mutual funds, stocks and bonds, and other liquid assets

- Personal property, including furniture and jewelry

Unofficially...
Between 1999 and 2006 the estate tax exemption will shift upward. In 2006 a husband and wife will be able to shelter a total of $2 million using the estate tax exemption of $1 million each, assuming proper planning.

- Collectibles, gold coins, and other precious metals

- Businesses and business assets

The value of some items may be difficult to determine. If a person has an asset that might be of significant value but doesn't know what it's worth, he or she should consider hiring an appraiser rather than letting the IRS make its own determination of worth, says Adam Rosier, CFP and senior financial advisor with American Express Financial Advisors, Inc., in Southgate, Michigan.

Estate planning is not only for the well-off or for people who own homes or insurance policies. You should consider estate planning techniques if you know your estate is not that valuable, but you're in a second marriage and you want your children to inherit everything, or if you have an heir with special needs, Rosier says.

You can create an estate plan using a number of different strategies:

- By naming beneficiaries of liquid assets, such as retirement plans, annuities, and life insurance, as well as Certificates of Deposit, brokerage accounts, and the like

- Titles

- Wills

- Trusts

The importance of estate planning if you have children

Sadly, there are situations in which people die unexpectedly. If there is a liability associated with the death, the estate may sue for damages and potentially receive a settlement. You should plan for such contingencies. It would be a tragedy to let your state of residence determine your distribution, says Christine Fahlund, CFP, of T. Rowe Price.

Fahlund describes what can happen if you or your spouse dies without a will using a real-life example: A father of several minor children was killed in an accident for which his estate received $3 million. He had no will stipulating where that $3 million should go, so the courts had to decide. They made a typical decision: His wife received half, and the children will receive the other half—$1.5 million plus interest—when they reach the age of majority.

Because the father died intestate, the children were left with hefty estate taxes (spouses are exempt) and will have access to a large sum of money when they reach the age of majority. Furthermore, the surviving parent will have to be appointed by the court to handle the minor children's money until they reach the age of majority. These problems could have been avoided if the father had set up a *revocable living trust*. This type of trust, like others, is used to control the distribution of the estate. It allows you to manage your money from the grave, Fahlund says. You decide how and when your money is distributed. See the section on revocable living trusts later in this chapter.

Fahlund also points out that accidents do happen, and accidental death indemnity insurance policies often pay out two to three times their face value. You don't want your state of residence to determine the split of the payout, she says. Most state laws give half to the surviving spouse and half to the children. "Why put yourself in that position?" Fahlund asks.

Bright Idea
If you and your spouse work and have children, consider buying life insurance so that if one of you dies, the surviving parent has a replacement income.

By establishing a trust on behalf of your children, you can determine who gets what and when. Dividing assets equally is a common court practice, but dividing property unequally may be better if the children are young. Fahlund suggests having a single trust until the youngest child reaches the age of 21, and then dividing the money equally into separate trusts. She suggests giving the trustee discretion to decide how much money each child gets during his or her upbringing. The amount is not necessarily going to be equal. It will depend on the child's individual needs.

In fact, it's crucial to recognize that each of your children may not require the same financial support. One child might have (or develop) special needs, for example, and require more than his or her siblings, sometimes, to an extreme. "Financial planning for a disabled individual focuses on identifying and providing a level of care to the individual for his or her lifetime, with particular consideration to when the primary family care givers are no longer available to provide support," says Lorri Crittenden, CFP at Dignum Financial Services in Fort Worth, Texas. "Planning for a disabled individual must integrate many legal and financial provisions including personal care, residential alternatives, estate planning for the extended family, insurance, legal trusts, guardianship, and government benefits such as Social Security and Medicaid," she adds.

Here are some things Crittenden says to consider when planning for the future of a disabled individual in the event of your death:

- Your vision for that individual's future: Do you want him or her to live in a small group home or on his or her own with assistance?

- Potential guardians, including a financial guardian (a financial advisor, an independent financial institution, a family member, or a friend) and a guardian of the person.

- Other family members: Integrate planning for all involved; evaluate the trade-offs.

"There may be ways to accommodate goals for other family members that are not obvious to the layman," Crittenden says. In addition, sometimes there are other family members who plan to assist during their lifetime or through a bequest in their will. "This information is important to know so that the plans of a well-intentioned family member don't thwart your planning," Crittenden says. "Assets given directly to a special needs individual may disqualify the individual for important government benefits," she notes, suggesting that in such situations, you should consider consulting a professional who specializes in estate planning.

Titles

How your property is *titled* (the legal structure of ownership) will affect you and your heirs, as well as creditors and tax collectors. Because title can be an important factor when dealing with estate taxes, it's an important aspect of estate planning.

Titles can:

- Reduce taxes.
- Protect against creditors.
- Ease the transfer of assets.

Individuals can own (titles) properties:

- In their own name, with the title just in their name or with a joint owner.

- Through a revocable trust (discussed later in this chapter)

The simplest way to hold property—securities and real estate, for example—is through sole ownership. Most single people own property this way, says Harvey Berger, associate partner with Grant Thornton, National Office of Federal Tax Services in Washington, D.C.

General title to real estate is called *fee simple*, which simply means you are the sole owner of the property. Married couples and other joint property owners may hold title as:

- Tenants in common
- Joint tenants with right of survivorship
- Tenants by the entirety

Tenants in common

Using this type of title, two or more people can own property together in any proportion of ownership, that is, 70:30, 50:50—however they decide to divide it. Owners can sell their portions independently or leave it to heirs without the other party's consent or knowledge. Property does not automatically pass to co-owners if one of the owners dies. Either owner can place his or her portion of the property in trust for a third party. This setup is commonly employed by unmarried people who co-own property, but have no interest in a partnership.

Joint tenants with right of survivorship

This type of title allows two people to own property jointly. Each owner has an undivided interest and neither can sell that interest without the other's consent. In this setup, the interest of one owner passes to the other in the event of the owner's death, without going through probate (hence, right of survivorship). The shared interest of one cannot be willed to an outside party.

This setup is often used by married couples who co-own bank accounts, stocks, and bond titles. It is also used for property owned jointly by parents and children.

This type of ownership also allows people who are not married, at least not to each other, to own property together. Both owners' consent is needed to sell the property.

Note, with tenants in common, a creditor can place a lien on that portion of the property that the tenant in common owns, and may force the sale of that portion of ownership of the property to collect its debt.

Note, too, that for property owned jointly by married couples, in the event of the death of one spouse, that spouse's portion automatically passes to the surviving spouse. If the couple has assets exceeding $650,000 in 1999 (the amount one can currently bequeath to one's heirs without having to pay federal estate taxes on it), the shift of the jointly held assets to the surviving spouse may increase the estate taxes. By passing all of the assets on to the surviving spouse, the spouse that died gave up the exemption (but the surviving spouse has the right to disclaim a portion of the assets).

The deceased spouse would have "given up" the exemption only if all of the assets were passed to the surviving spouse in this manner. In addition, disclaiming some of the assets passed to the surviving spouse would only make sense if they were placed in a trust instead. If the spouse did disclaim property equal to or less than the amount of the spousal exemption, and no previous trust was set up before the spouse's death, then the property would be passed back to the court for proper distribution. To avoid this, it would be better for the surviving spouse to take title to all of the property and then place all but the exempt amount in a trust, thereby giving him or herself full use of the estate tax exemption.

Some married couples have titled property as joint tenants with right of survivorship. But if one partner had kept some or all assets separate from the other spouse, and if there is no will, rather than passing these assets on to the surviving spouse (as most couples presume will be the case), most states' laws give half to the surviving spouse and half to the couple's children, Fahlund says. This is why title can be so important.

Tenants by the entirety

This type of ownership is specifically reserved for married couples; upon the death of one spouse, the other retains the right of survivorship, that is, the property passes to the survivor's estate tax-free and without probate.

The benefit of this setup is that a creditor cannot force the sale of the co-owned property to satisfy the debt of one spouse. (However, if both spouses are in debt to the same creditor for the same bills, this setup offers no protection.) Typically, homes are owned this way, which is why many mortgage lenders want both parties to sign the mortgage note. Since the recession in the 1970s, people started paying attention to the fact that you can title securities— mutual funds, stocks, brokerage accounts, bank accounts, for example—this way, too, says Fred J. Tansill, an estate planning attorney in McLean, Virginia.

You can use tenancy by the entirety to protect your assets from judgments if you're worried about being sued because of the nature of your profession (if you're a doctor or an engineer, for example). Going back to medieval law, creditors of one spouse cannot get to the other under a tenants by the entirety ownership, Tansill explains. To get this protection for bank accounts, brokerage accounts, mutual fund holdings, stocks, and other securities, you *must* title it "tenants by the entirety," he warns. Titling it "joint tenants" is simply not enough, he says, adding that a title of "joint tenants" doesn't have the same immunity. If you hold property as joint tenants, creditors of one spouse can probably get at least at 50 percent of the property, Tansill explains.

As noted earlier, for estate tax planning reasons it is desirable for wealthy couples to hold at least $1 million in each spouse's own name. But if you hold property as tenants by the entirety, you give up this tax planning opportunity. You must decide which you're more worried about—creditors or taxes.

There is a way to get around this dilemma when one dies, however, Tansill continues. Presuming the creditors are long gone, the surviving spouse can file a disclaimer on tenants by the entirety title, sending the property back to the deceased's estate. It's tax planning post mortem, he says.

There's another way out, as well. After retirement, when the threat of lawsuits decreases, you can switch to another type of title and place the property in a revocable trust.

How title affects estate taxes
The probate process only applies to assets that the deceased owned in his or her own name. Therefore,

jointly held assets, assets held by tenants by the entirety, and assets with named beneficiaries do not go through probate.

If you and your spouse own less than $650,000 in assets, typically the best thing you can do is to place property in the names of both spouses to avoid probate, Berger says. This is because estates valued at less than $650,000 are not assessed federal estate taxes.

Now let's consider estates worth more than $650,000. If you own your property as tenants by the entirety or as joint tenants with the right of survivorship, by definition all of it will pass to your surviving spouse in the event of your death. However, for tax purposes, half of the value of the property is included in your estate. Under the marital exemption rules, there will be no federal estate tax due on it, regardless of your estate's value. To avoid losing all of the benefits available to married couples, consider placing property equal to the amount of the marital exemption in a trust, which also will bypass probate.

For example, say a couple jointly owns property worth $700,000, and the husband dies. His estate would have $350,000 in it (half of the property), which passes to his wife free of any estate tax. But when the wife dies, her estate will total $700,000 (assuming there's no change in the property's value) and her heirs will owe estate taxes on the portion that exceeds the applicable exemption amount. "That's the pitfall of joint ownership from a tax standpoint," Berger says.

If you have more than $650,000 in your estate, consider separating the assets through title. By doing so, when one spouse dies, $650,000 of his or her assets can be placed in a trust (for protection from federal estate tax), with the income generated to be paid to the surviving spouse for the duration of his or her life. While the surviving spouse can collect income from the trust, the principal doesn't go into his or her estate on his or her death. Therefore, the heirs save in estate taxes.

This is why title becomes critical in estate planning. "You need to make sure each spouse's probateable estate is at least $650,000," Berger says. "You can then write the will [to include a trust] giving the surviving spouse the right to the income of all the property and some limited rights to use the principal without it being in his or her estate when he or she dies," Berger adds.

Some estate planning goals conflict, so you must give considerable thought to your decisions based on the outcomes. For instance, Berger is reluctant to place a primary residence in one name. "There are other risks there," he says, adding that "[t]itle becomes critically important [in a different way here]." What if the title was in the name of one spouse and that on his or her death, that spouse left the house to a child who decided to sell it, leaving the surviving parent without a place to live?

Here's another example: If you're a doctor or other professional vulnerable to lawsuits, you're more protected if your assets are held in tenancy by the entirety. However, as noted above, holding property in that way is not always good estate tax planning.

Wills

A *will* is a legal document that states how you want your property to be distributed in the event of your death. A will can also appoint an *executor* to your estate, which is the person in charge of distributing

Watch Out!
If a person indicates in his or her will that his or her entire estate be split evenly (or *per capita*) among his or her children, that provision will be unenforceable with respect to any bank accounts held jointly with any one of the deceased's children.

your assets, and can establish trusts for your children, name trustees for those trusts, and name guardians for your children. Wills deal, in part, with property subject to probate. In fact, wills deal with all types of property, including personal property that may be (financially) worthless. They do not offer protection from federal and state inheritance taxes.

If you're single and own nothing, estate planning is not so important, says Carrie Coghill, CFP and senior vice president at D. B. Root and Company in Pittsburgh, Pennsylvania. But if you own assets and you know to whom or where you want them to go, you should at least have a will. If you don't designate distribution through a will, state law determines who gets what.

A simple will takes care of estates under $650,000 and can be used to establish guardianship for minor children. It acts as a road map for a probate judge, determining who gets what assets.

As discussed above, some forms of title allow property to be excluded from a will and from probate. (Note that while joint ownership will allow assets to bypass probate, the inheritor, unless a spouse, would still have to pay estate taxes if the gross estate exceeds $650,000.) You can also avoid probate by designating a beneficiary for assets like insurance policies, bank accounts, stocks, mutual funds, and other securities. In fact, at some financial institutions you may designate a beneficiary on a money market account, savings account, CDs, and other bank deposits simply by adding a POD (Payable on Death) clause in the account registration. In these cases, accounts registered with this clause do not pass through your estate, but may be distributed directly to the beneficiaries listed.

You can also set up a will to form trusts in the event of your death so that you can avoid other problems. (Trusts are discussed in greater detail later in this chapter.) Say you have $500,000 in an IRA and $25,000 in a money market account. The IRA money isn't going to pass through your will (unless you set it up that way), because you will have probably designated a primary and secondary beneficiary for those funds (usually your spouse and then your children in equal shares), separate from your will. Note, however, that designating your estate as a beneficiary for an IRA is not a wise choice, as it makes the asset part of your estate, and may be subject to probate.

Now, say both you and your spouse are killed at the same time. What would happen to your two accounts is as follows: The $25,000 would pass through your will (as directed in your will) to your heirs and the $500,000 would go directly to your children (without passing through your will) in equal shares (because they are the secondary beneficiaries of your IRA), Fahlund explains. Your children would end up with a lot of cash once they reach the age of majority. The same thing often happens with life insurance policy proceeds, which begs the question, "How many 18-year-olds can wisely spend and invest that kind of money?" Fahlund asks.

The way to prevent this from happening is to make your spouse the primary beneficiary and the estate or trust under your will the secondary beneficiary. Then the money will go through your will or trust; in either case, you can include directions, for instance, that the children must have the money invested in certain types of funds and that they can take out a certain amount for college expenses at ages 18 through 22, and more for graduate school if

Timesaver
Having your assets distributed by will, as opposed to intestate, can be more time efficient if there's a chance your heirs might fight over them.

they attend, but that they cannot withdrawal any other large sums until they turn age 35.

At the very least you should consider having a will if you have a preference about who gets what of your material assets (say, your antique broach or heirloom linens). If you still don't want to, consider writing a letter to the family or to one member telling them specifics, for example, that your daughter should inherit your diamond ring and your cousin Jane should get your car, Fahlund suggests. However, she notes, such a letter is *not* a legally binding document; if you wanted your daughter to have your diamond ring, but it was sold to pay for your nursing home stay, your daughter will not legally be entitled to a replacement ring. If you made this request in your will, however, your daughter might have grounds to insist that the estate buy a diamond ring for her. On the other hand, by specifying your wishes in a letter rather than in a will, you may avoid having your family fight in court over lost or sold assets, Fahlund says. (Even if property has been sold, by writing your wishes in a letter, at least your loved ones will know what your intentions were, she notes.)

If you're between the ages of 35 and 60, consider reviewing your parents' estate plans (with their permission, of course), Fahlund advises. If your parents' plans aren't set up properly, unnecessary estate taxes may be incurred and otherwise avoidable complications may arise later, such as bitterness among siblings because of disappointing inheritances.

Making it legal

To make your will legal:

- The document must state that it's a will.

- It should be typed, though a handwritten, or *holographic,* will is valid in many states (keep in mind that handwritten wills are more easily challenged).

- It must be dated and signed in front of and by at least two witnesses (in some states three are required) who cannot be heirs and who do not need to read the will.

Before assets are distributed, a will must pass through probate court, which may take months to a year. Probate is used to accomplish the following:

- Prove that the will is valid

- Identify and appraise the property

- Pay all debts and taxes due

- Distribute the remaining property as directed in the will

If you have very little property, you can handwrite your will on a piece of paper, creating a holographic will (assuming this type of will is valid in your state). Sign and date it in your own handwriting. (State laws differ on whether you have to have others sign it, how many signatures are needed, and how long after your signature is placed on the document they can wait before signing it.) Note that these wills are more easily challenged and that courts will be extra strict in examining them.

If you want to know how to word your legal documents or simply want a quick way write them yourself, consider using a software program or buying a book that specifically covers the subject like *The Complete Idiot's Guide to Wills and Estates* (Macmillan) by Stephen M. Maple or *The Complete Will Kit* by F. Bruce Gentry. You can also see samples on the Web. For instance, you can see a sample

Unofficially...
Though a will doesn't have to be notarized, in many states, if you and your witnesses sign a sworn statement, called an *affidavit*, and get that document notarized, probate court procedures (which require the will to be proved valid) can be simplified.

Bright Idea

If you're worried about someone challenging your will, you may include a provision that states that anyone who challenges it forfeits his or her right to inherit under it. (Such a provision may not be enforceable in your state, however.)

living will at www.courttv.com/legalcafe/ health/ proxies/sample_livingwill.html.

If you're interested in estate planning, try reading *Beyond the Grave: The Right Way and the Wrong Way of Leaving Money to Your Children (And Others)* by Gerald M. Condon or a software program like Estate Planner by Parsons Technology, which gives you the outcomes for different estate planning options.

Living wills

In addition to what you think of when you talk about a traditional will, there is something known as a *living will*, also referred to as a health care power of attorney. In it you state how you should be treated in the event of a terminal disease, severe illness, or tragic accident. By giving such directions when you're healthy, your relatives won't have to make difficult decisions on your behalf, and you'll receive the type of care you desire.

Issues you might want to consider covering are:

- Organ donation
- Religious and faith issues
- Hospital, nursing home, and hospice arrangements
- Funeral arrangements

To carry out your living will, you'll need a *health care directive*, a written statement that expresses how you wish to be treated in advance of any incapacity. Make sure you're exacting and give comprehensive directions. If you omit any instructions in this document, a judge will determine (based on state law) what can and cannot be done. You'll also need *a health care proxy*, a person you designate to make your health care decisions based on the guidelines you provide in the directive, if you are incapacitated or unable to communicate your desires. The proxy will require a durable power of attorney. You'll also need a durable power of attorney to take care of financial matters like paying bills, making bank deposits, getting government benefits, for example, if you become incapacitated. (You may want to name alternates in case the ones you have chosen to fill these roles are not available at your time of need.) Typically, people choose their spouse or a sibling to act as an agent under durable powers of attorney. In the living will, you can specifically limit their authority and can state that the documents giving powers of attorney have no effect "unless and until [you] become incapacitated." All the documents discussed should be signed and notarized.

Revocable living trusts

Trusts bypass probate, which allows assets to transfer quickly and privately. Trusts are used to maintain control of assets after death, and some can be used to transfer property at minimum estate tax costs.

One of the most popular estate planning instruments is the *revocable living trust*, one which can be revoked or changed by the creator of the trust at any time during his or her life. Consider putting any amount over $650,000 into a revocable living trust because in 1999, $650,000 per individual is exempt from estate tax, though you can place any amount of money in one of these trusts. You can create a revocable living trust through your will.

Popular seminars tout revocable living trusts as estate tax–saving instruments. "Not true," Fahlund says. However, you can save taxes by creating a revocable living trust and, in that instrument, give instructions to create two separate trusts at your death: A *family trust* (also known as a *credit shelter*

Watch Out!
If you neglect to appoint a durable power of attorney, a judge may appoint someone to make personal decisions for you.

trust and *bypass trust,* an irrevocable trust that allows the transfer of your assets to your children to reduce or eliminate estate taxes) to save on taxes, and a *marital trust,* which provides financial or investment management for your spouse and may allow transferred property to qualify for the unlimited estate tax marital exemption—the trustee can pay bills, distribute income, and handle investments. (The family trust and marital trust can be created just as easily by writing a will and stating that you want those two trusts formed on your death.)

For a married couple who has more than $650,000 in assets in 1999 the living trust can be used to split up their estate because in they are entitled (in 1999) to have up to $650,000 each ($1 million per individual by 2006), pass estate tax-free to heirs. For example, if their collective worth is $1 million in 1999, Rosier says, split evenly, they'll each have $500,000. If one dies, no estate taxes are due. But if the surviving spouse inherits it all, $350,000 is exposed to estate taxes ($1 million less the $650,000 exemption) when that spouse dies.

So what are the benefits of using a revocable living trust? There are actually several. First, it provides for your financial protection in the event you are no longer able to manage your financial affairs yourself. You can be trustee while you're healthy, but if you have a stroke or become otherwise incapacitated, your successor trustee would manage your assets in the trust. As people age, their interests change, as do their intellectual abilities, Fahlund says, pointing out that the transfer of power over the trust assets can be gradual.

Another benefit of revocable living trusts is continued privacy because the instrument will bypass probate. The trust can function like a will, dictating at what age children are to receive trust assets and the percentage shares of the distribution. The trust can be linked to a *pour-over will*, a short document that names the executor and that determines how taxes, creditors, and final expenses will be paid. The pour-over will directs the executor to gather all assets not included in the trust and pour them over into the trust. Once that happens, the trustee will follow the directions included in the trust. The pour-over will must be filed with the probate court, but because it doesn't say much, it doesn't reveal much. The world is full of vendors selling information, Fahlund says. Your will is public information, but using this strategy, the details of how your assets are distributed (as well as what those assets are) aren't included. The living trust has allowed you to keep your private matters private, even after your death.

Regarding probate, living trusts offer another useful feature—if you own property in a state other than your state of residence, when you die, that property must go through what's known as an *ancillary probate*. So, for those owning two homes, for example, putting that out-of-state property in your revocable living trust will avoid probate in another state. Many people think it's worth setting up the trust just to avoid the out-of-state probate hassle, which necessitates hiring a lawyer in that other state, Fahlund says.

The living trust can be used as a tool to manage your property, and can be especially helpful if you become incapacitated because the successor trustee can manage your property, rather than a court-appointed trustee, which takes time. The benefit of

Bright Idea
Revocable living trusts are popular with some because they are a tool for avoiding probate and probate fees. But in a lot of states, probate is inexpensive and quick. Ask an estate planning attorney if your state's probate procedures make it worthwhile for you to create a living trust for the purpose of avoiding probate.

having an immediate successor can be especially important if you own a business or other assets that need to be managed seamlessly.

Finally, you can include provisions in the trust that preserve the use of your estate and use the gift tax exclusion to set up other trusts that will help reduce estate taxes.

Unofficially...
Because the terms of the revocable living trust are not subject to probate review, it is generally more difficult to protest the provisions of a living trust.

There are disadvantages to using a revocable living trust, as well. You must retitle assets into the trust name, which entails a lot of paperwork. And, although creditors only have a limited time after your death to make claims against your estate while it's being probated, there is no time limit within which creditors may go after assets in a living trust.

If your goal in using a revocable living trust is only to avoid probate, there are easier ways to accomplish that goal. As noted earlier, you can hold property jointly and name beneficiaries for other assets.

There are many other types of trusts and other estate planning tools, including gifts and bequests you can use to reduce estate taxes. For more information, read the books suggested earlier in the chapter and consult a financial planner and attorney who specialize in estate planning.

Selecting trustees, an executor, and a guardian for your children

In the event of your death, the executor steps in and pays your estate's bills and accounts for the property in your will. A trustee oversees the finances for your trust. A guardian will become responsible for your minor children's financial and emotional well-being.

Particularly if your estate is substantial, you may want to think about appointing more than one executor or trustee, as well as more than one guardian—one who'll retain physical custody of your children, and one who'll oversee your children's money. If you have set up provisions to leave your estate to your minor children in a trust in the event of both your and your spouse's deaths, this second guardian can be a bank or other financial institution. But if you do choose a bank or other financial institution, keep in mind that it *must* invest the trust assets conservatively to be certain they are preserving the principal. If your intention is to have the money grow to cover your children's college expenses and get them started out on the right foot financially, this strategy will probably backfire. And, if you die without a will, the courts, fearful of not preserving the principal, will place your money in CDs, which don't always keep up with the rate of inflation, Coghill says.

Though you clearly don't want money intended to take care of your children in your absence to be placed in high-risk investments, you don't want your funds tucked away under a mattress either. Financial planners advise directing that your funds be invested in mutual funds that will outpace inflation, cover taxes, and still provide growth of the principal. Over time, based on historical S&P 500 stock market performance, risk diminishes.

Therefore, you may want to consider choosing a trusted financial planner or investment savvy friend or relative, and you may want to consider leaving general investment directions in your will. In any event, you should seriously consider designating two unrelated guardians (or trustees or executors) to build in some checks and balances.

Another reason to name two trustees, executors, or guardians is that in case one dies or is otherwise

Bright Idea
Make a list of the locations of your important documents, including your and your children's wills, birth certificates, marriage certificates, military records, insurance policies, income tax, real estate, credit card records, investments, and bank accounts. Note outstanding debts, safety deposit box and key locations, and the names of your attorney and your financial planner, if any.

not able to perform his or her duties, there is another one standing by.

Beware of conflicts of interest, though. A financial institution directing the investments for your trusts shouldn't also be administering the trusts or distributing the trusts' assets. If the trust returns are poor over an extended period of time, who's going to notice? Who will fire the trustee? Appoint a relative to oversee the professionals.

If you decide to appoint one individual as trustee, be aware that there's no way to check if the person you've chosen is following the guidelines you set forth for investing and spending the money you've left to secure your children's future. It's best to choose two people who aren't particularly close to each other to ensure checks and balances.

(Note: While many trustees and executors are close relatives of the deceased and don't want to be paid, be aware that by statute, trust and will administrators are entitled to be compensated for their efforts on behalf of your estate or trust. This fee is usually a percentage of the trust or estate assets, Coghill says.)

With proper estate planning you can manage your money from the grave, Coghill says. This definitely requires appointing the right people to manage your money on behalf of your heirs when you're gone. So think carefully before choosing—you wouldn't appoint just anyone to watch over your children. You shouldn't appoint just anyone to watch over their money.

Insurance and estate planning

To ensure that you'll have an estate for your heirs, you might want to consider getting insurance to shield your assets from lawsuits (like slips and falls)

Watch Out!
Think twice if you're a trustee and you're tempted to handle the trust assets in a way that conflicts with the wishes of the deceased. The trust beneficiaries can sue you if they find out the assets are not being invested as instructed. It's your fiduciary responsibility to handle the funds as specified in the trust.

and to protect against errors and omissions by attorneys and financial advisors.

"Nobody enjoys buying insurance," explains Pam Senk, director of retirement planning at Retirement Foundations in Tampa, Florida. But if you become sick or injured or die prematurely, it could protect your family and yourself from losing everything you've acquired. Don't make yourself "insurance poor," she says, but do get adequate coverage.

The purpose of insurance is to make sure your assets are protected in case of a tragedy. It's to cover your necessities. Health insurance is the most important type of coverage you can have. Understand how your deductibles and your plan work.

Disability insurance coverage is also important, but is often overlooked, Coghill says. It is especially important to single people because if they become disabled, they don't have a spouse to help foot the bills. This type of coverage is also important if you're married. Your spouse might find him- or herself in a real bind without this insurance if something happens to you, Coghill notes.

If your employer offers you disability insurance, it's usually less expensive than getting an individual policy. Try to protect at least 60 percent of your salary. If your employer doesn't offer this type of coverage, go out and get insurance to cover at least your fixed expenses, like your mortgage and car payments, Senk advises.

Most people don't think about long-term care insurance coverage until they're in their 50s, Coghill notes. But your insurability becomes an issue as you get older or if you get sick. The benefit of buying this type of coverage when you're young is

Moneysaver
If you're young and considering buying long-term insurance, you should consider how much your premiums will total for years prior to, say, age 50 to see if it's a worthwhile investment for you or if your money would be better invested in the stock market. It's more likely that term insurance will be more suitable and cheaper.

that your premium remains the same as long as you have the policy, unless the insurance company raises premiums across the board.

If you're considering buying life insurance, figure out how much money your family will need and for how long. Then pick the type of policy that will best meet their needs.

(For a more detailed discussion on how to protect your assets with insurance, the benefits and drawbacks on specific types of insurance, and what to watch out for, see Chapter 5.)

Legal representation

Do you need an estate attorney? That depends. Many people, even if they have small estates, want their intentions made crystal-clear.

It's not so much the size of the estate that dictates whether you should consult an estate attorney, but the importance of both the assets to your heirs and how they're handled, according to Fahlund. So, even if your estate is small, you may want to have an attorney review your will to make sure it's legal and that there is no room for challenge.

Furthermore, if your total estate exceeds $650,000 (in 1999), you should consider meeting with an estate attorney to see if setting up a trust is a good option for you. Bear in mind that even if your estate requires no more than a simple will, your executor will need a lawyer to get through probate court and to help decipher the tax code. You may therefore want to name an attorney for such purposes.

It's important to use an attorney who specializes in estate planning. Experience is also important. Your survivors won't find out if the attorney you chose knew his or her stuff until it's too late.

How do you find a good estate attorney? To get started in your search, consult The American College of Trust and Estate Council (www.actec. org). Membership in this organization is by invitation only, and members must be approved by their peers. Another good source is *The Best Lawyers in America*, which can be found in the reference section at your local public library and at www. bestlawyers.com. You should also considering getting recommendations from friends and family.

Fahlund says to make sure that the attorney you select specializes in estate planning. Well-intentioned general practitioners may be able to draft a will or a trust, but they may not know enough to ask the right questions; for example, they may never find out if your assets are titled or even the nature of your assets, Fahlund says. They go through software packages and forms books to get standard language, she notes, which often isn't enough to do the job right.

An attorney who specializes in estate planning will know to ask thorough questions, like if both you and your spouse die simultaneously, do you want to leave your money to pay for construction to add onto your children's guardian's house so that your children can live more comfortably and their guardian doesn't have to relocate? Expert estate planning attorneys can help you accurately and thoroughly assess your needs and those of your family, Fahlund says.

An estate attorney's fee is not based on the size of your estate (as is the case with executor's or trustee's fees), Fahlund says, but compensation does vary based on location.

Just the facts

- If you have minor children, you should have a will in order to name a guardian for them in the event of your death; if you don't, a judge may do it for you.

- Titled property and property with a named beneficiary bypasses the probate process.

- In 1999, estate and gift tax rates range from 37 percent to 55 percent, but you can pass up to $650,000 estate-tax-free to your heirs.

- Setting up a revocable living trust with your spouse as the income beneficiary can help your children (or other heirs) avoid estate taxes on up to $650,000 of your estate when your spouse eventually dies.

Financial Threats

GET THE SCOOP ON...
Unemployment benefits ▪ Protecting your assets
▪ Strategies for finding a new job ▪ Getting
back on your feet financially

PART VII

Dealing with Job Loss

Chapter 14

Losing your job can create a financial disaster, especially if you're in a competitive market and particularly if you live paycheck to paycheck. Two missed mortgage payments can lead you down the road to foreclosure; unpaid insurance premiums can leave you vulnerable to financial collapse as well, if, for instance, you cause a car accident or have an acute medical problem.

While some people feel secure in their jobs, no job is guaranteed, and there aren't always signs warning you when the ax is about to fall. Many people have come into work to find their desks cleaned out and a pink slip waiting for them. (The always present, albeit not always noticeable, possibility of job loss is a good reason to have at least six months of expenses put away in an easily accessible savings account.)

In this chapter I'll tell you what services your state Employment Commission may be able to offer you if you lose your job, give you strategies financial planners suggest using to protect your assets, and offer information that may help you get a new job.

Unemployment benefits

The first thing to do when you lose a job—besides pick up your severance check—is to march right over to your local Employment Commission office and register. This way you can have a little money coming in while you hunt for a job. Consider it your first line of defense.

Collecting unemployment is not the same as collecting welfare, so you shouldn't feel at all guilty. Unemployment is insurance. It's an entitlement, not a welfare fund, says Dave Mormon of the U.S. Department of Labor. Only people who have worked and earned the money are eligible. In addition, you must be out of work due to no fault of your own, so don't think you can tell your boss off, get fired, and collect unemployment benefits while he or she foots the bill. (If you want to quit your job, make sure you have at least six months of expenses put away to help tide you over if you don't have another job lined up.)

Unemployment benefit payments are intended to prevent you from experiencing major financial distress while you search for a job equivalent to the one you lost. Benefits are paid as a right; they are not based on need.

The unemployment insurance system is administered under state laws by state officials, so how much you qualify for varies from state to state.

Approximately 121 million Americans, or 97 percent, have jobs that are covered by unemployment insurance, according to the Department of Labor. An estimated $20 billion in state unemployment benefits was paid in 1998 to 7.4 million unemployed workers.

To qualify for benefits in most states, you must have worked during the past 12 to 18 months. You

Watch Out!
If you had your paychecks directly deposited into your account while you were still employed, take a careful look at your last paycheck stub. It might be a check. Many employers do not deposit last checks electronically.

must also meet minimum earnings requirements set by the state. If you qualify, the amount of benefits you'll receive will be based on your previous work and wages; weekly benefits average $190. Most states will permit you to collect benefits for up to 26 weeks (6 months). Most people—two thirds—find work before they receive their maximum entitlement. The national average amount of time people collect benefits varies from about 13 to 17 weeks, depending on the economy.

If you qualify for benefits, in most states you must prove that you are looking for a job in order to collect them. Here's what it takes to qualify in most states:

1. You must have lost your job through no fault of your own.

2. You must meet the requirements for earned wages or time worked in your state prior to your unemployment.

3. You must be able to work.

4. You must be available for work.

5. You must actively seek work and have proof of your job search.

The Unemployment Commission offers:

1. Help finding a job

2. Search assistance—helping you help yourself

3. Job development services

4. Claims services

To help you with your job search, local offices may offer:

- Access to a computerized job bank

- Internet access

Moneysaver
File for unemployment benefits as soon as you become eligible; you won't receive any payments for any week before you filed the claim even though you were unemployed.

- Access to computers with word processing software (Microsoft Word and Corel WordPerfect) to use to update your résumé and write cover letters
- Access to fax machines
- A resource library with books on career development
- Workshops on interviewing skills
- Workshops on résumé writing
- Business magazines
- Job search technique videotapes
- Information on occupational training providers
- Skills assessment tests
- Additional training to change fields
- Access to job opportunities posted by local employers

Unofficially...
During periods of high unemployment, you may qualify for an additional 13 to 20 weeks of benefits, depending on the state. If Congress acts during that time, you may qualify to receive benefits for an even longer period of time.

In any one day the Unemployment Commission has access to one million jobs, according to Mormon. When you register, they'll take information on your background and skills and will try to give you a referral to an employer who has posted a job.

There are 1,600 local Unemployment Commission offices throughout the country. The people who work at each office know employers in their community, Mormon says. Although there may not be any job opportunities posted in your field at their office, they may be able to phone an employer and ask him or her if there's a position available for you.

Protecting your assets

The best time to plan for job loss is before it occurs, says Elissa Buie, a CFP in Falls Church, Virginia, and president of the Institute of Certified Financial Planners.

Have an emergency fund set aside, preferably containing three to six months worth of living expenses. If you have an emergency fund, you can add any severance and vacation pay that you receive to that pot. "This creates an entirely different job search situation," Buie says. Then you don't have to take the first job that comes along. You can view your situation as a chance to take a look at all the available opportunities or to take the next step up on your career ladder.

Next, know what you own in terms of investments. "[T]hat [knowledge] also adds a measure of comfort," Buie notes. Finally, know your expenses, both fixed and variable, and you'll know where to tighten your belt, she says.

If you don't have an emergency fund set aside, you've got to do some quick math. Assess your financial situation. Figure out your net worth by adding up all of your assets and subtracting all of your liabilities like taxes, auto loans, school loans, your mortgage, credit card debts, bills due, etc. See how much money you have in assets, and liquidate enough to tide you over for a month. Then take action. Cut out or cut back on luxuries, such as dining out, magazine subscriptions, and movies, for example. Don't incur more debt on goods and services that aren't necessities.

Buie suggests these strategies to protect your assets:

- Take advantage of some of the winners in your portfolio and liquidate them. This can be especially useful if your income tax bracket falls and you need to draw on short-term gains, which are taxed at your income tax rate, versus long-term gains, which are taxed at 20 percent.

- Offset taxes by selling some of the losers in your portfolio. (However, if you're unemployed for a long time, your tax rate may be lower, so the offset wouldn't be as valuable.)

- Roll your 401(k) out of your company plan and into an IRA, which gives you control over your retirement funds and provides you with a last line of defense. You can borrow against that money for a brief period of time during the rollover period, but you'll pay taxes and penalties if you don't get it into an IRA account within 60 days (see below). Of course, paying a penalty is better than losing your home to foreclosure. (Note: You can only roll over retirement funds once a year.)

In addition to these strategies, Jim Bruyette, partner with Sullivan, Bruyette, Speros & Blayney in McLean, Virginia, offers another rule of thumb: Keep track of your job-hunting expenses because many of them are deductible if you're searching for a job in the same trade or business as your last job. Expenses to log include:

- Typing
- Postage
- Fax services
- Copying
- Travel

Things that aren't covered include, for example, buying a new suit for interviews.

Finally, Bruyette says to avoid tapping into your retirement plans as a resource for short-term income. He says it's more advantageous to borrow against your Visa card (or other credit card) at 18 percent interest, taking a year to pay it off because he believes it's less expensive than paying taxes and penalties and incurring loss of tax-deferred growth from dipping into your retirement plan. But if you're going to do this, get a credit card offering a low introductory rate. Those sometimes last for a year. (See Chapter 2 for more information on credit cards.)

Postemployment insurance options

The most important action you can take to protect your assets is to manage financial risk, and you risk losing whatever you have if you or a member of your family gets seriously sick or injured and aren't insured.

The only thing worse than being out of a job is being out of a job and having a load of medical bills, Bruyette says.

"Don't give up your right to COBRA," Buie warns. (COBRA is discussed in detail below.) Shop around for other health insurance policies, too. You may, however, run up against roadblocks getting health insurance if you or any member of your immediate family insured on your health insurance policy has a preexisting condition. In that case, you may be better off going with COBRA, even if it's more expensive, Buie says. Be aware of your rights under HIPAA as well, also discussed below.

Health continuation coverage benefits under COBRA

The Consolidated Omnibus Reconciliation Act (COBRA) allows for the provision of health benefits to terminated employees or those who have lost health insurance coverage due to a reduced work-load to buy group coverage for themselves and their families for up to 18 months. You'll have 60 days after termination (or other qualifying event) to accept the coverage. COBRA coverage is retroactive if elected and paid for within that 60-day period.

You'll probably have to pick up the tab for the coverage, including the portion your employer used to kick in, but health coverage under COBRA is still generally a lot less expensive than most individual policies and has the added benefit of not excluding preexisting conditions. The premium can't exceed 102 percent of the cost to your previous employer.

Under COBRA, your health coverage will remain identical to that provided by the plan under which you had been previously covered. Premiums are generally fixed for each 12-month cycle, but may be increased if the costs of the plan increases. (Note: Disabled beneficiaries may receive an additional 11 months of coverage after the initial 18 months, but the premium for those additional months may be increased to 150 percent of the plan's total cost of coverage.)

The initial premium payment must be made within 45 days after the date of the COBRA election by the qualified beneficiary and will include the premium costs for the first two months of coverage if you wait that long to pay. Premiums are due every 30 days thereafter.

Some employers are exempt from COBRA—generally, the law covers group health plans maintained by employers with 20 employees or more. It doesn't apply to plans sponsored by the federal government or some church-related organizations.

To qualify for COBRA, you must have been either terminated (voluntary or involuntary) for reasons other than "gross misconduct" or have lost your health benefits because of a reduction in the number of hours of employment.

In addition to those factors, spouses qualify in cases of divorce or legal separation, death of the covered spouse, or if the covered spouse becomes entitled to Medicare. For these events, COBRA coverage is available for 36 months for both you and your dependent children.

Qualifications for dependent children are the same as those for spouses. In addition, when a child loses his or her "dependent child" status under the plan rules, he or she can qualify under COBRA for 36 months of coverage.

Special rules apply to extend COBRA coverage for 11 months for those who qualify for Social Security disability benefits.

Employers are obligated by law to provide new employees with general information regarding their rights under COBRA when they are hired. They must give you and qualified beneficiaries specific notice within 14 days of being hired of your right to elect COBRA coverage when a qualifying event occurs. However, it's your responsibility to notify the plan administrator of a qualifying event within 60 days after that qualifying event occurs (for example, divorce, legal separation, or a child's ceasing to be covered as a dependent under plan rules).

Vision and dental services are not offered for continued coverage under COBRA, except where mandated by law. But if a plan provides these non-core benefits, under COBRA you may generally elect either the entire package or just the core benefits.

COBRA coverage begins on the date that your health insurance coverage would otherwise have been terminated. It ends when either you stop making premium payments, the last day your coverage is reached, your (former) employer ceases to maintain a group health plan, you obtain coverage with another employer group health plan that doesn't have any exclusions or limitations on any preexisting conditions you or your family may have, or a beneficiary is entitled to Medicare benefits.

For more information on COBRA, contact the U.S. Department of Labor, Pension and Welfare Benefits Administration, Division of Technical Assistance and Inquiries, Room N-5619, 200 Constitution Ave., N.W., Washington, D.C. 20210, or go to www.dol.gov/dol/pwba/public/pubs/ COBRA/cobra95.htm on the Web.

Guaranteed individual health coverage under HIPAA

The Health Insurance Portability and Accountability Act (HIPAA), also known as the Kassebaum-Kennedy law, may help you keep health coverage, as well. It guarantees the availability of individual health coverage if you've had employment-based coverage for at least 18 months, are ineligible or have exhausted your COBRA coverage, and are not eligible for coverage under any other employment-based health plan.

HIPAA limits exclusions for preexisting conditions, though you might have to wait up to 12 months to get full coverage if you change jobs or health plans. (Note: Credit is provided for prior continuous coverage.)

The legislation also makes it possible to make penalty-free withdrawals from IRAs for medical insurance if you're unemployed for at least 12 weeks and for other medical expenses if they exceed 7.5 percent of your adjusted gross income.

Bright Idea
Join a professional, religious, or civic group. Some offer group health insurance, which is usually much less expensive than an individual policy.

To take advantage of HIPAA, you must apply for a health insurance policy within 62 days of the end of your previous coverage.

If you decide to purchase a health insurance policy, see what the policy covers and at what percentage of reimbursement. Make sure that the plan will cover the physicians that you see or that you're willing to change providers. Also, make sure that you're covered at hospitals out of your area in case you or your family members travel and get sick or are injured. Make sure the deductible isn't so high that it would only pay to be insured if you incur extremely high bills. "Small" bills can add up very quickly in a family. (The same goes for percentage of reimbursement because out-of-pocket expenses can also add up.)

Finally, make sure you buy enough coverage and that the coverage is flexible enough for you to get the care you need if you (or a member of your family) are diagnosed with a condition or disease. Buying a less expensive policy may limit your access to specialized medical care and may cost you a lot more money in the long run. Health insurance is not the place to try to cut expenses.

Life and disability insurance coverage

As with health insurance, don't panic and be tempted to lapse your life insurance coverage, Buie says. If you have group coverage under your former employer, shop around for an individual policy, which tends to be less expensive. In any event, Buie stresses, it's better to pay increased premiums for a month or two—until you get a new job—then let your insurance lapse and take a risk.

Life insurance cash values can be a good place to get money if you deplete all other funds, Buie says.

You're not making your cash flow situation worse like you would be if you used a line of credit. However, you will be missing out on any tax-deferred gains.

Savvy investment strategies for periods of unemployment

People who have lost their jobs and those that have retired have to make similar types of investment decisions. "You have to balance your need for liquidity with your desire to get higher long-term rates of return," Bruyette says.

Bruyette is not a proponent of "live off the interest and preserve the principal" because, he says, it will lead you to the wrong types of investments—those with high interest, like junk bonds or risky stocks, but not those with long-term return potential.

Junk bonds and risky stocks are exactly what you *don't* need in situations where you've lost your job and need a steady cash flow to make ends meet. Instead, Bruyette prefers to divide the investor's portfolio into three levels of investments. This investment strategy is called *laddering*. Laddering is a process. Each year (during long periods of unemployment or for retirement), you take one year's worth of expenses and roll them down to the next level. (Level 3 replaces funds taken from level 2. Level 2 is used to replenish funds spent from level 1. Level 1 is comprised of easy-to-access liquid assets. See Table 15.1 below.) This strategy gives you the greatest chance of taking advantage of the stock market without jeopardizing your day-to-day financial needs, Bruyette explains. When you get a job, all of the money (except for an emergency fund, that is, 6 months of level 1 funds) should go into long-term investments (level 3) until you start nearing retirement.

TABLE 15.1 THE LADDERING PROCESS

Level 1.	Funds that are going to be needed immediately or in the near future	Risk-free investment—liquid bank savings account
Level 2.	Money not needed for a year or two	Limited risk investments—1 to 2 percent higher returns than Level 1—longer-term bonds
Level 3.	Money not needed for four years or more	Long-term investments—equity mutual funds/stocks

Source: Jim Bruyette, partner with Sullivan, Bruyette, Speros & Blayney in McLean, VA

Victoria Collins, CFP and executive vice president of Keller, Collins, Hakopian and Leisure in Irvine, California, offers another financial planning method that may be more palatable for those with a lower tolerance for risk. She says because you want to be sure your investments are more liquid than they would be if you were working, shift them to no-load, short-duration bond funds for an income stream. This type of investment has lower volatility than equities. Once you're working, though, she suggests repositioning your portfolio to include more equities.

Strategies for finding a new job

Finding a new job can be challenging. What steps should you take to get a new job? Here are a few suggestions:

1. Assess your skills, knowledge, and experience, and see how you can apply them to positions that are currently open.

Watch Out!
In certain markets, your principal in bond funds may diminish even though the fund is paying a steady stream of income.

2. Do your homework. If you've targeted a company you'd like to work for, find out more about it. You can go to the library and review its annual report, and you can visit the company's Web site (if they have one) to search for employment opportunities and find out about benefits. Or you can look for corporate information, such as corporate cultures, opportunities, and recruiting processes, at www.wetfeet.com, which has independent research on a variety of different companies. (The company can be reached by phone at 800/926-4JOB.)

3. Search for jobs on the Internet, in newspapers, in trade magazines, and through networking.

4. Go to job fairs. There's a free, downloadable guide on making the most of a job fair at www.wetfeet.com.

Timesaver
Purdue University offers an index of more than 1,000 online job-search resources: www.ups. purdue.edu/ Student/ jobsites.htm.

Although recruiters say that most jobs are gotten through networking, that may be changing. More and more résumés are being submitted by e-mail and fax. And more and more recruiters and employers are paying a lot of money to access résumés electronically through job search Web sites. People looking for jobs are taking notice. So are entrepreneurs. Job search Web sites are popping up all over the Internet.

Consider visiting these cyberspace job banks:

- Career Mosaic (www.careermosaic.com)

- The Monster Board (www.monster.com)

- CareerWeb (www.careerweb.com)

- Yahoo!—click the employment section link (www.yahoo.com)

- America's Job Bank (www.ajb.dni.us)

- Career Path (www.careerpath.com)
- Online Career Center (www.occ.com)
- Best Jobs USA (www.bestjobsusa.com)
- Job Bank USA (www.jobbankusa.com)
- Boldface Jobs (www.boldfacejobs.com)
- Jobsource—for college students (www.jobsource.com)
- JobSpot (www.jobspot.com)
- JobCenter.com (www.jobcenter.com)
- Job Web (www.jobweb.com)
- HelpWanted.com (www.helpwanted.com)
- JobOptions (www.espan.com)
- Nonprofit Career Network (www.nonprofitcareer.com)
- U.S. Office of Personnel Management (www.usajobs.opm.gov)
- Job Trak (www.jobtrak.com)
- Career Magazine (www.careermag.com)
- CareerCity (www.careercity.com)
- Careers OnLine (www.careersonline.com)
- 4Work (www.4work.com)
- Hot Jobs (www.hotjobs.com)
- NationJob Network (www.nationjob.com)
- TOPjobs USA (www.topjobsusa.com)
- Attorneys at Work (www.attorneysatwork.com)
- MedSearch (www.medsearch.com)
- Green to Gray—this Web site is tailored to those leaving the military and entering the civilian work force (www.greentogray.com)

Using the Internet to help you in your job search can speed up the whole process. Here are some tips for using the Internet as a useful job search tool:

- Narrow down your search by geographic location, job category (Internet security, for example), and keywords (firewalls and encryption).

- Use links to connect to related sites.

- Compose a standard cover letter. Copy and paste it to create an e-mail message. Make slight changes to tailor it to each job posting. Note the job for which you're applying in each letter, as well as the company name and address.

- Send résumés saved in a text-only format, so the receiver can read it regardless of the software and hardware that company uses.

- Keep a log of companies to which you apply. Have it handy by the telephone for when recruiters call. You'll want to have notes about the company and the position(s) you applied for to illustrate that the specific job is important to you.

If you are in a pressured situation and need to get a job right away, consider temping. No longer just secretarial and clerical positions, these jobs range from managerial leadership positions to technical positions, with both salaried and hourly pay schedules.

Temping lets you get a taste of the corporate culture and gives you an opportunity to showcase your skills, perhaps leading to a permanent job at that company. It's a way to get your foot in the door. Look for a temp agency in the Yellow Pages under

> 66
> I went to print a résumé sent in Word and 30 printed pages later realized that in the conversion process, the résumé had become 2,000 pages of gibberish.
> —Fairfax, Virginia based Human Resources Manager.
> 99

Employment or find them in job postings at Web sites like the Monster Board.

Being forced to get a new job can be an opportunity—in terms of both new job responsibility and increased salary—for climbing the corporate ladder. In fact, many job switchers get an instant 15 percent "raise" according to one Washington, D.C.–based recruiter.

Just the facts

- Your state Unemployment Commission and its local offices can provide job search help as well as workshops on interviewing and résumé writing.

- Continuing all your insurance coverages is important to protecting your assets; COBRA and HIPAA may make it easier for you to afford health coverage while you're unemployed.

- You may need to change your investment strategies during periods of unemployment, depending on your financial situation.

- The Internet, which contains numerous job-search sites, is a useful resource for finding a job.

Bright Idea
Over 50, out of a job, and ready for a change in careers? For senior citizen career switchers, the American Association of Retired Persons (AARP) has a career development segment at its Web site (www.aarp.org). There's also a discussion on age discrimination and what you can do to combat it.

GET THE SCOOP ON...
Preventing your children from having to pay for
your divorce ▪ How to limit the price tag of
divorce ▪ Why women often come out behind ▪
How to figure out your assets
to get your fair share

Dealing with Divorce

While getting married can be easy and fun—several months or maybe even a year of wedding planning from Cloud Nine—untying the knot, especially one with frayed edges, is difficult and a lot less pleasant.

Being single won't be as simple as it was before. Your finances will probably remain tangled for years to come, or perhaps forever if you don't remarry. If you have children, your ties to your ex will remain intact, no matter how tattered.

In this chapter I'll tell you things you probably won't want to hear about—for instance, how children suffer when money is used as a weapon on the divorce battlefield—and I'll tell you things you need to know about to make the divorce process move along more quickly and fairly. I'll tell you how to assess your combined net worth, how to make the divorce process easier, how to make divorce less taxing on both of you, and much more.

The cost of divorce

The true cost of divorce is the loss of love and family, and those who often pay the biggest price are the children. Every child wants his or her family to remain intact, and children often blame themselves for the unhappiness that caused their parents to part ways. So give the children due concern. Consider them a peace zone amidst the warring sides.

Watch Out!
When money is used as a weapon, it can have detrimental effects on the children.

One reason this nasty tug-of-war erupts is because money has a symbolic meaning—it can be used as a weapon, a tool for people to express anger, says Dennis Moore, a school psychologist in Newtown, Pennsylvania. For instance, the father might say that the mother uses child support to buy herself things, and the mother might say that the father is making his new family more of a priority, Moore says.

While those accusations may be derived from and fueled by bitterness, according to Moore, fathers *have* been known to purposefully reduce their incomes prior to getting divorced in order to pay less in support—blinding themselves to the deprivation they cause their children—just to get back at their wives. Likewise, mothers have been known to lose or quit their jobs prior to the divorce decree to get higher settlements, regaining employment after the decree is handed down, he says.

Sometimes mothers whose ex-husbands default seek revenge by withholding children from visitation. Children come to resent mothers who do this, Moore says, adding that he strongly advises against this type of behavior. Though already deficient by not paying support, such a father may still provide positive experiences for his children, Moore says, though he adds that it's better for the custodial parent not to make excuses for the other parent not living up to his obligations. Moore says that fathers also need to be aware that although they may think they'll enjoy more financial independence by not paying child support, what they end up doing is depriving and traumatizing their children, who are being swept up helplessly into the conflict. Meanwhile, as the war ensues, the mother gets caught up in court battles to get the father to pay, thus draining her own finances. Now the mother can't give enough time, money, and emotional support to the children, Moore says, adding that the money fathers save by not paying child support "may ultimately be spent paying for their child's psychotherapy."

Fathers should know that reneging on financial obligations intended for the welfare of their children is neglect. They should also know the deprivations and the associated psychological trauma they might be causing their children. While mothers should attempt to get what they're entitled to, Moore says, when they hit roadblocks, they should resist pursuing matters through years of litigation. Know when to give up, he says. Not wanting to let your ex have "the satisfaction" is not a good enough reason to continue the battle, he argues. The children suffer. And nothing could be more costly than that.

Of course, there is no doubt that divorce is expensive, financially. Viewed as an investment, divorce is like a dip in the Dow. It's a short trade with bad market timing. Don't expect to come out ahead. "There's nothing pretty or attractive about divorce when it comes to finances," says Steve Rhode, co-founder of Debt Counselors of America, a nonprofit organization.

If you want to know what you're entitled to, you'll first have to know what you're worth, and that can be costly, but necessary. There are legal fees and

Unofficially...
Watch what you say about your soon-to-be or current ex-spouse. That's your child's father or mother you're talking about.

other expenses associated with finding out. Selling your house in the settlement? Real estate agent commissions, a property appraiser, a termite inspector, perhaps a few points to close the deal—these fees alone can easily add up to $10,000 and more. Add in moving expenses for a few hundred or even a thousand more, depending on how much stuff you get to take and where you're heading. Then the two of you have to have places to live. One of you may have to pay alimony. Don't forget child support. Alas, you've created your own personal Black Monday. Even an amicable divorce can wind up costing you several thousand dollars.

Myths about divorce settlements

"About half of all U.S. marriages will end in divorce, statistics show. Still, many people are misinformed about the financial consequences of a breakup," says Linda Lubitz, a CFP in Miami, Florida.

Lubitz dispels these common myths about divorce:

- *Everything is divided 50-50.* Actually, the standard in most states is "equitable distribution," the interpretation of which varies from state to state and even from judge to judge. Division of assets can be tied to the length of the marriage, income, age, education, earning capacity, and other factors.

- *All assets are equal.* When taxes, sales costs, and investment gains are factored in, not all assets are equal. A $100,000 house and $100,000 in a pension fund probably won't have the same value in 20 years.

- *The wife should get the house.* In reality, the wife's income may be too small to cover mortgage payments, taxes, repairs, and maintenance.

- *"No problem—I'll get alimony."* Most divorce settlements don't include alimony. When alimony is awarded, it generally goes to women who have been married for a long time and have never—or not since the marriage—worked outside the home.

- *"My ex-spouse will pay child support."* According to a 1991 U.S. Census Bureau study, only half of the women awarded child support received the full amount; of the remaining half, about 25 percent received partial payment and 25 percent didn't receive any payments at all.

Bright Idea
Usually, one spouse is the primary carrier of health insurance coverage for the entire family. Consider including continuous health insurance coverage as an obligation in the separation agreement.

"You will be involved with negotiations and, as in most business negotiations, the better prepared you are and the less emotional you are, the greater the chance of your achieving your objective," Lubitz says.

Now the question is how do you pick up the pieces and start over again? First, you must figure out how to protect your assets.

Figuring out what you own

If you thought your wedding was expensive, it pales in comparison to the price tag dangling on your divorce. While it would be unwise to enter marriage preparing for divorce, it's always smart to keep abreast of your finances; that way you'll at least know your financial standing in the event of divorce. Though perhaps more convenient to have just one spouse deal with all the bookkeeping and oversee investments, such an arrangement leaves the other partner in the dark. In the event of divorce, if you're the one in the dark, you'll need to strike a match and light the lantern—quickly. And you're going to have to distance yourself from the emotional devastation to come away with what you deserve.

Start by understanding the cost basis of the assets your considering taking, and look at the tax consequences. "There's a difference between the legal reality and the financial reality [of the value of assets]," says Victoria Collins, CFP and executive vice president of Keller, Collins, Hakopian and Leisure in Irvine, California. "The legal reality for most assets is fair market value minus debt." Whatever is left over is what's divided.

The financial reality of the cost basis of the assets, on the other hand, takes into account tax consequences, repair costs, cost of sales (closing costs and commissions for real estate, transaction costs for stocks), and similar costs. The financial reality is broader and is based on what you will net versus the gross number, which may be very different that what you actually get, Collins explains.

During divorce when spouses are dividing assets, they "generally think of the major assets, like the house and the retirement plan," Collins says. "They forget about other assets that they may have built up, such as cash value in life insurance policies, stock options, tax refunds, accumulated vacation pay, frequent-flier miles, season tickets, [and] time shares." They also may forget about outstanding notes (that is, loans). "Those are things you'll want to include in your settlement planning," Collins says. Sometimes artwork, antiques, tools, and collector's items are undervalued or overlooked, she adds.

Marital property "is typically defined as all property acquired during the marriage," according to Lubitz. It doesn't include gifts and inheritances by either spouse. "But [it] can include intangible

property, such as the right to receive pension benefits, the goodwill value of a business, [and] the value
of a professional license or degree, depending upon
the case law or statutes of your state," she says.

Issues that get in the way

Collins, who also has a Ph.D. in psychology, finds
that there are three things that get in the way of pru-
dent financial decisions during divorce. She refers
to them as the three "get" attitudes:

1. People want to "get it over with," so they're willing to sell out.

2. The desire or need to "get back together." In
   this case, one spouse doesn't want to ask about
   certain assets, for instance, a retirement plan,
   because he or she doesn't want to lose the relationship for good.

3. The need or desire to "get even" or "get back at"
   the other spouse.

"Recrimination and anger simply make the
attorney wealthy," Collins points out. They don't
make for an ongoing relationship.

Divorce is an important financial transaction—
more important than buying a home and more
important than retirement planning, Collins says.
Don't assume the attorneys will get the best deal for
you. "Their job is not to do the financial planning
for you," she says.

The difference between men and women

As a general rule, men and women approach
divorce with different perspectives, according to
Judi Martindale, CFP and head of Martindale and
Associates in San Luis Obispo, California. "Men see
divorce as a business decision, [a financial deci-
sion]," she says. They view it in terms of financial

Watch Out!
A final divorce decree automatically cuts you out of your ex-spouse's will in most states.

consequences. Women, on the other hand, see it as an emotional decision. "Consequently, men usually come out better," she says.

The gender differences don't stop there. In Martindale's experience, women most often want to keep the house. But they can't afford it because they often don't have the income to make the mortgage payments. So they end up selling it a couple of years down the road. What's the problem? First, and most obviously, the payments are draining. Second, women accept this property in lieu of cash or investments. A house is not liquid like other assets are, and as an investment, it generally doesn't grow in value as much or as quickly as other assets do.

Another problem: "[Women] get worse investments [in a divorce settlement, but] won't know it," Martindale says. "That happens a lot." Women generally just don't know about money matters, she continues. They don't understand the tax consequences of different assets, nor do they understand the financial planning consequences.

In contrast, men frequently deal with money, keep abreast of their entire financial picture, and will pay for financial advice. Women, who need it more, often won't, Martindale says. "A lot of women have a 'poor' mentality," she adds. They have a limited income and don't know the value of getting advice. They see getting professional advice as one place to cut back on spending.

Women need to learn about what money can do for them besides buy things; it can give peace of mind, buy the best medical or nursing care, and more. "We think of [money] in terms of materialistic things," she says, but it also can be used to buy comfort.

Buying comfort means not spending money, but investing it, so it will be there for you when you need it most.

Dividing assets when you're splitting up

Divvying up the assets during divorce is one of the biggest financial decisions one can make. Unfortunately, "we make it at a time when we're least able to cope," Martindale says, and women tend to have a harder time coping than men.

How your assets are divided is decided in part by the laws of the state in which you reside. The same goes for future alimony payments. (Note that large property settlements can reduce or eliminate alimony in some states.)

"In most states, an equitable distribution does not require an 'equal' distribution," Lubitz says. A trial court may consider factors such as:

- The standard of living established during the marriage
- The duration of the marriage
- The age of the spouses
- The physical and emotional condition of each spouse
- The financial resources of each spouse
- The time necessary for one or both spouses to acquire an education that will enable him or her to find appropriate employment
- The financial contribution of each spouse to the marriage

"The court's failure to consider these factors or to make any equitable distribution of the marital assets can result in reversal," she notes.

"In community property states, it is generally recognized that each spouse acquires a present, vested, undivided, and equal interest in property acquired by either [spouse], or both, during the marriage. Upon divorce, the community property would generally be divided equally between the spouses," Lubitz says.

Community property states include Arizona, California, Idaho, Louisiana, Nevada, New Mexico, Texas, Washington, and Wisconsin. In contrast, in the 40 equitable distribution states, assets and earnings accumulated during marriage are divided fairly (equitably), at least in theory. In practice, though, more of the assets reportedly go to the higher wage earner.

Making the best financial decisions during divorce is difficult. "Once you're in [the thick of things], you can't see very well," Martindale says. "That's why you need help so much, for other people to give their perspective."

At the very least, with fewer assets and less money, you'll each have to amend your budgets and come up with new financial plans with revised goals and timelines. Probably, the standard of living for both you and your spouse will be reduced, especially considering that you'll have two residences, a luxury you probably wouldn't have considered as a married couple.

If you've invested a lot of time in your marriage, you may be worried about your retirement nest egg. It is likely that your spouse will be entitled to an equitable share of the retirement savings—at least that portion accumulated during your marriage—because it is considered a marital asset. In deciding how retirement savings are to be distributed, the

Unofficially...
There are financial advisors who specialize in financial counseling for people who are going through divorce. One way to find one is to look in *Worth* magazine's annual listing of top financial advisors. Specialties are listed.

court may consider such factors as the length of your marriage, your ages, your health, your income, contributions you made to the marriage, and futures prospects (for example, a new job, promotions, and/or big bonuses). Remember, however, that if you live in a community property state, all marital assets—all earnings during marriage and all property acquired with those earnings—are split 50-50.

You may want to get a qualified domestic relations order (QDRO)—a judgment, decree, or court order issued in part to protect your rights to receive benefits from a qualified retirement plan (such as most pension and profit-sharing plans) or a tax-sheltered annuity. A QDRO can specify the amount or portion of the participant's benefits to be paid to a child or former spouse. It also can address payment of child support, alimony, or marital property rights. Benefits paid under a QDRO to a spouse are generally included in the spouse's or former spouse's income for taxation purposes. If you receive an eligible rollover distribution, as the ex-spouse you may be able to roll it over tax-free into an IRA or another qualified retirement plan. Refer to IRS Publication 575 for more information, which can be downloaded from www.irs.gov or received by mail (call the IRS at 800/829-1040 to request a copy).

Lubitz says to make certain that if a QDRO is drafted for a pension plan distribution, certain requirements set forth in IRS Code Section 414(p) and ERISA Section 206(d)(3) are met. She suggests the following:

- The QDRO should specifically state the provisions of the treatment of the retirement assets

Watch Out!
In some community property states, if one spouse is determined to be the cause of the breakup, he or she may be awarded less than 50 percent of the community property.

vis-à-vis the spouse and must be entered and recorded at the courts.

- Insist that the retirement plan documents be amended to provide for distribution. Unless the plan documents specifically provide for lump-sum distribution of assets before normal retirement, the funds must be left under the current administration. The plan could be disqualified if a distribution due to a QDRO is made.

- Be aware of your spouse's rights pertaining to an IRA and qualified plans. Unless your spouse specifically waives his or her right to any retirement plans, he or she has a beneficial interest in the funds. Prenuptial agreements do not necessarily release a spouse's claim to these assets.

Asking for help

To save a few bucks, you and your spouse might want to consider sitting down peacefully and deciding on who gets what yourselves. However, if you can't agree on things, you might have to consider hiring some outside help.

Mediation versus arbitration

You might, for instance, consider using a mediator, a kind of referee, to help you see each other's side. If you can come to an agreement this way, you'll only have to use an attorney to make the agreement legal.

Unofficially...
You have the legal right to full disclosure of your family's entire assets and your spouse's income.

If you think your spouse is too persuasive or you just want things settled according to law but don't want to litigate, consider using an arbitrator. Either way—using a mediator or an arbitrator—you'll probably save money, and that's what you're both trying to do.

Both mediation and arbitration avoid court. But they are very different methods for resolving differences. In mediation, the mediator serves to help you and your spouse resolve differences so that you are both satisfied with the results. It's an amicable process. The mediator has no power to impose or enforce a decision. In arbitration, an arbitrator in certain circumstances does have the power to impose a settlement. The arbitrator listens to arguments from both sides, then renders a ruling. The arbitrator's ruling becomes public information. If you want to keep your private affairs private, consider resolving the issues yourself or through mediation.

There are, of course, other differences between mediation and arbitration:

- The mediation process is typically faster than the arbitration process.

- In mediation, you and your spouse control the outcome; in arbitration, you relinquish control to the arbitrator, who may make legally binding decisions, depending if you and your spouse have both decided it will be binding or non-binding arbitration.

- In mediation, the outcome is based on perceptions and needs; in arbitration, decisions are based on facts, evidence, and law.

- Mediation is less expensive than arbitration.

There's also a hybrid of the two dispute resolution techniques called "med/arb." This process begins with mediation, but the role of the mediator changes to that of an arbitrator if the spouses cannot come to an agreement. Take note: If a person has served as mediator, he or she is privy to information that may not have been entered into arbitration arguments. Therefore, his or her ruling could be unintentionally swayed.

Mediators don't have to be licensed, according to Carol Ann Wilson, CFP, certified divorced planner at Quantum Financial, and president of the Institute for Certified Divorce Planners in Boulder, Colorado. Most often they are attorneys or psychologists, but they come from many other professional backgrounds as well, including the clergy, accountants and other financial professionals, social workers, marriage counselors, and family counselors, all of whom receive specialized training in mediation. Arbitrators come from all fields as well and don't have to be licensed. Their roles vary by state. Note: Some states use both terms interchangeably.

To find a mediator in your area, contact the Academy of Family Mediators in Lexington, Massachusetts; www.mediators.org; 781/674-2663. To find an arbitrator, contact the American Arbitration Association at www.adr.org.

Calling a lawyer

If you opt to do your own divorce to save big bucks, you'll need to contact an attorney to review the papers you'll need to file in court. Or, if the battle lines already have been drawn, you may have decided it's worth it to duke it out in court. Either way, to find a matrimonial attorney, you can contact the National Women's Law Center, the American Academy of Matrimonial Attorneys, the American Bar Association, or look one up in *The Best Lawyers in America*, available in the reference section of your local library.

Timesaver
Have your attorney bill your spouse directly. That way, if your spouse fails to pay the bill, the attorney can sue him or her directly, leaving you out of it.

Above all, be prepared

Before going to a divorce mediator, arbitrator, or attorney:

- List all marital assets and get an appraised value of them. Check tax returns for investments and bank accounts. Art, antiques, and similar assets will have to be appraised for current market value.

- Figure out how much you'll need in child support; include food, camp, school supplies, after school activities, tuition, and other expenses.

- Confirm through written documentation your spouse's income, including bonuses; check tax returns.

- Research your spouse's income potential by looking at what his or her profession pays for more experience and what benefits are typically offered.

Once you are in the heat of negotiations, make sure to:

- Tie mandatory increases in alimony and child support payments to cost-of-living index increases.

- Require in the settlement an annual review of your spouse's income via tax returns to see if his or her income has increased; base alimony and child support payments on those increases.

Looking out for number 1

What can you do to protect yourself from being taken to the cleaners during a hostile divorce? For the best outcome, a little preplanning is always helpful. This is often a sticky subject because most people do not enter into a marriage thinking they'll

Moneysaver
Sometimes marital assets are frozen during settlement negotiations, leaving spouses with little cash. Occasionally, this may result in credit problems. If this happens to you, contact your affected lenders and the credit bureaus and inform them of your circumstances. Your lenders may waive late payment fees, and the credit bureaus can help you clean up your record once the payment issues are resolved.

end up divorced. Martindale suggests having separate accounts as well as a joint account. If all your money is in joint accounts, one spouse can empty out the couple's entire savings.

Martindale tells the story of a client who was engaged and set up a joint account for honeymoon expenses. One of the two broke off the engagement and the other emptied the account. If that relationship wasn't over before, it certainly was over then, Martindale notes.

Rhode makes the point that you're divorcing your spouse, not your creditors. As long as you have joint obligations you will be jointly responsible for them. If one spouse doesn't pay the bills, the other one is adversely affected until the debt is paid off. A divorce decree means nothing to your creditors; even if their records say your spouse is the one responsible for payment, you still have legal obligations to your creditors.

Some people think they can avoid this problem by keeping their bills separate. One person is responsible for the mortgage, and the other has to pay the gas and electric and all credit card bills, for instance. Rhode doesn't think that's such a great idea. He says he gets letters all the time complaining that one spouse is in debt and afraid to tell the other. This strategy could lead to credit debt disaster.

"There's always a division of labor in a marriage, and oftentimes men get the money," Martindale says. She suggests altering that responsibility every year, noting that sometimes women are under the false impression that they're familiar with their family's financial situation because they do the daily budget. Meanwhile, men are doing the investing—and it's the investments that hold the power.

Bright Idea
You may want to consider reducing the amount of your bequest in your will to your spouse to the minimum amount required by law until your divorce is final. After your divorce is final, you'll probably have to rewrite all of your estate planning documents, changing the beneficiaries and trustees.

It's important for women to educate themselves about finances. Understand what a tax return says— it can give you a wealth of information. By reading it you can get a good idea of all the investments you hold, with the exception of your retirement accounts. Your tax return lists investment account and bank account numbers. "[Of course the best] time to learn all this is not when you're in the midst of panic about it," Martindale points out.

In the meantime, get an agreement in writing detailing who is the responsible party for what debt, advises Kathy Balzan, a credit counselor at American Credit Counselors Corporation, a non-profit organization that offers free credit counseling services. "Cancel any joint bank accounts and open up individual accounts. Cancel all credit cards and get new ones. Close all unused credit card accounts. Call all creditors and advise them of your new marital status. Also, don't forget to change the names, if necessary, on car titles, deeds of trust, and stocks and bonds," she says. Remember to get everything in writing.

Lubitz makes another suggestion: "Make sure that the spouse responsible for making alimony and/or child support payments has sufficient disability income insurance to pay the required money if disability occurs," she says. "Also, make sure that adequate life insurance is purchased and maintained to ensure present value of future payment obligations. Decreasing term [insurance] could be a good choice for this."

Everyone knows that divorce can get nasty sometimes. To get a better settlement, some spouses hide assets, and they're pretty tricky about it. Collins shares some tricks of the trade to watch out for:

Watch Out!
Some lenders call in mortgage notes once a final divorce decree is issued. This means you'll owe full payment immediately on your home. Check your contract carefully!

1. A spouse may be in collusion with his or her employer to delay bonuses and stock options until after the divorce. (You might have to take a deposition of your spouse's boss or the person who handles payroll to find out, though. Or you might have to hire a forensic accountant, one who does cash-flow analysis. This type of accountant starts with the end and works back to the beginning.)

2. A spouse who owns his or her own business may pay a salary to a fictional employee and cancel the checks after the divorce is final. Again, you may have to take depositions in order to find out if this behavior is occurring.

3. A spouse may delay signing a long-term business contract until after the divorce is final. This lowers the value of his or her business.

4. A spouse may be paying money to others (like a girlfriend or boyfriend or parent) for services not rendered, with the understanding that the money will be returned after the divorce is finalized.

5. A spouse will say he or she is paying off a debt, but it's a phony debt to a friend, and any money paid will be returned to that spouse after the divorce. (Money to pay off the debt is taken from the community pot.)

6. A spouse may have invested in government bonds, which don't appear on account statements and aren't registered with the IRS.

7. A spouse may buy and cash traveler's checks on a regular basis, storing up cash reserves that look like expenses paid by checks or credit cards.

Watch Out!
If your spouse's lifestyle is high, but his or her income is low, you should wonder where all the money is coming from. High living may be a sign of hidden assets.

Getting back on your feet

Divorce is tough stuff. Even in the boxing ring, no amount of fancy footwork is going to get you back on your feet again if you're busy giving and taking punches. So you'll have to take some time out, head to your separate corners, and come up with a plan of action that doesn't involved the other player.

Consider making these moves:

- Locate all your important legal documents, including the title to your home, insurance policies, military records, income tax records, real estate title/deed and mortgage papers or lease, credit card records, investment records, bank account numbers, birth certificate, will and/or trust documents, Social Security card, marriage certificate, and any prenuptial agreement.

- Take inventory of all your outstanding debts.

- If you're not used to investing, give yourself time to settle into your new life before making investment decisions. You don't want to sell off stocks and bonds in a panic—which could increase your losses over time—if you can afford not to do so. Nor do you want to be suckered in by commission-hungry salespeople or listen to well-intentioned, but possibly uninformed friends and family. Take some time out to learn about investing. Read *The Unofficial Guide to Investing in Mutual Funds, The Unofficial Guide to Investing, The Complete Idiot's Guide to Managing Your Money, The Complete Idiot's Guide to Making Money on Wall Street, The Complete Idiot's Guide to Making Money in the New Millennium,* or similar reference books. (See Appendix C for more information about these and other books.) Take a course on investing.

- Invest in computer software like Intuit's Quicken or Microsoft's Money to keep track of your expenses and investments. Personal finance software can also help you keep tabs on your budget, bank account balances, debt, and upcoming and paid bills.

- Make a new budget. Pick a routine time each month to pay bills.

- Get copies of your credit report and check for errors (and for your ex-spouse's shopping sprees if you haven't closed your joint accounts).

- Retitle your home, savings accounts, and investments. Change beneficiaries on your savings accounts, investments, retirement plans, life insurance policies, and trusts.

- Rewrite your will; you'll have to get together with your ex-spouse to decide on guardianship for your children.

- Reevaluate your disability insurance and life insurance needs.

Saving on taxes: keeping Uncle Sam a distant relative

While divorce can be emotionally taxing, there are financial tax implications to consider. Understanding them might permit both you and your ex to walk away from your marriage with a little more money in your pockets.

If you and your spouse can agree that the money one pays to the other will be used as intended (to keep a roof over your head, the family clothed and fed) and that it doesn't matter what you call it—child support or alimony—together, you can save a lot of money, Bruyette says.

Consider this: Alimony is tax deductible to the payor; however, it's considered income to the receiver and is therefore taxed as such. In contrast, child support is not tax deductible to the payor, nor is it considered income to the receiver. "In many cases it make sense to classify the ongoing support payments as alimony," Bruyette explains. If you can waive the white flag and increase alimony in lieu of child support, you both save.

Here's how it works: The person in the higher tax bracket wants to be able to deduct support payments. So say one ex-spouse is in the 40 percent tax bracket. The other ex-spouse is not working outside the home. If the employed ex-spouse, say the husband, was to pay his former wife $100,000 in total support, he would be able to deduct $40,000 (40 percent), provided the payment is for alimony. The ex-wife's taxable income is now $100,000, which would result in a federal tax obligation of $23,000. But together the couple will save $17,000 in taxes.

What happens in many cases, according to Bruyette, is that the spouse who earns less doesn't want to pay taxes on any of the support so he or she ends up with a large amount of child support being paid. When the children get older, the child support ends. With the set up described above, however, the ex-spouses could agree that the higher earner pays his or her ex more in alimony than he or she would have in child support. The key is cooperation. "When personalities get involved sometimes it gets expensive," Bruyette points out.

There are a couple of caveats to consider. If the IRS determines the money is for the benefit of the child, you might have to pay back taxes. (See Chapter 11.) Also, by taking alimony in lieu of child support payments, you're taking a risk. The courts are quicker to enforce child support payments. And the Internal Revenue Service will pay child support out of the paying spouse's tax refund if he or she turns out to be a "deadbeat."

Moneysaver
If one party is in a low enough tax bracket to make use of education-related tax credits, pass on any education costs to him or her.

Despite what you and your spouse agree to—alimony, child support, or a combination of the two—there's still good news tax-wise: As a newly single person you'll get a tax break, courtesy of the marital tax penalty. Here's an example of tax savings using Quicken calculations: If you and your spouse each earned $50,000, your income tax bill would have been $18,981 if you filed jointly as a married couple. That's $9,491 each. If you maintain the same income, as a single filer your federal income tax bill will be only $8,746—that's a savings of $745. If you take that savings every year and invest it in a security with a 10 percent annual rate of return, in 10 years that income tax savings would add up to $12,049.05, excluding capital gains taxes and any management fees or sales commissions. (Of course, on the other hand, the second income would have allowed you both to save and invest even more.)

Doing your homework

If you are contemplating or going through a divorce, do some research. There are plenty of books out there on divorce. In addition, there are some Internet sites that contain helpful information; consider visiting www.DivorceOnline.com, www.DivorceNet.com, and www.DivorceCentral.com (which also has a bulletin board filled with personal ads, if you're ready to take the plunge again and start dating).

Just the facts

- Using money as a weapon can have a strong adverse impact on the children.

- You should consider the tax, maintenance, repair, and similar costs of any asset you want to keep in order to fully assess its value.

- Be sure to re-title your property and choose new beneficiaries for your life and other insurance policies once your divorce is final.

- You can save money and time by using a mediator or arbitrator to help you divide your assets instead of going through the court system.

Chapter 16

GET THE SCOOP ON...
Protecting yourself from identity theft ▪
Protecting your assets while making transactions on the Internet ▪ Protecting yourself
against check-writing fraud ▪ Identifying
unscrupulous telemarketers ▪ Gaging your
financial advisors honesty

Fraud Protection

Most businesses are legitimate and so are most salespeople. But there are a few people out there who set up shop to steal your money. Their methods vary. Some use the phone, some the mail, and others the Internet. But they all take your money and run.

Other thieves steal your money by stealing your identity. All they need is your name and Social Security number. Then they can spend you deeply into debt and leave you with a bad credit rating, a lot of clean-up work, and sometimes a criminal record.

In this chapter I'll tell you how thieves get access to your private information, how they operate, and how you can protect yourself. I'll also tell you about Internet fraud and give you tips from a computer security expert on how to protect yourself if you decide to use the Internet for shopping, banking, or investing.

Protecting yourself from identity theft

Imagine someone—a total stranger—going on shopping sprees with your credit card, taking a loan out in your name to buy a sporty new car, and getting an apartment with your squeaky clean credit, which a few weeks later is a dirty mess that you're left to clean up at your own expense. To add insult to injury, you're considered the guilty party by your creditors until you're proven innocent. Until then, you might be labeled a bad credit risk, which may affect your attempts to buy anything with credit or even secure a new job. Depending on the scheme, you might even be labeled a criminal. But what are your options? You need credit to function.

"Increasingly, our system of commerce depends on personal identification information to facilitate transactions," says James Bauer, deputy assistance director, office of investigations at the U.S. Secret Service, in testimony before the senate committee on banking, housing, and urban affairs, subcommittee on financial services and technology on April 1, 1998. (The U.S. Secret Service is the law enforcement bureau of the U.S. Department of the Treasury.)

Identity theft—where a criminal assumes your identity by using your name and Social Security number and in some cases other identifying factors to charge up huge bills at your expense—reportedly costs billions of dollars every year and has already happened to tens of thousands of people.

Although you may only be responsible for the first $50 on each credit card charged by the thief and the first $500 on debit cards, you'll have the added expense of calling creditors, filing police reports, and preparing for court.

On October 30, 1998, President Bill Clinton signed H.R. 4151, the "Identity Theft and Assumption Deterrence Act of 1998," into law. "This legislation will make identity theft a federal crime, with penalties generally of up to three years' imprisonment and a maximum fine of $250,000," the president said in a statement released by the White House. The president's statement continues:

Specifically, the legislation would penalize the theft of personal information with the intent to commit an unlawful act, such as obtaining fraudulent loans or credit cards, drug trafficking, or other illegal purposes. It would also direct the Federal Trade Commission to help victims deal with the consequences of this crime.

Impostors often run up huge debts, file for bankruptcy, and commit serious crimes. This legislation will enable the United States Secret Service, the Federal Bureau of Investigation, and other law enforcement agencies to combat this type of crime, which can financially devastate its victims.

Thieves get access to your identity in a variety of ways. Stealing your wallet or purse is the easiest and quickest method. But they've been known to dig through trash to get personal information from bank statements and bills, not to mention all those preapproved credit card offers. Sometimes they steal those credit card offers and statements, as well as boxes of new checks, right from your mailbox. They can also get information from an "insider," someone who has direct access to your credit records, credit applications, bank documents, and personnel records; usually this information is given out by a thief working at a company or institution that has these records.

Besides digging in trash, stealing mail, and bribing bank employees, criminals can get information

> **"**
> The idea of identity theft as a violation would enable law enforcement to prevent the fraud before it starts.
> —James Bauer, deputy assistance director, office of investigations at the U.S. Secret Service.
> **"**

from rifling though co-workers' desk drawers, soliciting identifiers through false job application schemes, and retrieving information through the Internet, according to Bauer.

Make sure you choose an Internet service provider that has security measures in place. In his report, Bauer tells of an incident where hackers accessed personal information and credit card numbers of 10,000 clients. The hackers were in Germany. (See below for more information on Internet theft.)

In addition to these means, "criminals also can obtain information, such as property deeds and court case data, which often contain personal information," Bauer noted in his statement. These records often include unlisted phone numbers, Social Security numbers, and physical descriptions like height and weight. While this information has always been a matter of public record, access to it has been made easier by the Internet.

Other easy sources through which criminals can access your personal information are data mining and data warehouse companies. These companies sell information (legally) obtained from credit card applications.

"Through the use of sophisticated 'desktop publishing' equipment, such as computers and color laser copiers, criminals are easily able to create falsified documents based on some else's identity," Bauer says in his statement.

Unofficially...
Information you provide on various motor vehicle department applications, as well as that on credit card applications, can be sold legally.

While sometimes the impersonator takes the money and runs by getting cash advances off your credit cards and buying things they can return for cash, other times, to string the theft out and bring the tab up even higher, the impersonator will make a few payments on the new bill, delaying the time before you're alerted by creditors.

Although you may not be able to prevent identity theft, there are things you can do to protect your finances and your reputation:

- Rip up preapproved credit card and loan offers, receipts, bills, checks for advances, canceled checks, and bank statements before tossing them into the garbage.

- Don't carry all your credit cards in your wallet.

- Keep a list of all your credit cards and the phone numbers to contact if they are lost or stolen.

- Don't carry your Social Security card in your wallet; memorize the number.

- Don't carry your birth certificate, passport, or visa with you.

- Don't leave your ATM receipt at the ATM machine.

- Don't give out or write down any of your PINs; memorize them.

- Shield your hand when entering your access code at a public phone and when entering your account number and PIN at an ATM.

- Don't give out your credit card number or any other personal information to phone solicitors, even if you recognize the name of the company they say they're calling from.

- Don't list your full name in the phone book; leave out your address and prestigious titles like "M.D." or "Atty." Better yet, get an unlisted phone number.

- Send an e-mail to the Internet phone/address locator Web sites (www.switchboard.com, www.four11.com, www.555-1212) requesting an

Timesaver
As an alternative to listing your credit card numbers and emergency phone contacts for lost or stolen cards, make a photocopy of each card, front and back, instead.

edited version of your information or simply have it deleted.

■ Pick up your new checks at the bank, or at least be on the lookout for them after you've placed the order; if they don't arrive when expected, notify the bank.

■ If your Social Security number is also your driver's license ID number, request a new number from the motor vehicles department.

Bauer notes that information also can be taken from your voter registration card and alien registration card.

If you're still worried, you can take further protective action. Stop the unsolicited, preapproved credit card offers by preventing the three credit reporting bureaus from selling your name to lenders. Write to them with your request. For addresses call Equifax at 800/556-4711, Experian at 800/353-0809, and TransUnion at 800/680-7293. You also can have them put a fraud alert in your file to prompt creditors to contact you before they open an account in your name.

While you can reduce your risk of being a victim of identity theft, you cannot eliminate that risk entirely. If you find that you're being impersonated, you must take action quickly to protect your finances:

■ Notify your creditors, banks, credit union, and investment companies immediately.

■ Call the fraud units of the three major credit bureaus (Equifax 800/525-6285; Experian 800/301-7195; TransUnion 800/680-7289).

■ Make a police report.

- If the impersonator opened a checking account in your name or if your checks have been stolen or lost, call one of the check verification companies: CheckRite 800/766-2748; Chexsystems 800/428-9623; Equifax 800/437-5120; National Processing Co. 800/526-5380; SCAN 800/262-7111; or Telecheck 800/710-9898.

- Contact your gas and electric companies.

- Notify your phone companies, both local and long distance.

- Notify the Social Security Administration (800/772-1213); ask for a new Social Security number.

- Notify the Department of Motor Vehicles; ask for a driver's license with a new number.

- Contact the U.S. Postal Inspector Service if mail was used or if the impersonator filed for a change of address.

- Contact the U.S. Secret Service.

   If you need support or further guidance, there's help available:

- Privacy Rights Clearinghouse at 800/773-7748 or www.privacyrights.org gives assistance to victims.

- The Federal Trade Commission also provides information on privacy at www.ftc.gov, or contact the FTC Consumer Response Center, Room 130, 6th St. and Pennsylvania Ave., N.W., Washington, D.C. 20580; 202/382-4357.

❝
Unless a bank is notified within two days of check card fraud, customers are exposed to $500 in liability.
—Consumers Union.
❞

Protecting your finances on the Internet

Protecting your finances in cyberspace takes more common sense than technology. If you decide to use the Internet for shopping sprees, banking, investing, or finding at-home work, you'll have to learn to recognize online danger signs just as you would in the offline, 3D world. For instance, if you were going down a street and saw a bank sign hanging over a hotdog stand, you'd get a clue about that "business" and would hurry along with your wad of cash still tucked safely inside your wallet.

While there may not be such obvious tip-offs in cyberspace, there are plenty of cues out there, if you look closely. M. E. Kabay, Ph.D., CISSP, director of education at ICSA, Inc., gives these tips:

Watch Out!
Wild claims can be found in the real world, too. If someone tells you that he or she has secret information that no one else has on how to strike it rich on Wall Street, you have to ask yourself, why would this person tell you this incredible secret for only $19.95? Don't be gullible or greedy.

- Know with whom you are dealing. Don't assume because someone has an animated, professional-looking Web site that they are what they appear to be—the Web site itself doesn't prove anything about the business.

- If a site has spelling mistakes, a lot of exclamation points, or a lot of capital letters, move on—these are the signs of an adolescent mentality or an illiterate, both of which you want to avoid dealing with.

- If the site makes wild claims like they'll give you twice the normal interest rate with no risk or you can earn $200,000 a year grooming poodles, move on. "This is a test to see if your IQ is higher than 75," Kabay says. If you sign on, you've failed the test.

Kabay provides these tips for protecting your finances online:

- Check phone numbers. If the business claims to be in a certain state, check to see if the area code is in that state. Or, if you call information using the area code and they can't give you a phone number, that should make you suspicious. If it's a large company, they should have a toll-free phone number starting with 800, 888, or 877.

- Look at the e-mail address. Check to see if it has a domain name in it, for example, www.icsa.net (ICSA, Inc.).

- Call and ask for written documentation. Look at the postmark and make sure it's coming from the city the company claims to be located in.

None of these protections gives complete certainty that the business is legitimate. They're just cyberspace cues, Kabay says.

E-mail advertisements

"Don't ever, ever respond to junk e-mail. Period," Kabay warns. "Unsolicited commercial e-mail is a violation of the terms of service of almost every Internet service provider in the world." So, by the very act of sending an advertisement, the company is fundamentally dishonest. "But it gets worse," he continues. "Many, many of these message are sent with either temporary user identities or they are outright fraudulent addresses."

For instance, scammers sometimes use free AOL or CompuServe trial offers. They create a screen name and send out as much junk e-mail as they can. Then they close the account because many people send these e-mails straight to abuse@aol.com or other service provider abuse hotlines.

Bright Idea
Check with the Better Business Bureau to see if there have been complaints about a particular company. If you have trouble pinning the company's location down to a city, consider it a warning bell.

Kabay also warns that if a junk e-mail instructs you to reply to an address if you don't want any more junk e-mail, don't reply. These people use old lists, Kabay says. This is their way of updating them, their way of knowing if your address is a good address.

Additionally, don't attack or spam (overwhelm the end user's computer by inundating him or her with e-mail) people in the junk mail reply address. The reply address often is different from the sending address. They may be totally innocent and unaware of the scam. Kabay tells of a case in which an 18-year-old set up a junk mailer program using flowers.com as a reply address for complaints and bounces ("return to sender—address unknown"). That happened to be a real business. The owner sued and won $19,000 in damages for the thousands of bounces and angry e-mail messages the owner received from other victims of the spammer. Sometimes junk e-mail includes a phone number for complaints. Again, don't call and harass that person. He or she may be completely innocent. After all, what scammer is going to welcome complaints?

Kabay says to delete all junk e-mail or send it to the service provider for investigation.

Protecting your online transactions

If you decide to invest or shop or just surf on the Internet, you'll enter Web sites through a browser, such as Netscape Navigator or Microsoft Internet Explorer. If you're investing, you'll click on the icon for trading or transferring mutual funds. If you're shopping, you'll click on the icon for the item that you want to add to your shopping cart. The site should send a message saying that you're entering an encrypted area, and you'll begin a secure sockets layer (SSL) encrypted session.

The SSL encryption is necessary because the information you provide—your credit card number, for instance—may hop in and out of many computers (servers) along the way to its final destination.

Using an SSL-encrypted session guarantees that your information can be read only by an authorized user at the specified Web server's address. Both Internet Explorer and Netscape support SSL sessions. Check to see if the Web site you want to do business at uses the SSL.

To determine if you have an SSL-enabled session, look for the padlock icon in Microsoft Internet Explorer, which will appear closed (locked) if the SSL is enabled. In Netscape, the icon is a key, or a padlock in more recent versions. If the key is broken or the padlock unlocked, the SSL is not activated.

Another way to tell if the Web site is secure is to look for the ICSA TruSecur seal. The TruSecur Process provides security guidelines, a remote test (a vulnerability analysis), an on-site inspection, at least two random spot checks, and a twice-monthly vulnerability awareness report to companies that contract for their aid and meet their high standards for security.

Before providing sensitive information to a Web site, look for three things:

1. A message or other indicator that you're entering an encrypted session.

2. The ability to cancel a transaction that contains sensitive information.

3. A privacy statement disclosing how the information will be used and how the site is secured.

In general, it's safe to buy over the Internet, provided, of course, you're at an authentic site. "There is no known case … in which a credit card number

Watch Out!
Don't send sensitive information, like your credit card or bank account numbers, via e-mail. Hackers can gain access to e-mail messages. They also can access your information if you give it to a site that is not secure or one that has a security hole. (Typically, sites that deal with money have firewalls in place to prevent outside hackers from accessing their servers.)

has been picked off the network in transit," Kabay says.

Before you do business on a Web site, check its privacy policy and see if you agree with what it will do with your name, Kabay suggests. Some sites sell your registration information. You might end up with a lot of junk paper mail.

Also, there have been complaints about lost orders, Kabay notes. Before you press the send button, use your browser's print option to get a paper copy of what you send. If you get a confirmation of the order from the site, print that, too, or save it as an HTML file. If something goes wrong, you'll need it.

Protecting yourself against fraud on the Internet

The Web provides a cheap and easy way to set up shop for both legitimate and fraudulent companies. All it takes is a professional-looking Web site and a company name. Some scammers bank on the popularity of other businesses. They bring surfers to their site by using an address that closely resembles a legitimate site by using, for instance, .org instead of .com as an extension or by using an address similar to a legitimate company but with a common typographical error. For example, instead of "bankonit.com", a scam company might use "bankonti.com" or "bnakonit.com."

Investing online

If you're investing online, take action to protect your finances:

- Verify that the brokerage or mutual fund (or other investment opportunity) is licensed by your state's department of commerce, division of securities. The North American Securities

Administrators Association (NASAA) Web site (www.NASAA.org) has links to state department of commerce sites.

- Don't buy investments strictly on the basis of chat room hype. Although it is illegal to try to manipulate stock prices, some people talk up or talk down stocks to persuade potential investors, boost the price of shares, or increase their own profit.

- Don't take advice from people who hide their identities (which is exactly what a screen name does).

- Download and print a hard copy of any online solicitation that you are considering. Note the Internet address and the date and time that you saw the offer.

- If you want to invest in a security online, verify its legitimacy by calling a broker or the company holding the investment.

- Ask a librarian for information about the company, including a credit report, pending or previous lawsuits, liens, or judgments.

- Check Public Citizen's Web site (www.publiccitizen.org) for information on scams deployed by so-called creditors and car dealers.

- Check the National Fraud Information Center's Web site (www.fraud.org) to get educated on scams. Call 800/876-7060 to file a complaint.

To report fraud and other complaints on investments, contact the Securities and Exchange Commission (www.sec.gov) at 202/942-7040.

The National Association of Securities Dealers (www.nasdr.com) will follow through on consumer complaints; they can be reached by telephone at

66

The Secret Service has investigative jurisdiction over credit card and other access device fraud, fraudulent identification, and financial fraud involving computer access.
—James Bauer, deputy assistance director, office of investigations at the U.S. Secret Service.

301/590-6500. Consumers can register a request for free arbitration at the Web site.

Fraud and your financial planner or salesperson

The unprecedented bull market of the past decade has attracted many new, unsophisticated investors to Wall Street. These people make easy prey for online and real-world fraud. Because of the market's high returns, it's relatively easy to mask sales practice problems such as unsuitable investments, high fees and excessive commissions, and *churning* (excessive trading). With market returns in the double digits—and some investments returning 20 percent or more—many investors aren't paying close attention to commission rates and fees. Churning pushes both of these higher, increasing the salesperson's profits and reducing yours.

There are two levels of fraud. The first level is improprieties by brokers. These sales practice violations are also referred to as *front-office fraud*. The second, more serious level is blatant fraud by so-called promoters.

The first level includes:

- Unauthorized transactions
- Unsuitable recommendations
- Failure to execute a transaction
- Churning (excessive trading to increase commission)

The second, more serious, level of fraud includes:

- Misrepresentation of facts
- Making promises that are impossible to fulfill
- Omission of material information

■ Outright lies

Fraudulent salespeople work in different fields using different tactics. There are several indications, or red flags, you can look or listen for:

■ "Guaranteed return." There are *no* guarantees in investing.

■ "Limited offer." This strategy is designed to give you a sense of urgency to get you to sign on the dotted line before giving the investment thoughtful consideration.

■ "Limited number available." This is another tactic used to make you act quickly.

■ "Risk-free." *All* investments carry risk.

■ "High returns." High returns are often associated with high risk.

■ Veil of secrecy. This strategy is designed to deter you from asking questions, making it easier for the scam artists to sell their "product."

■ High-pressured sales tactics. This strategy is used to get you to invest without thoughtful consideration. If someone is selling a legitimate investment, that person should have no reason to insult you or pressure you.

While most financial planners are decent, honest people, some are dishonest and unethical. Here are some signs to watch out for and some tips to protect your finances:

■ Your financial planner urges you to move your money to a similar investment. This can be an unscrupulous method of generating sales commissions, increasing the planner's profits while decreasing yours. Not only will you have to pay added commissions, but you'll probably have to pay added transaction fees. Because all this money comes out of your investment, and you don't have to write a check for it, it can go unnoticed. Check your brokerage statements carefully.

▪ Your financial planner dismisses an error in your account without thoughtful consideration. Ask the manager for a written explanation, and check to see if the problem was corrected in your next statement.

▪ Don't purchase an investment through a cold call.

▪ Don't deal with brokers who refuse to send you written information.

▪ Don't give your bank account number(s), your mother's maiden name, or any PINs (personal identification numbers) or other security codes over the phone, unless you made the call.

▪ Make sure you get and read all disclosure information.

▪ Check to see if the investment and broker are registered with your state's securities regulator. Check to see if the state has received or knows of any complaints about the broker or the brokerage firm, and if either has a disciplinary history.

▪ Don't write a check to the sales representative. Make it out to the investment company.

▪ Check to see if the address to which you're asked to send the check differs from the address of the brokerage firm or that listed in the prospectus.

▪ Make sure your receive account statements each month or quarter, whichever is standard for that company. Such statements serve as your record of all transactions, so make sure all information contained in each statement is correct. Have any errors explained in writing and corrected immediately. Check the next statement to verify that the change was made.

- Hang up on aggressive cold callers, and never allow yourself to be pressured into making an investment over the phone.

- If you don't understand the investment, don't invest in it. You might not understand it because it might not make any sense.

Protecting your assets from telemarketers

Nationwide, hundreds of telemarketing "boiler rooms" are filled with salespeople using high-pressure tactics to sell illegal or fraudulent investment products and vacations. They're also quick to sell you chances to win prizes.

Although some telemarketers are selling legitimate investments or long-distance phone service, others are more than just annoying—they're fraudulent. They may use pressure to sell you their product, or the product itself might be a scam.

Legitimate cold callers must follow certain rules set forth by the Securities and Exchange Commission (SEC):

- Calls to private residences must be received between 8:00 A.M. and 9:00 P.M. (Note: time restrictions don't apply if you're already a customer of the firm, if you've given them permission to call you at other times, or if they're calling you at work.)

Watch Out!
Telemarketing isn't the only way scammers contact you. Illegal franchise investment offerings are often marketed through business opportunity and franchise shows, and scammers use the mail as well as the Internet to pull off their schemes.

■ The caller must identify him or herself and the nature of the call. He or she must also tell you the name of the firm and the firm's address and telephone number.

■ At your request, cold callers must add your name to their "do not call" list. (You must use those exact words in order for them not to be able to get around the letter of the law.)

■ The caller must not threaten you in any way, try to intimidate you, use offensive language, or call you repeatedly in an effort to annoy, abuse, or harass you.

■ Before taking money directly from your bank account, brokers must get your permission in writing.

■ The salesperson must tell you the truth about the investment.

Unscrupulous telemarketers use tried and true selling strategies. Cold call warning signs include:

■ High-pressure sales tactics. Telemarketers work from scripts. The salesperson will have retorts readily available to respond to every objection you make, if you manage to get a word in edge-wise.

■ A sense of urgency. By telling you it's a limited offer, whether by time constraints ("today is the last day the offer will be available") or by numbers ("there's only three left"), the salesperson is trying to get you to act immediately without investigating the legitimacy of the company or product.

■ Appealing to your self-esteem. The telemarketer might tell you that some big name with a good reputation bought this product or they might even tell you not to be stupid by giving up such a great opportunity.

■ An offer of stellar profits or "guaranteed" returns on an investment product.

A telemarketing tactic used to sell investments is the "three-call" technique. During the first call, the salesperson touts the firm's strengths to build up your trust. Then he or she closes the call by saying he or she will call you back if something "hot" comes along. Low and behold, he or she calls you again. During the second call—the "set up"—the caller tells you about some sure-fire deal. During the third call—"the close"—he or she really lays on the pressure.

Yet another sales tactic is called the bait-and-switch technique. Using this method, the broker actually sells you a good investment. But after gaining your trust, he or she tries to sell you high-risk investments, which will probably result in high commissions for the broker and big losses for you.

If you're concerned about the validity of the investment, ask the salesperson the risks involved and how appropriate the investment is to your financial plan. Rather than a direct, honest answer, you'll probably get more hype about the investment's high returns.

If you have a problem, write to your sales representative's manager or the firm's compliance officer and ask for a written explanation. Of course, if it's a scam, you won't get an answer, or at least not a valid one.

If your problems relate to an investment, contact the SEC's Office of Investor Education and Assistance (U.S. Securities and Exchange Commission, Office of Investor Education and Assistance,

Timesaver
You can reduce unwanted calls from many telemarketers by contacting the Direct Marketing Association's Telephone Preference Service and asking them to put you on their "do not call" lists. Write to: Telephone Preference Service, P.O. Box 9014, Farmingdale, NY 11735-9014.

Mail Stop 2-13, 450 Fifth St., N.W., Washington, D.C. 20549; phone: 202/942-7040; fax: 202/942-9634; e-mail: help@sec.gov). After receiving a complaint, one of their specialists will contact the firm, company, or individual that is the subject of the complaint. If the problem is not resolved, the SEC will tell you about your legal options.

In addition, this SEC office provides research and answers to your questions. The SEC will tell you if a broker or investment professional is licensed and if a company is registered with the SEC. They also offer publications and hold periodic investors' town meetings around the country.

You also can contact your state's securities regulator. The North American Securities Administrators Association (toll free: 888/846-2722; Internet address: www.nasaa.org) will help you locate the address and phone number for your state's office.

Protecting your assets from check fraud

Moneysaver
Avoid leaving any blank spaces (and room for alteration) when you write in the amount of a check.

Technology has made it possible for criminals to create realistic renditions of your checks as well as fake IDs to use to cash in on your savings. Check fraud schemes vary. Some of the more popular ones include altering checks you've written—either by changing who the check is made out to or the amount of the check, counterfeiting the check, forging your signature or endorsement, and/or drawing on a closed account.

Criminals may be bank insiders or outsiders. They use a variety of methods to get your personal information. Sometimes they have links to financial institution insiders; sometimes they steal financial institution statements and checks from your mail or trash. Other times they work with dishonest employees of merchants who accept payments by checks.

Here are some common check fraud schemes:

1. You make out a check. A criminal intercepts the check, either at your mailbox as it waits for pickup, from your wallet, or otherwise, and using chemicals or other methods, erases the amount or the name of the payee and enters new information.

2. A criminal steals your wallet, takes a blank check from it, and forges your signature by copying it from your driver's license. Using the diver's license or an altered version as ID, the criminal cashes the check at your bank.

3. You make a check out to a company for, say, $70. The criminal then adds a "9," making the check payable for $970.

There are other variations on check fraud. Identity assumption occurs when the criminal learns information about your name, address, Social Security number, bank account number, home and work phone numbers, and employer and uses this information to misrepresent him- or herself to the bank as you. The scheme may involve changing account information (like your address), drawing funds, and using checks. When state motor vehicle departments use Social Security numbers for identification numbers, this scheme becomes even easier for the criminal. Remember, criminals can buy department of motor vehicle information. The information also can be used to order checks from a check printer.

Here's how identity assumption works: You pay a bill using a check. A bank employee copies the

Timesaver
Report stolen checks to your financial institution at once. After calling and speaking to the manager, send a written statement by fax rather than mail to ensure that it's received immediately.

check and hands the copy over to a partner in crime, who contacts the bank pretending to be the customer—you. The impersonator tells the bank he or she needs new checks right away because he or she has moved—which means that you won't get the checks because they're going to be sent to the impersonator's address. The impersonator then writes forged checks against your account.

Closed account fraud is another common scheme. In this case, the checks are written by the criminal against an account you've closed. The scheme depends on the float time allowed by your financial institution. (Destroy all checks from closed accounts and close accounts rather than abandon them if you no longer want them.)

Some check schemes are committed by or with the help of bank insiders. Telemarketing fraud is based on the creation of "demand drafts" rather than checks. Drafts resemble a check, but carry no signature. Here's an example of how this scheme works: A telemarketer calls you and tells you that you've won a cash prize, but in order to deposit it into your account, he or she needs your account information. Once you provide that, the criminal prepares the demand drafts and withdraws funds from the account. A variation of the scheme is when a criminal tries to sell you something, like a magazine subscription, to get your account information. Or the caller promises to issue a credit card, but needs your account information to do so. (Note: your bank should check to see if you've provided written authorization for the drafts.)

Remember, you work hard to earn your money. You must also put some effort into protecting it.

Watch Out!
Don't leave a blank check in your wallet.

Just the facts

- All a criminal needs to steal your identity is your name and Social Security number.

- A criminal can legally buy your personal information from a warehouse.

- Shopping, banking, and investing on the Internet is safe at legitimate sites—just make sure that when you perform transactions online, you do so in an encrypted session.

- Legitimate companies selling their products via telemarketers will always be able to back up their claims with written documentation.

Glossary

Actual cash value: Insurance policies reimburse based on replacement value, what the lost item costs in today's dollars, or actual cash value, the depreciated value of the lost item.

Adjustable-rate mortgage (ARM): With this type of a mortgage, the lender can adjust its interest rate periodically based on changes in a specified index.

Amortization: The gradual repayment of your mortgage, both principal and interest, over time.

Annual fee: A flat, yearly charge.

Annual percentage rate (APR): An interest rate based on the cost of credit and expressed as an annual percentage.

Annuity: Sponsored by insurance companies and other financial institutions, this type of investment guarantees payment of specific amounts at set times or a single lump sum payment. Annuities can be either fixed or variable. Fixed annuities work similarly to Certificates of Deposit (CDs)—you invest a lump sum and receive a guaranteed fixed rate of interest for a specified amount of time. With variable annuities you invest in a portfolio of stocks, bonds, and cash equivalents, so your return depends on the portfolio's overall performance. Variable annuities often have annual charges.

Appraisal: The written estimate of a property's value. It is prepared by an appraiser.

Appraised value: The appraiser's professional opinion of value based on fair market value and analysis of the property.

Assessed value: A public tax assessor's appraisal of the value of a property to calculate property tax.

Back-end load: This is the sales commission charged when you sell shares from a back-end fund.

Bankruptcy: A court proceeding in which a debtor can relieve him- or herself of massive debt obligations, in part or in whole, depending on the type of bankruptcy filed.

Beneficiary: The person designated to receive the assets (title to a property, income from a trust, and so on) in the event of the holder's death.

Bequeath: To transfer personal property to named heirs through a will.

Bond funds: These mutual funds have portfolios primarily made up of corporate, municipal, or federal government bonds. Bond funds are considered income funds because they often pay out dividends. Many of these funds are tax-free.

Cap: A cap limits how much the interest rate can increase or decrease on an adjustable-rate mortgage.

Capital gains distributions: When a fund sells a stock at a profit, it passes the profit along to shareholders in the form of capital gains. These gains are usually realized annually at the end of the year and are subject to short-term (held 12 months or less) or long-term (held more than 12 months) taxes.

Capital growth: This occurs when the value of the mutual fund's securities increase in value. The result is a rise in the net asset value of the mutual fund shares.

Certificate of title: A legal statement that discloses the property's current owner.

Closing: Also called *settlement*, the buyer of a home signs the mortgage documents and pays closing costs to finalize the sale of the property.

Closing costs: These are fees and other expenses that must be paid by buyers and sometimes sellers when transferring ownership of a property. They typically include a loan origination fee, attorney's fee, an advance on taxes (which is placed in an escrow account), title insurance fees, and other fees.

Contingency: Often placed in a real estate contract, this is a condition that must be met before a contract is legally binding. Buyers and sellers often each add several contingencies.

Credit card: This type of card allows you to purchase items without cash and delays the payment for about 25 days. Some credit cards carry annual fees, and all assess interest for charges that are not paid by the end of the grace period. Other charges and fees may apply. Credit cards often come with perks like cash back on purchases and frequent-flyer miles. You also can hold off on payments of any disputed charges if you put the cause of your dispute in writing and send it to the credit card company.

Credit history: Kept by a credit bureau, this record details a person's line of credit and debt repayment history. It is used by lenders to help determine if a potential borrower is a good risk.

Credit report: A report of a person's credit history prepared by a credit bureau.

Debit card: This type of card gives you electronic access to your money by taking it straight from your bank accounts, so there is no float period nor is there protection on your purchase as there is for credit cards. Both ATM and check cards are debit cards.

Deed: A legal document that conveys title to a property.

Diversification: Spreading an investment among a variety of securities to reduce risk.

Dollar cost averaging: Investing a fixed sum at regular intervals. This investment technique has two advantages: You don't have to time the market to invest at market lows, and it generally compensates for investments made at market highs.

Down payment: The part of a property's purchase price the buyer pays in cash.

Earnest money deposit: A deposit made by the person who bids on a home to show that he or she is serious about buying it. This deposit is refunded if the seller backs out, but not if the buyer backs out.

Equity: The homeowner's financial interest in his or her property. It is defined as the difference between the property's fair market value and the amount still owed on the mortgage.

Escrow: A deposit held by a third party to be delivered on the fulfillment of a stated condition.

Estate: All property owned by an individual at time of death.

Estate planning: Arranging to make sure your assets pass to those who you want to have them after your death.

Executor: A person named in a will to oversee the distribution of an estate as directed in the will.

Finance charge: The costs incurred for using credit. It includes interest and may include other charges.

401(k) plan: Many employers offer this type of retirement plan. Often, the employer matches all or part of your contribution, making this an especially good investment tool. In addition to salary reduction, depending on the company, contributions can be made by a "cash election" profit-sharing or stock bonus plan.

Front-end load: This is the sales fee charged when you buy a fund with a front-end load.

Global fund: Also known as a *world fund*, this type of mutual fund invests in both U.S. and foreign securities.

Grace period: A period of time, usually about 25 days, during which you can pay your credit card bill without incurring a finance charge. Typically, the grace period applies only if you pay your balance in full.

Growth fund: This type of mutual fund's objective is long-term growth of capital. The portfolio is made up of mostly stocks.

Health maintenance organization (HMO): A type of health care plan that offers patients medical coverage with low or no copayments for visits to doctors and hospitals that belong to that HMO network.

Home inspection: An inspection of the condition of the structure, electrical and plumbing systems, and other mechanical systems of a property and its conveying contents.

Homeowner's insurance: An insurance policy that covers the dwelling (and sometimes other structures on the property) for certain types of damages. It also covers the owner personally against lawsuits from people injured while visiting.

Homeowner's warranty: An insurance policy that covers repairs to specific parts and contents of a house for a specific period of time after the purchase.

HUD-1 statement: Also known as the *settlement sheet*, this is an itemized listing of the costs that must be paid at closing, including real estate commissions, loan fees, points, and initial escrow amounts. The seller's net proceeds are also disclosed on this statement. The form is provided by the U.S. Department of Housing and Urban Development.

Income fund: The objective of these mutual funds is to seek current income rather than capital growth.

Index fund: These funds seek to mirror a broad-based index, most often the S&P (Standard & Poor's) 500-stock index. Because they are not actively managed, these funds usually have low management fees.

Individual retirement account rollover: An individual may withdraw all or part of an IRA and exclude the withdrawal from income if it is deposited to another or the same IRA within 60 days after the withdrawal. Any portion not returned to IRA format within 60 days will be taxed as ordinary income and may be subject to the additional 10 percent penalty. Only one rollover is permitted per year. A rollover technically means that the money has touched the hands of the owner. A direct transfer from one IRA custodian to another (broker to broker) is not a rollover.

Individual retirement arrangement (IRA): These are personal, tax-sheltered retirement accounts that you can invest in if you meet certain requirements. Contributions are tax-deductible for some, depending on circumstances. Earnings in these plans can grow tax-deferred or, in the case of the Roth IRA, tax-free.

Inflation: Inflation is the rise in prices of goods and services caused by an increase in spending and a decrease in production and supplies. Inflation decreases spending power.

Interest rate: Interest is an amount earned on an investment or an amount charged on a loan. The interest rate is the exact percent being earned or charged. Interest rates on credit cards are either fixed rate (they remain the same over time), or variable (they are tied to changes in other interest rates, such as the prime rate). The interest rate may start out as fixed, but increase as a result of a condition being met (a lack of card use for a certain amount of time) or a condition not being met (carrying a balance versus paying it in full each month).

International fund: These mutual fund portfolios are made of foreign securities and carry more risk than domestic funds because of political volatility and the difficulty in researching companies outside the United States.

Intestate: Without a will.

Joint tenancy: A form of co-ownership designated in the property title. Under this form of ownership, each tenant has an equal interest and equal rights in the property, including the right of survivorship.

Keogh plan: This is a tax-deferred retirement account. You can set one up if you're self-employed or own a partnership business.

Liability insurance: Insurance coverage that protects against claims against a property owner for injuries or property damage sustained as a result of the property owner's negligence or inappropriate actions.

Living will: A legal document that voices your medical decisions if you are unable to speak for yourself as a result of medical incapacitation.

Load: About one third of all mutual funds carry a load, or sales commission. Loaded funds can carry commissions as high as 8.5 percent of the fund's offering price.

Lock-in period: The time during which a lender agrees to guarantee a specific interest rate on a specified mortgage.

Money market fund: These low-risk funds pay money market interest rates by investing in safe, liquid securities like bank Certificates of Deposit (CDs) and U.S. government securities.

Negative amortization: A gradual increase in the mortgage debt that occurs when the monthly payment is too small to cover the principal and interest due. The amount of the shortfall is added to the remaining balance. This situation occurs on some mortgage loans that have fixed monthly payments, but variable interest rates.

Net worth: The value of all of a person's assets minus liabilities.

No-load fund: A mutual fund that has no sales commission.

Origination fee: A loan processing fee paid to the lender. The fee is expressed in the form of *points*. One point equals 1 percent of the mortgage.

Point of service (POS): Point of service health plans combine the features of an HMO with those of out-of-network, fee-for-service coverage. Out-of-network usage typically has a per person cap and POS options or products that may be offered by managed care programs or indemnity insurers.

Power of attorney: A legal document that authorizes a specific person to act on your behalf. It can give complete authority or be limited to specified acts and/or periods of time.

Preapproval: A thorough process used to assess the prospective borrower's ability to pay back the loan. It determines how much money a prospective homebuyer can borrow.

Preferred provider organization (PPO): A type of health care plan that gives patients a choice of using doctors and hospitals in a network and paying a copayment or using physicians and hospitals outside the network and being responsible for paying an annual deductible and a percent of the bill for the visit.

Prequalification: A process used to determine how much money a prospective homebuyer could be eligible to borrow.

Private mortgage insurance (PMI): Mortgage insurance used to protect lenders against loss if a borrower defaults on the loan. Most lenders require PMI for loans exceeding 80 percent of the cost of the home (or property).

Probate: The process of distributing a deceased person's estate.

Probate court: Referred to as surrogate court in some states, probate court is a division of a state trial court or a specialized court that only hears cases concerning the distribution of deceased persons' estates.

Qualified plan rollover: Any part of a taxable portion of a distribution from a qualified plan may, within 60 days, be rolled over to another qualified plan or an IRA. Rollovers from qualified plans are subject to a mandatory 20 percent federal tax withholding. A direct transfer from a qualified plan to another qualified plan or IRA will eliminate this tax withholding.

Qualified Domestic Relations Order (QDRO): This court order uses pension or retirement benefits to divide marital property or to provide alimony or child support. It is necessary during divorce to comply with federal law governing retirement pay.

Remaindermen: The person or people who will inherit property in the future. For instance, a property may be left to a spouse for life and after the spouse dies the property may be inherited by a son. The son, therefore, is the remainderman because he will inherit the home in the future, after his parent dies.

Replacement value homeowners' or renters' insurance: This type of coverage pays the amount it would cost to replace the covered item today (rather than what it cost when you originally bought it).

Reverse mortgage: Rather than paying into a mortgage, certain qualified homeowners can tap into their equity for retirement support using a reverse mortgage.

Sector fund: This type of mutual fund invests in a specific industry, like health care or technology.

SIMPLE IRA: A Savings Incentive Match Plan for Employees is a tax-deferred retirement plan that may be used by a sole proprietor or offered by a small business that doesn't contribute to any other retirement plan.

Simplified Employee Pension (SEP): This type of pension allows you to make contributions to your own retirement plan if you're self-employed, and to your employees' plan. You can make contributions if you're the head of an S-corporation or a C-corporation, as well.

Specialty fund: This type of mutual fund invests in securities of a specific industry or group of industries or special types of securities.

SSL-encrypted session: An Internet site may use a secure socket layer (SSL), which protects the information the user provides by encrypting the data so it cannot be read as it is sent from your computer to the designated site or back from the site to your computer.

Tenancy by the entirety: A type of joint tenancy of a property designated by title that mandates the right of survivorship and is available only to a husband and wife.

Tenancy in common: A type of joint tenancy, as designated in the property title, that does not include the right of survivorship.

Term life insurance: Life insurance that covers you for a fixed period (term) of time.

Title: A legal document evidencing property ownership or a right of ownership.

Title insurance: Insurance that protects against loss arising from disputes over the true ownership of a property.

Title search: Completed before settlement, this is an examination of the title records to ensure that the seller is the legal owner of the property and that there are no liens or other claims on the home.

Universal life insurance: This kind of insurance provides coverage throughout your entire life and builds up savings over time. You can use the interest from your savings to help pay your premiums.

Variable life insurance: This type of insurance provides coverage for your entire life and builds up savings over time. You can invest your savings in a menu of mutual funds, which generally are managed by the insurance company.

Whole life insurance: This kind of insurance provides coverage for your entire life. Part of the premium payments are used to build up savings over time.

Will: A legal document that specifies legal guardianship for your minor children and how assets in your name will be distributed after your death.

Worker's compensation: Insurance required by law that compensates employees who are injured on the job.

Resource Guide

Cars and Trucks

Auto-by-tel
www.autobytel.com
Publishes dealer invoice prices.

Autopedia
www.autopedia.com
Automotive information, including rebates and incentives, insurance checkup, loan payment calculators, and more.

Consumer Reports
www.ConsumerReports.com
Publishes car and truck value ratings and safety test results.

Edmonds
www.edmonds.com
Publishes dealer invoice prices.

IntelliChoice
www.intellichoice.com
Publishes best overall values in automobiles.

National Highway Transportation Safety Administration

www.nhsta.gov

Publishes safety test results.

Financing College

AmeriCorps

www.cns.gov

The Corporation for National and Community Service

1201 New York Ave., N.W.

Washington, DC 20525

800/94-ACORPS

Information on financing college through community service.

College Board

www.collegeboard.org

College cost calculators, financial aid information, and more.

College Savings Plans Network, an affiliate of the National Association of State Treasurer

www.collegesavings.org

2760 Research Park Dr.

Lexington, KY 40511

606/244-8175

Information on state college savings plans.

fastWEB

www.fastweb.com

Has a database search of more than 400,000 scholarships; information on other financial aid.

Federal Student Aid Information Center

www.ed.gov

800/4-FED-AID

Financial aid assistance.

FinAid

www.FinAid.org

Information on financing college and scam alerts.

***Money Magazine* Online**

www.moneymag.com

College savings calculator.

Nellie Mae

www.nelliemae.org

Information on financing college.

Sallie Mae

www.salliemae.com

Information on financing college.

Complaints

Banks

Comptroller of the Currency, Administrator of National Banks

www.occ.treas.gov/customer.htm

800/613-6743

Customer Assistance Group

1301 McKinney St., Suite 3710

Houston, TX 77010

Supervises many national banks.

Federal Deposit Insurance Corporation (FDIC)

www.fdic.gov

Lists consumer rights. Locate complaint filing process at www.fdic.gov/consumer/fdiccr.html.

The National Credit Union Administration

www.ncua.gov

Links to regional offices by e-mails.

The Office of Thrift Supervision
www.ots.treas.gov
202/906-6237
Consumer complaints: 800/842-6929;
consumer.complaint@ots.treas.gov

State Banking Authorities
Lists contacts for all 50 states.

State bank regulators
www.pueblo.gsa.gov/crh/banking.htm
Lists state banking authorities.

The Web Investor
www.thewebinvestor.com/online-bank-assoc.html
Lists national and state bankers associations.

Businesses

Better Business Bureau
www.bbb.org
Alerts on businesses plus a BBB locator.

Cars and trucks

Autopedia
www.autopedia.com
Lemon law summaries.

The Lemon Aid Stand
www.pond.net/~delvis/lemonlinks.html
Lists attorneys who will fight dealers who sell cars
with defects not covered under the lemon laws.

Online complaint forms can be found at
www.pond.net/~delvis/lemonlinks.html.
Complaints can be filed by e-mail.

Credit ratings

Victims of Credit Reporting
pages.prodigy.com/ID/vcr/vcr.html
Contacts to credit agencies, information on how credit blemishes can affect you, and links to credit laws.

Fraud

National Association of Securities Dealers
www.nasdr.com
301/590-6500
Improper business practice complaints against investment salespeople, financial advisors, and brokers can be filed here; you can also file tips on fraudulent behavior or abusive conduct.

The National Fraud Information Center
www.fraud.org
800/876-7060
Information on fraud and scams.

Securities and Exchange Commission
www.sec.gov
202/942-7040
Investor assistance and complaints; has information on Internet fraud.

U.S. Postal Inspection Service
www.usps.gov/websites/depart/inspect/credit.htm
Information on credit card schemes.

Unemployment claims
National Association of Insurance Commissioners
www.naic.org
State insurance commissioners contact information.

U.S. Department of Labor
www.dol.gov
202/219-8776
Unemployment information.

Investments

National Association of Securities Dealers
www.nasdr.com
301/590-6500
Complaints against investment salespeople, financial advisors, and brokers can be filed here.

Credit Cards
Bank Rate Monitor
www.bankrate.com
Information about credit cards.

CardWeb
www.CardWeb.com
Information on credit card rates, fees, and bonuses.

The Consumer Law Handbook
www.law.cornell.edu/topics/consumer_credit.html
Full text of federal consumer credit laws.

The Federal Reserve System
www.bog.frb.fed.us/pubs/shop/tablwb.pdf
Publishes a report on credit card plan terms every six months.

Credit Reporting Bureaus
Equifax
800/525-6285 (to report fraud)
800/685-1111 (credit report orders)

Experian
800/397-3742 (credit report orders)

Trans Union
800/680-7289 (to report fraud)
800/888-4213 (credit report orders)

To find out if there's been any activity on your account as a result of fraud call:

CheckRite: 800/766-2748

Chexsystems: 800/428-9623

Equifax: 800/437-5120

National Processing Co.: 800/526-5380

SCAN: 800/262-7771

Telecheck: 800/710-9898

Debt

American Bureau of Credit Services
800/SAVEME2
Credit counseling.

Consolidated Credit Counseling Services, Inc.
www.debtfree.org
Credit counseling.

Consumer Credit Counseling Service
800/388-2227
To receive a free copy of *Managing your Debts: How to Regain Financial Health,* mail your credit card, cut in half, along with a self-addressed, stamped business envelope to CFA, P.O. Box 12099, Washington, DC 20005-0999.

Debt Counselors of America
www.GetOutOfDebt.org
800/680-3328
Debt counseling.

Divorce

The Academy of Family Mediators
www.mediators.org
781/674-2663
Referrals to mediators.

American Academy of Matrimonial Attorneys
www.aaml.org
Referrals to divorce attorneys.

The American Arbitration Association
www.adr.org
Referrals to arbitrators.

Divorce Central
www.DivorceCentral.com
Information on divorce.

DivorceNet
www.DivorceNet.com
Information on divorce.

Divorce Online
www.DivorceOnline.com
Information on divorce.

Employment

WetFeet.com
www.wetfeet.com
Information on companies and tips on job searches.

Changing careers

American Association of Retired Persons (AARP)
www.aarp.org
Information on how to get a job when you're older.

Corporate Gray Online
www.greentogray.com or www.bluetogray.com
Tailored to those leaving the military and entering
the civilian work force.

Family Friendly
www.familyfriendly.com
Lists companies with family-friendly work places and other programs by category searches.

Job banks on the Web

America's Job Bank: www.ajb.dni.us

Best Jobs USA: www.bestjobsusa.com

Boldface Jobs: www.boldfacejobs.com

CareerCity: www.careercity.com

Career Magazine: www.careermag.com

Career Mosaic: www.careermosaic.com

Career Path: www.careerpath.com

CareerWeb: www.careerweb.com

Careers OnLine: www.careersonline.com

4Work: www.4work.com

HelpWanted.com: www.helpwanted.com

Hot Jobs: www.hotjobs.com

Job Bank USA: www.jobbankusa.com

JobCenter.com: www.jobcenter.com

JobOptions: www.espan.com

Jobsource: www.jobsource.com (for college students)

JobSpot: www.jobspot.com

Job Trak: www.jobtrak.com

Job Web: www.jobweb.com

Monster Board: www.monster.com

NationJob Network: www.nationjob.com

Nonprofit Career Network:
www.nonprofitcareer.com

Online Career Center: www.occ.com

Purdue University (an index of more than 1,000 online job search resources):
www.ups.purdue.edu/Student/jobsites.htm

TOPjobs USA: www.topjobsusa.com
U.S. Office of Personnel Management:
www.usajobs.opm.gov

Yahoo!: www.yahoo.com (click the employment section link)

General Consumer Protection

Consumer's Resource Handbook
www.pueblo.gsa.gov/crh/respref.htm
Tips on car purchase and repairs, shopping from home, avoiding consumer and investment fraud, choosing and using credit cards wisely, and more.

The Federal Trade Commission
www.ftc.gov/ftc/consumer.htm
Information on investments, cars, credit, employment, and more.

Insurance

AccuQuote
www.AccuQuote.com
800/442-9899
Gets price quotes for life insurance policies.

Georgetown University's Institute for Health Care Research and Policy
www.georgetown.edu/research/ihcrp/hipaa
Information on the Health Insurance Portability and Accountability Act (HIPAA).

National Association of Insurance Commissioners
www.naic.org
Industry information.

Quicken InsureMarket

www.insuremarket.com

Gets price quotes on auto, home, life, disability income, small business, medical, supplemental health, and long term care insurance.

Quotesmith.com

www.quotesmith.com

Gets price quotes on term life, auto, medical, and medicare supplement insurance.

RightQuote

www.rightquote.com

Gets price quotes on life insurance policies.

Investing

Barrons

www.barrons.com

Detailed information on specific stocks and mutual funds.

BestCalls.com

www.bestcalls.com

Investor conference call listings and times.

Dow Jones University

www.dju.wsj.com

Online classes on investing.

Money Magazine

www.moneymag.com

General financial news and information.

Morningstar

www.morningstart.com

Detailed information on specific stocks and mutual funds.

Motley Fool
www.fool.com
Stock investment information.

Smart Money
www.smartmoney.com
General financial news and information.

Wall Street Journal
www.wsj.com
Detailed financial information.

The Washington Post
www.WashingtonPost.com
Investment information and advice from James K. Glassman, Albert B. Crenshaw, and others.

Yahoo!
www.yahoo.com
Information finance links include investment picks, mutual funds, stock quotes, message boards, and more.

Lawyers

American College of Trust and Estate Counsel (ACTEC)
www.actec.org
310/398-1888
3415 South Sepulveda Blvd., Suite 330
Los Angeles, CA 90034
Referrals.

The Best Lawyers in America by Steve Naifeh and Greg Smith
www.bestlawyers.com
Reference book for peer-selected referrals.

Real Estate

American Society of Home Inspectors (ASHI)
www.ashi.com
Referrals for affiliated home inspectors.

Mortgagecalc.com
www.mortgage-calc.com
Mortgage calculator.

National Association of Exclusive Buyers Agents (NAEBA)
800/986-2322
Referrals.

The National Center for Home Equity Conversion
www.reverse.org
Information on reverse mortgages.

Finding an agent

The National Association of Realtors at REALTOR.COM
www.realtor.com
Referrals for Realtors.

For sale by owner

The Abele Owner's Network
www.owners.com
Homes for sale by owner postings.

United Homeowners Association
www.uha.org
Information on how to sell your home without an agent.

Home loans

Bank Rate Monitor: www.bankrate.com

E-loan: www.eloan.com

GetSmart.com: www.getsmart.com

HomeShark: www.homeshark.com

Liberty First Financial: www.LoanGuide.com

Microsoft HomeAdvisor: www.homeadvisor.com

Mortgage Market Information Services Inc.:
www.interest.com

Mortgage-net: www.mortgage-net.com

Quicken Mortgage: www.quickenmortgage.com

The Lending Tree: www.lendingtree.com

Homeowners insurance

InsWeb
www.insweb.com
Gets price quotes on homeowners' and renters' insurance (as well as auto, life, and health).

House hunting

Coldwell Banker
www.coldwellbanker.com
Searches for listed homes.

Homescout
www.homescout.com
Searches for listed homes.

National Association of Realtors
www.realtor.com
Searches for listed homes.

Relocation on the Web

Coldwell Banker: www.coldwellbanker.com

Homefair.com: www.homefair.com/home

MapQuest: www.mapquest.com

REALTOR.COM: www.realtor.com

Relocation Central: www.relocationcentral.com

Relocation Online: www.relocationonline.com

Virtual Relocation.com: www.virtualrelocation.com

Taxes
H&R Block
www.hrblock.com/tax
Tax information.

Internal Revenue Service
www.irs.gov
Publications, forms, and information.

Strong Funds
www.strong—funds.com
Tax advice.

T. Rowe Price
www.troweprice.com
Tax advice.

Wegner's Online Tax Encyclopedia
www.wegnercpas.com/encyclop/content.htm
Tax information.

Trusts
The American College of Trust and Estate Council
www.actec.org
310/398-1888
Referrals to lawyers specializing in trust and estate planning.

Council on Foundations
www.cof.org
202/466-6512
Information on estate planning and philanthropy.

Recommended Reading List

Car and Truck Buying

The Complete Car Cost Guide (serial)
The Editors of IntelliChoice
Price: $45.00
Paperback (1998)
IntelliChoice
ISBN: 0941443973

The Complete Small Truck Cost Guide (serial)
Steven Gross, Vincent Mendolia, Eds.
Price: $45.00
Paperback (1998)
IntelliChoice
ISBN: 0941443981

The Complete Idiot's Guide to Buying or Leasing a Car
Donna Howell
Price: $15.95
Paperback—484 pages (1998)
Macmillan General Reference
ISBN: 0028625242

The Unofficial Guide to Buying or Leasing a Car
Donna Howell
Price: $15.95
Paperback—484 pages (1998)
Macmillan General Reference
ISBN: 0028625242

College

10 Minute Guide to Paying for College
William D. Van Dusen
Price: $10.95
Paperback—144 pages (1996)
Arco Pub
ISBN: 0028606140

The Guerrilla Guide to Mastering Student Loan Debt:
Everything You Should Know About Negotiating the
Right Loan for You, Paying It Off, Protecting Yourself
Anne Stockwell
Price: $14.00
Paperback—352 pages (1997)
HarperCollins
ISBN: 0062734350

Barron's Complete College Financing Guide
Marguerite J. Dennis
Price: $14.95
Paperback—288 pages (4th edition, 1997)
Barrons Educational Series
ISBN: 0812095235

America's Best College Scholarships 1998–1999
(annual)
John Culler
Price $19.95
Paperback (1998)
John Culler & Sons
ISBN: 1887269371

Bears' Guide to Finding Money for College 1998–1999
(serial)
John Bear, Ph.D, Mariah P. Bear
Price: $8.95
Paperback—208 pages (1998–1999 edition 1997)
Ten Speed Press
ISBN: 0898159334

Divorce

The Dollars and Sense of Divorce
Judith Briles, Edwin Schilling, and Carol Ann
Wilson
Price: $17.95
Paperback—248 pages (1998)
Dearborn Trade
ISBN: 0793127637

*Divorce and Money: How to Make the Best Financial
Decisions During Divorce*
Violet Woodhouse, Victoria F. Collins, M. C.
Blakeman
Price: $26.95
Paperback—296 pages (4th edition, 1998)
Nolo Press
ISBN: 0873374622

The Complete Idiot's Guide to Surviving Divorce
Pamela Weintraub, Terry Hillman, Elayne
Kesselman
Price: $16.95
Paperback (1996)
Alpha Books
ISBN: 0028611012

Employment

The 1999 What Color Is Your Parachute?: A Practical Manual for Job-Hunters and Career-Changers
Richard Nelson Bolles
Price: $16.95
Paperback—366 pages (Revised edition, 1998)
Ten Speed Press
ISBN: 1580080081

The Complete Idiot's Guide to Getting the Job You Want
Marc A. Dorio, Rosemary Maniscalco
Price: $16.95
Paperback—346 pages (2nd edition, 1998)
Alpha Books
ISBN: 0028627237

The Complete Idiot's Guide to the Perfect Interview
Marc A. Dorio
Price: $14.95
Paperback—288 pages (1997)
Macmillan General Reference
ISBN: 0028619455

101 Great Answers to the Toughest Job Search Problems
Ollie Stevenson
Price: $11.99
Paperback—214 pages (1995)
Career Press
ISBN: 1564141586

10 Minute Guide to Job Interviews
Dana Morgan
Price: $10.95
Paperback—152 pages (1998)
Macmillan General Reference
ISBN: 0028621360

*Change Your Job, Change Your Life: High Impact
Strategies for Finding Great Jobs in the 21st Century*
Ronald L. Krannich, Caryl R. Krannich
Price: $17.95
Paperback (6th edition, 1997)
Impact Publications
ISBN: 1570230668

101 Ways to Power Up Your Job Search
J. Thomas Buck, William R. Matthews, Contributor
Price: $12.95
Paperback—222 pages (1997)
McGraw-Hill
ISBN: 0070410437

Estate Planning

*J. K. Lasser's Estate Planning for Baby Boomers and
Retirees*
Stewart H. Welch III
Price: $15.95
Paperback—305 pages (1998)
Macmillan USA
ISBN: 0028625293

*Estate Planning Made Easy: Your Step-By-Step Guide to
Protecting Your Family, Safeguarding Your Assets and
Minimizing the Tax Bite*
David T. Phillips, Bill Wolfkiel
Price: $21.95
Paperback—248 pages (2nd edition, 1998)
Dearborn Trade
ISBN: 0793127122

Plan Your Estate: Absolutely Everything You Need to Know to Protect Your Loved Ones
Denis Clifford, Michael Phillips, Cora Jordan
Price: $24.95
Paperback—496 pages (4th edition, 1998)
Nolo Press
ISBN: 0873373901

The Complete Idiot's Guide to Wills and Estates
Steve Maple
Price: $16.95
Paperback—352 pages (1997)
Macmillan General Reference
ISBN: 0028617479

Finances

Get a Financial Life: Personal Finance in Your Twenties and Thirties
Beth Kobliner
Price: $12.00
Paperback—283 pages (1996)
Fireside
ISBN: 0684812134

Get a Financial Life: Personal Finance in Your Twenties and Thirties
Beth Kobliner
Price: $12.00
Audio cassette (1997)
Simon & Schuster Audio
ISBN: 0671575570

Get Rich Slowly: Building Your Financial Future Through Common Sense
William T. Spitz
Price: $12.95
Paperback (1996)
Macmillan Books
ISBN: 0028608453

Kathy Kristof's Complete Book of Dollars and Sense
Kathy M. Kristof
Price: $19.95
Hardcover—327 pages (1997)
Macmillan Books
ISBN: 0028608526

Making the Most of Your Money
Jane Bryant Quinn
Price: $30.00
Hardcover—944 pages (Revised and updated
edition, 1997)
Simon & Schuster
ISBN: 0684811766

*Savvy Investing for Women: Strategies from a Self-Made
Wall Street Millionaire*
Marlene Jupiter
Price: $14.00
Paperback—352 pages (1999)
Prentice Hall Trade
ISBN: 0735200807

*Couples and Money: A Couples' Guide Updated for the
New Millennium*
Victoria Collins, Suzanne Brown
Price: $13.95
Paperback—220 pages (2nd edition, 1998)
Gabriel Books
ISBN: 1891689983

Investing
The Unofficial Guide to Investing in Mutual Funds
Stacie Zoe Berg
Price: $15.95
Paperback—400 pages (1999)
Macmillan General Reference
ISBN: 0028629205

The Unofficial Guide to Investing
Lynn O'Shaughnessy
Price: $16.00
Paperback—612 pages (1998)
Macmillan General Reference
ISBN: 0028624580

The Complete Idiot's Guide to Making Money on Wall Street
Christy Heady
$18.95
Paperback—358 pages (2nd edition, 1997)
Macmillan General Reference
ISBN: 0028619587

Barron's Guide to Making Investment Decisions, Revised and Expanded
Douglas Sease and John Prestbo
Price: $16.00
Paperback—416 pages (1998)
New York Institute of Finance
ISBN: 0735200440

Everything You Need to Know About Money and Investing: A Financial Expert Answers the 1,001 Most Frequently Asked Questions
Sarah Young Fisher and Carol A. Turkington
Price: $18.00
Paperback—400 pages (1998)
Prentice Hall
ISBN: 0735200416

How the Stock Market Works
John M. Dalton, Ed.
Price: $17.95
Paperback—352 pages (2nd edition, 1993)
New York Institute of Finance
ISBN: 0130978663

Jonathan Pond's Financial Management Guide:
Retirement Planning for Asset-Rich Individuals
Jonathan Pond
Price: $19.95
Paperback—448 pages (1993)
Prentice Hall Trade
ISBN: 0130312207

Real Estate

Brincefield's Guide to Buying a Home—The 21 Biggest
Mistakes People Make When They Buy a Home
Price: $29.95
Brincefield & Hartnett, P.C.
526 King St., Suite 423
Alexandria, VA 22314-3143
Phone: 703/836-2880
Fax: 703/549-1924

How to Save Thousands of Dollars on Your Home
Mortgage
Randy Johnson
Price: $14.95
Paperback—256 pages (1998)
John Wiley & Sons
ISBN: 0471192538

Taxes

Complete Idiot's Guide to Doing Your Income Taxes
Gail A. Perry, Paul Craig Roberts
Price: $12.95
Paperback—502 pages (1998)
Alpha Books
ISBN: 0028626826

Tax Havens
Anthony S. Ginsberg, CPA
Price: $55.00
Hardcover (2nd edition, 1998)
Prentice Hall
ISBN: 0735200408

Vest-Pocket Tax Advisor 1999: Tax Facts at Your Fingertips (serial)
Terence M. Myers, J.D., Dorinda DeScherer, J.D.
Price: $49.95
Hardcover—547 pages (1998)
Prentice Hall Trade
ISBN: 0139596771

The *Unofficial Guide*™ Reader Questionnaire

If you would like to express your opinion about managing your personal finances or this guide, please complete this questionnaire and mail it to:

The *Unofficial Guide*™ Reader Questionnaire
Macmillan Lifestyle Group
1633 Broadway, floor 7
New York, NY 10019-6785

Gender: ___ M   ___ F

Age: ___ Under 30   ___ 31–40   ___ 41–50
___ Over 50

Education: ___ High school   ___ College
___ Graduate/Professional

What is your occupation?

_____

How did you hear about this guide?
___ Friend or relative
___ Newspaper, magazine, or Internet
___ Radio or TV
___ Recommended at bookstore
___ Recommended by librarian
___ Picked it up on my own
___ Familiar with the *Unofficial Guide*™ travel series

Did you go to the bookstore specifically for a book on personal finances?   Yes ___   No ___

Have you used any other *Unofficial Guides*™?
Yes ___   No ___

If Yes, which ones?

_____
_____
_____

What other book(s) on managing your personal finances have you purchased?

_____

_____

_____

Was this book:
___ more helpful than other(s)
___ less helpful than other(s)

Do you think this book was worth its price?
Yes ___   No ___

Did this book cover all topics related to managing your personal finances adequately?
Yes ___   No ___

Please explain your answer:

_____

_____

_____

Were there any specific sections in this book that were of particular help to you?   Yes ___   No ___

Please explain your answer:

_____

_____

_____

On a scale of 1 to 10, with 10 being the best rating, how would you rate this guide? ___

What other titles would you like to see published in the *Unofficial Guide*™ series?

_____

_____

Are *Unofficial Guides*™ readily available in your area?   Yes ___   No ___

Other comments:

_____

_____

_____

_____

About the Author

Stacie Zoe Berg can tell you everything you need to know about managing your personal finances. Ms. Berg, author of *The Unofficial Guide™ to Investing in Mutual Funds,* is a freelance journalist who contributes articles to *The Washington Post, The Washington Times,* and several trade magazines. She covers personal finance, residential real estate, computer technology and information security, and more.

Ms. Berg is a member of the American Society of Journalists and Authors and Washington Independent Writers. Over the years she has been associated with other professional organizations, including Women in Communications, for which she is a former board member and newsletter assistant editor, and Women in Museums (sponsored by the Smithsonian Institution). Ms. Berg also is an award-winning Toastmaster.